Great Cricketers

GREAT CRICKETERS

EDITED BY
Denzil Batchelor

EYRE & SPOTTISWOODE
LONDON

© *1970 Eyre & Spottiswoode (Publishers) Ltd*
First published 1970 by
Eyre & Spottiswoode (Publishers) Ltd
11 New Fetter Lane, London, EC4

SBN **413 26510 2**

Printed in Great Britain by
Ebenezer Baylis and Son Ltd
The Trinity Press, Worcester, and London

Contents

6 CONTENTS

Illustrations

1*

Acknowledgements and thanks for permission to reproduce photographs are due to

The Mansell Collection: Grace, Spofforth, Woods, Fry, Ranjitsinhji, Warner, Barnes

Mrs Christine Beldam: Grace (bowling), Trumper

M.C.C.: Spooner, Douglas, L. S. Constantine, Macartney, Mead, Mailey, Woolley

Sport & General Press Agency Ltd: Bailey

The Lancashire County Cricket Club: C. H. Parkin

The remaining photographs are reproduced by courtesy of Central Press Photos Ltd

Editor's Introduction

It is about time somebody said it: there is no such thing as a team game. In this bad world the player is the thing, not the team. Association Football, which if spectator figures are the gauge, has every right to consider itself our national sport, proves that to the hilt. It is nice to know that the club you have visited ever since your father held your hand to cross the road, is on top of the division or leading in the race for promotion; it is galling to know that they seem doomed to relegation – but all this interest is largely fanned up by press reports; the really dominant figures are Nobby Stiles and George Best, Peter Osgood and Johnny Haynes.

So it is, and always has been, with cricket. In the far away old days, the game rather than the League mattered. One remembers that the great S. M. J. Woods on being asked how Somerset was faring in the Championship table, urbanely asked: 'What is the Championship table?' (In those days a generation purer in heart than the present one considered the match in question was all that mattered. When Jessop won the Oval Test in 1902 nobody remembered that we had already lost the rubber. Today, the most important thing of all is the Ashes. You must win them and hold them. Next in importance comes the Rubber. That must be won or drawn. It is all nonsense, really.)

But underneath it all, it is the individual who matters. It was W.G. whom everyone wanted to see – not London County. Which of us could put his hand on his heart and name five other members of that side?

Sussex *was* Sussex because it was the county of C. B. Fry and K. S. Ranjitsinhji. Taking the argument right down to today, what member of a Trent Bridge crowd makes haste to get

there in time for the toss to see what happens to Nottinghamshire? He goes to watch Sobers. Just as, to be frank, the
Worcestershire and Warwickshire crowds go to watch
Graveney, Kanhai and Gibbs rather than to see how the old
county is faring.

Cricket is a game we remember – by and large – because of
the stars. What is remarkable too is that we remember individual performances far more vividly than results. One of
the greatest innings I ever saw was Donald Bradman's double
century on the Sydney Cricket Ground against Learie O'Brien
Xavier Fleetwood-Smith. I can't tell you who won that
match – I suppose New South Wales, but I really don't
know.

Well, here is a book then to the popular taste. It is, if you
like, a Galaxy. You will find W.G. and F. R. Spofforth here,
C. B. Fry, Hobbs, Lord (Learie) Constantine, Walter Hammond, Frank Woolley, Philip Mead, of the Old Brigade. But
here too are Bill Lawry (specially written by Jack Fingleton),
Tom Graveney, Lance Gibbs and Graeme Pollock.

I love the personalities behind the men as much as I love
the cricketers themselves. As a schoolboy I used to visit The
Oval with my father. It was there that my sister, A.W.O.L.
from school, once asked him, half-drugged from watching
Hobbs and Sandham, 'Who was Isosceles?' They were not
just batsmen averaging 37.23 or bowlers needing seventeen for
their 100 wickets, or the best 'keeper in the country.

One of them was a game-keeper, one was a lunatic asylum
attendant, this one was a fishmonger, that one a variety entertainer. We knew all their Christian names and what they had
done in their past lives: such as grown crops in West Africa.
We all thought of Shepherd (not P. A. Perrin) as the greatest
batsman who had never played for England.

This book is an attempt to do for you what the Surrey team
did for my boyhood.

I suppose the time will come when somebody will bring out
a book dealing with the thirty greatest performances in the

history of cricket: Alletson's quick-scoring innings; McCabe's 187 against Jardine's team; Laker's 19 wickets in a Test. All very fine, but as I grow older I become less and less interested in technique and more and more interested in the man behind the leg-drive or the yorker. I wish, for instance, that I knew all that there was to know about Warwick Armstrong. I know that when he first played for Australia he weighed eight stone and that when he last played he weighed twenty. I know that when Mailey saw him on his death-bed, Arthur reproached him with reducing the dignity of a Test Match at The Oval in 1921 by picking up a piece of wind-blown newspaper and reading it in the deep field. 'I wasn't selling the Test Match short,' said Warwick, 'I was finding out whom we were playing.'

Until someone writes such a book, this selection of *Great Cricketers* will fill the gap for me.

1969   DENZIL BATCHELOR

Great Cricketers

W. G. Grace

BERNARD DARWIN

'W.G.,' said an old friend of his, 'was just a great big schoolboy in everything he did.' It would be difficult in a single sentence to come nearer to the clue to his character. He had all the schoolboy's love for elementary and boisterous jokes: his distaste for learning; his desperate and undisguised keenness; his guilelessness and his guile; his occasional pettishness and pettiness; his endless power of recovering his good spirits. To them may be added two qualities not as a rule to be found in schoolboys: a wonderful modesty and lack of vanity; and invariable kindness to those younger than himself, 'except,' as one of his most devoted friends has observed, 'that he tried to chisel them out l.b.w.'

If one had to chose a single epithet to describe him, it would, I think, be simple. 'I am not a psychologist,' he says in one of his books, and his estimate was doubtless accurate. He did not think very deeply or very subtly about anybody or anything; perhaps not even about cricket, although his knowledge of it was intuitively profound, his judgment of a cricketer unique. Of all the stories about him none is better known than his answer to a question as to how a particular stroke should be made: 'You put the bat against the ball'. It may be read in one of two slightly different senses, and in either it seems to reveal something of his character. Take it as a serious attempt to explain the whole secret of a stroke, an earnest endeavour to help the learner, and in that sense it shows his essential simplicity. Again it may be taken as a reflection on those who want to be too clever and abstruse, and I imagine that W.G. did not want people to be clever. He was too modest to have the contemptuous arrogance of the unlearned towards learning; that belongs to the lout, and he had no trace of it, but for his own part he liked best the other simple folk like himself. His interests were all of the open air. If people wanted to read books, no doubt they got pleasure from it, but it was a pleasure that he could not really understand. *Wisden*, yes, perhaps, to confirm a memory or refute an argument, or in winter as an earnest of the summer to come; but in a general way books were bad for cricket. 'How can you expect to make runs,' he said to one of the Gloucestershire side, 'when you are always reading?'; and added, almost gratuitously, 'You don't catch me that way.' I have searched in vain for anyone who ever saw him take the risk, except in the case of a newspaper or a medical book in which he wanted to look up a point.

W.G. was not an intellectual man, and even as regards his own subject his was not an analytical brain, but by instinct or genius – call it what you will – he could form a judgment of a cricketer to which all others bowed. One who played much with him has given me two instances to which many more might, of course, be added. A schoolboy who had made innumerable runs for his school, and was generally regarded as an extraordinary cricketer, played in his first first-class match with W.G., and made a respectable score. Everybody crowded round the oracle to hear the verdict, and expected a favourable one. 'He'll never make a first-class cricketer' – that was all, and it turned out to be entirely true. Here is a converse example. When Mr Jessop first appeared for Gloucestershire, those who now realize that they ought to have known better were struck only by the more rough-hewn and bucolic aspects of his batting. 'What have you got here, old man?' they asked W.G. rather disparagingly. 'Ah, you wait and see what I've got here,' he answered with a touch of truculence, and went on to say that in a year or so this would be the finest hitter that had ever been seen. That this verdict also turned out true is hardly worth the saying.

Moreover, if W.G. did not possess what is generally called

cleverness, he had, within certain precise limits, a remarkable acuteness. He might not think deeply, but on his own subjects he could think quickly. 'A man must get up very early in the morning,' said the Game Chicken, 'to get the best of John Gully,' and many a cricketer might well have said it of W.G. He had that sort of quickness of apprehension that may, without disrespect, perhaps be called cunning, and is often to be found, a little surprisingly, in those who seem at first sight simple-minded and almost rustic. He had plenty of shrewdness too in judging the qualities of men, so far as they interested him and came within his sphere. He might occasionally do ill-judged things in the excitement of the moment, but at the bottom of everything there was a good hard kernel of common sense.

We are told that when W.G. first appeared in first-class cricket he was shy, and we can picture him a tall, gawky, uneasy boy. He had not been to a public school; he came from a small country doctor's family; he had met few people except in his own country neighbourhood, and he suddenly found himself among those who had had a different sort of up-bringing. It is no wonder that he was silent and uncomfortable; but fame and popularity are wonderful softeners of that agony of shyness, and, if he perhaps kept a little of it deep down inside him, there was no external trace of it. He was perfectly natural with all whom he met, and if he liked them he was soon friendly and hearty with them. He was helped by a wonderful unself-consciousness. He seemed to take himself for granted, at once a supreme player of his game, and, off the field, as an ordinary person, and did not bother his head about what impression he made. He was far better known by sight than any other man in England. Long after his cricketing days were over, he had only to pass through a village street in a motor-car for windows to be thrown up and fingers to be pointed, but he seemed, and really was, as nearly as possible unaware of it, unless perhaps his admirer was a small child, to whom he liked to wave his hand. This unselfconsciousness pervaded his whole existence. He had come, as has been said, from a home comparatively countrified and uncultivated; he kept, to some extent at least, its manners and its way of speech all his life. He mixed constantly with those who were, in a snobbish sense, his superiors and had other ways and other manners, and I do not believe that he ever gave such things a thought. He recognized different standards in the houses he stayed at, to the extent that there were some to which he ought to take his 'dancing-pumps', and that was all. He liked friendliness and cheerfulness wherever he met it; he was ready to give it himself, and never thought of anything else that could be demanded of him.

I do not know if I am right, but he gave me the impression that the one thing that would not go down with him was any elaborateness of manner, any too formal politeness. I remember a little scene on a golf-course. I was playing with him in a foursome, and someone unintentionally drove into us from behind. W.G., always jealous of his rights in any game, resented it, but the driver of the ball apologized with extreme politeness, and surely all would now be over. But it was not; the more careful the apologies the less did W.G. let the poor man alone, until he made the rest of the foursome feel very uncomfortable. I thought then, and I think now, that if the offender had come up, and said cheerfully, 'Doctor, I'm awfully sorry,' and had even clapped him on the back, all would have been well, but he was of the sort that cannot for the life of them clap people on the back, and nothing could atone.

It has been said that W.G. liked simple jokes, and if they were familiar ones of the 'old grouse in the gun-room type' so much the better. There seems to me something extremely characteristic about a story, very small and mild in itself, told by Mr C. E. Green in the *Memorial Biography*. Mr Green was Master of the Essex Hounds, and had the hounds brought for W.G. to look at after breakfast. He liked the hounds, and he liked the Master's big grey horse, and, Mr Green goes on, 'For years afterwards whenever we met he would sing out 'How's my old grey horse?' That is perhaps hardly worthy of the name of joke, but, whatever it was, it was the kind of friendly chaff that pleased W.G. He liked jokes to do with conviviality, for he was a convivial soul. Essentially temperate in his everyday private life, he enjoyed good things on anything in the nature of an occasion; he had, as I fancy, a kind of Dickensian relish for good cheer, not merely the actual enjoyment of it but also the enjoyment of thinking and talking about it, and he combined with this, of course, a much greater practical capacity than Dickens ever had. A whole bottle of champagne was a mere nothing to him; having consumed it he would go down on all fours, and balance the bottle on the top of his head and rise to his feet again. Nothing could disturb that magnificent constitution, and those who hoped by a long and late sitting to shorten his innings next day often found themselves disappointed. His regular habit while cricketing was to drink one large whisky and soda, with a touch of angostura bitters, at lunch, and another when the day's play ended; this allowance he never varied or exceeded till the evening came, and, despite his huge frame, though he never dieted, he ate sparingly. His one attempt at a weight-reducing regimen was the drinking of cider. As he believed in a moderate amount of good drink, so he disbelieved strongly in tobacco. He had been brought up in a non-smoking family (though his brother Alfred became a backslider), and stuck to its tenets religiously all his life. It was an aphorism of this that 'you can get rid of drink, but you can never get rid of smoke'. He constantly proclaimed it as his own private belief, but he never made any attempt to put his team on any allowance of tobacco.

from W. G. GRACE *1934*

F. R. Spofforth

A. G. MOYES

Spofforth stood a couple of inches over six feet, was long and lean, weighing only eleven stone, and able to run 100 yards in less than eleven seconds. All these natural advantages helped him in the style of bowling he had made his own. He studied the batsmen, saw their weaknesses, developed the art of deceit to the limit. And he had faith in his own ability, just as when as a lad he had ignored those who urged him to change his ideas. He had the spirit that would not admit defeat. At the Oval in 1882, when England, needing only 85 to win, seemed certain of victory, he told his colleagues 'This thing can be done'. And he went out and did it – fourteen for 90 in the match. He was the master bowler. When he bowled the wind was in the east and gave the batsmen an uncomfortable feeling – a man with an art that can immortalize.

Lord Harris, who played so often against him, has emphasized this quality in his tribute in the 1927 *Wisden*: 'I was playing for ten years at home and abroad against those great medium-paced Australian bowlers Allan, Garrett, Palmer, Giffen, Turner, and Ferris, as well as Spofforth, and I have, of course, also played such great English bowlers as Shaw, Watson, Jim Lillywhite, Lohmann, C. T. Studd, and W. G. Grace, and I am quite satisfied and always have been, that Spofforth was the most difficult of them all, because he concealed so well the pace of the ball. . . . What we must judge performances by are the circumstance and conditions of the time when they were done, and, taking those as the criteria, I do not see how any bowler can be held to be better than was F. R. Spofforth.'

Now turn to another English opinion, published, like that of Lord Harris, in 1927 – a date which is important, because the speaker had seen, among others, England's mighty bowler S. F. Barnes. Lord Darnley, who, as the Hon. Ivo Bligh, led a victorious English side in Australia, said this: 'The long arms seemed to be whirling round at much the same speed whether the ball was coming fast or slow, and he had practised these disguises of pace to perfection.' And again: 'Incomparably the best stayer of any fast or medium-paced bowler that I can remember.' Lord Darnley also wrote of his delivery: 'No bowler I ever saw had a more graceful, spacious sweep of the arm, and his delivery gave a most satisfactory sensation of perfection of pace and power combined.' And, in conclusion: 'One of the very best bowlers the last fifty years have seen, unquestionably; possibly the best of all.'

Now for W. G. Grace, the champion batsman of the day: 'It is difficult to express all one feels about Spofforth,' he wrote in *W. G. – Cricketing Reminiscences and Personal Recollections*: 'He was unique as a fast bowler, and practically established a school of bowlers. His pace was terrifically fast, at times his length excellent, and his break-backs were exceedingly deceptive. He controlled the ball with masterly skill, and if the wicket helped him ever so little was almost unplayable. A good many batsmen funked Spofforth's bowling, and a great many more found it impossible to score off him.'

Here, then, was a master of the art of bowling, possessing all the basic requirements, plus a deadly yorker, and a delivery which seems to have been almost frightening in its intensity. The 'Demon', they called him after that famous match in which the Australians beat the M.C.C. in one afternoon, and the name in itself is an indication of the state of mind of those who pinned it on to Spofforth. Some have doubted his right to stand at the top of the list, either alone, or in company with others, because they have claimed that he did not turn from the leg. One hesitates to accept that, or to agree that he did not. A bowler of such brains and skill would scarcely fail to realize the value of

the ball that runs away from the bat. Lord Harris referred to
the fact that Spofforth could turn from the leg 'though I cannot
remember his doing so', and the *Sydney Morning Herald*, in its
report of the famous M.C.C. match of 1878, states that the
'Demon' bowled Grace with such a ball.

The majesty of the man can be estimated by his deeds and
by the effect he had on his opponents. In 1878 and 1880, years
when he must have been in his prime, he did not play in a Test
in England – in 1878 because there were none, and in 1880 because of injury. And yet he took ninety-four wickets at 18.41
runs apiece. Had he been able to play against England in those
years he would without doubt have been the first bowler to
take 100 Test wickets. In all matches which might be considered first-class Spofforth had 1,146 wickets at 13.55 runs
apiece. Seven times in first-class games he and his partner
bowled unchanged through an innings – three times with
Palmer, twice with Boyle, and once each with Evans and
Garrett. One such performance was for New South Wales
against Victoria, one for Australia against the Rest, and the
others for Australian teams in England.

Spofforth's mightiest deeds in England, listed in the yellow-
covered pages of the 1927 *Wisden*, were:

> 10 for 20 (including hat-trick), Australians
>   *v*. M.C.C., at Lord's, 1878.
> 9 for 53, Australians *v*. Lancashire, at Manchester, 1878.
> 13 for 110 (including hat-trick), Australia
>   *v*. England, at Melbourne, 1878-9.
> 13 for 85, Australians *v*. Derbyshire, 1880.
> 9 for 51, and 4 for 34, Australians *v*. Somerset, 1882.
> 14 for 90, Australia *v*. England, at the Oval, 1882.
> 8 for 11, and 6 for 47, Australians *v*. Scotland, 1882.
> 5 for 15, Australians *v*. Alfred Shaw's XI, 1882.
> 7 for 3, and 7 for 34, Australians *v*. An England XI, 1884.
> 13 for 123, Australians *v*. Players, 1884.
> 7 for 16, Australians *v*. Middlesex, 1884.
> 14 for 96, Australians *v*. Players, 1884.

13 for 85, Australians
   v. Cambridge University Past and Present, 1884.
15 for 36, Australians v. Oxford University, 1886.
7 for 19, Australians v. North of England, 1886.
15 for 81, Derbyshire v. Yorkshire, 1889.
9 for 56, and 5 for 58, Derbyshire v. Leicestershire, 1890.
8 for 74, M.C.C. v. Yorkshire, 1896.

Some of his averages in minor games were fantastic, such as these:

19 for 109, Australian team v. Fifteen of New South Wales.
17 for 125, Australians v. Eighteen of South Australia.
14 for 25, Australians v. Twenty-two of Southland (N.Z.).
15 for 41, Australians v. Wellington (N.Z.).
22 for 69, Australians v. Hawke's Bay (N.Z.).
19 for 31, Australians v. Eighteen of South Australia.
16 for 112, Australians v. Fifteen of Victoria.

In England he took nine wickets in 20 balls against Eighteen of Hastings in 1878, and in a match in 1880 he took twelve wickets in 18 balls. For Hampstead, after he went to live in England, he took all ten wickets in an innings against Marlow twice in successive years, for 20 runs in 1893 and for 14 runs in 1894. He was thirty-eight years of age when he began to play for that club, yet he took 951 wickets for seven and a half runs apiece. He also appeared for Derbyshire, where he lived as a director of the Star Tea Company, and also for the M.C.C., and even at the age of forty-three could win high praise from such a master as C. B. Fry.

This man possessed genius, and, as Neville Cardus put it, he brought bowling under the control of mind. He had a burning zeal, was a modern Saul 'breathing out threatenings and slaughter'. When he bowled he looked, as S. M. J. Woods wrote, 'all legs, arms and nose,' and 'he had more guile than any bowler I ever saw; a perfect follow-through, and he delivered every ball with the same action, so that it was hard to distinguish what ball was coming next'. Spofforth was also shrewd. He mostly bowled his deadly yorker on the off-stump, 'because the batsmen expect it on the leg-stump'. He flourished in days when wickets were smaller than now, and when the off-spinner had to pitch the ball on the line between wicket and wicket to get a l.b.w. decision. Pitches were doubtless a bit easier; more helpful to spin, but not so much different as to alter the view that Frederick Robert Spofforth, first of the moderns, has had few equals and probably no superior. He bequeathed to cricket a rich legacy.

from AUSTRALIAN BOWLERS *1953*

S. M. J. Woods

ALAN GIBSON

Samuel Moses Joshua Woods, for such were his prophetic names, was born in Sydney, Australia, in the year 1868. He came to England, to complete his education, in 1883. From then until his death at the age of 63, he made his home in the West Country, which he called 'the dearest in the world', and Somerset, particularly her sportsmen, came to think of him as one of her own. But he also remained very much an Australian, with the forthrightness, the zest for living of the early digger. I think the combination of these two influences was partly responsible for the richness and variety of the man, and is also the reason why from his contemporaries one gets so many differing impressions. Even his voice has been variously described as a high-pitched Australian twang, and a rolling West Country burr. The truth in that instance seems to have been that as life went on, more and more Somerset turns of phrase were overlaid on the original Sydneyside, sometimes with striking results.

Much of his character emerges in his reminiscences, a splendid, mixed-up collection of anecdote and history and opinion, often ungrammatical, often repetitive, but flavoured with a quality you will not often find in cricketers' books today, trimly compiled from a book of press-cuttings by a practised journalistic hand. Woods comes into the conversation whenever we start deploring, vainly but truthfully, the passing of the great characters from the game of cricket. Mr Denzil Batchelor has described modern cricket as a game played by civil servants against civil servants, for the amusement of civil servants. Averages are its god, and its prophet the statistician. There is a

minimum of statistics in Sammy Woods' book, and then he
frequently gets them wrong. (Of course he could easily have
looked them up, but clearly did not consider it worth the
trouble.) This alone shows how different our approach to the
game has become. One of his most famous remarks was that
draws were only any use for swimming in. Once he was
captain of the Gentlemen against the Players at Lord's, at a
time when it was the biggest match of the season, and a source
of intense rivalry. He set the Players 500 to win, and when
time was up they had tied the scores, with two wickets left,
Tom Hayward and J. T. Brown of Yorkshire getting most of
the runs. The umpires were about to take off the bails, when
Woods took the ball himself for an extra over. The Players
won. He was criticized, even in those days: but criticism had
about as much effect on him as a peashooter on the Great
Pyramid. One trembles to think what he would say of the
present-day situation, when a Test captain is expected to hold
a press conference after every match or be branded as stand-
offish and unco-operative.

It was at Cambridge University that Woods first made a
heavy impact on English cricket. He played four years against
Oxford and took 36 wickets. Cambridge won three of the
matches and the fourth was rained off. He was principally a
bowler then, very tall and very fast in an era which had high
standards for fast bowling. 'I always maintain,' he says 'it is
time enough to get runs when the ball is round your throat on a
little blue or pink ribbon.' When in due course, the ribbon
came along, so did the runs. He shared rooms at Cambridge
with his close friend Gregor MacGregor, also a Cambridge
captain and later an England wicket-keeper. The University
were once playing an eleven of almost international standard,
raised by C. I. Thornton. Woods and MacGregor invited
Thornton and about half a dozen of his team to breakfast. The
bill of fare was headed by draught beer and hot lobsters. The
visitors were horrified. So they were duly provided with coffee
and bacon and eggs, while Woods and MacGregor ate the

lobsters and drank the beer between them, after which they started cricket and Woods took all ten wickets in an innings.

Their rooms at Cambridge must have borne a strong resemblance to those which Sir Pelham Warner found on a visit, many years later, to two other distinguished Cambridge cricketers. When he sought pen and paper, there were none to be found in the place, and, as he reports, the only two books on the shelves were *Wisden's Cricketers' Almanack* and *Ruff's Guide to the Turf*. At any rate, Woods had been some terms at the University before some officious authority pointed out that he had still omitted to pass the entrance examination known as Little Go. The academic requirements were not onerous, but there was some doubt whether they were within the hero's capacity. A contemporary – that delightful writer who used the pseudonym 'A Country Vicar' – has described the awe and alarm with which the University viewed his solemn progress, in the majesty of academic dress, to the examination schools. What would happen at Lord's without the fast bowler? At the rugby match without the leader of the forwards? Fortunately the examiners were wise in their generation – or Sam had been misjudged – and when the results were published, Woods, S. M. J., was safely in the pass list. I cannot vouch for the story that he was asked only one question: the name of the first king of Israel. 'Saul,' he answered triumphantly, and then spoilt the effect by adding, as he was leaving the room, 'also called Paul.'

In 1888 the Australian cricketers were over here, and called on Woods for the three Test matches. Later he played for England, against South Africa, and played for England at Rugby football as well. But his cricketing associations after Cambridge days were chiefly with Somerset. He played for them for twenty years, and was captain for twelve or fourteen ('I can't remember which,' he explains). Somerset were given first-class status in 1891, and confirmed it with a famous victory over Surrey, then as recently the giants, at Taunton. He tells this story of the game's dramatic conclusion: 'Surrey batted well in the last innings, Maurice Read and Lohmann making a fine stand. I got them both out at five o'clock; we were to draw at half-past five. Five wickets to fall in half an hour. We got four more, and ten minutes to go when Sharpe joined Wood. I was going to bowl the last ball of the match when Wood said to me, "Keeps his end up well for a man with one eye, eh?" I said, "Which one?" "Left one." I bowled my first round-arm ball of my life, and hit his off-stump. Had I not had the information we wouldn't have won.' 'I must say,' he says, 'I consider this game made Somerset cricket. Our spectators went barmy, flung their hats in the air, and hit each other about.' Woods was captain of Somerset in their two famous victories over Yorkshire in the early 1900s, the only two matches Yorkshire lost in three seasons. In one of them Somerset were bowled out for 87, Yorkshire scored over 300, but Somerset still won by 279 runs after one of the most remarkable transformations ever seen in a game.

King Richard I is said to have taken more pride in his dentistry than his crusading. I suspect Sammy Woods was no more pleased by a good haul of wickets than an opportunity to demonstrate his wide and assorted, if amateur, medical knowledge. An emergency on the field never found him wanting. He sadly describes his failure to assist J. T. Brown, who had put his shoulder out in bowling. 'I took off my boot,' he says, 'and tried to put it in at once, but couldn't manage it, although I had someone to sit on his head and others to hold him down. He was very sweaty from bowling, I couldn't get a firm grip of his arm, so he had to go to hospital and have it done. I am certain to this day that had he kept still it would have saved a lot of trouble. Poor fellow, I don't think he ever bowled again.' Bathing at Sydney on a visit home, he came to the aid of a friend of his, whom he describes as a 'little parson', and who had 'nearly severed his big toe with an oyster shell. . . . I took a plug of tobacco out of his mouth which he had been chewing, stuck it in the cut and tied his handkerchief round it. "It'll soon be all right, I think" '. His only comment on the efficacy of the cure is that 'he didn't walk for a week'. The same day, when they were leaving for home, one of the horses wouldn't start. Sam stuck a quid of tobacco in the horse's ear, or so he says, and off he went at once. 'Wonderful thing, tobacco!' he concludes. His remedy for cramp in the legs was to rub them with whisky; though it is said that Brockwell, the famous Surrey professional, refused this treatment on conscientious grounds: and then revolutionized medical science by making a swift recovery after applying the healing fluid internally. Squire Notley of Coombe Sydenham taught Woods to relieve lumbago by carrying a new potato about with him. On one occasion – they were out beagling – the Squire completed the cure by going to a hollow tree, producing some bottles from it, and offering a choice of whisky, brandy, or gin. I am sure this must have been the inspiration for a practice of Sam's own, which he does not mention in his book, but which is usually the first thing anybody in Taunton or Bridgwater will tell you about him. When nothing more active was required of him (and he played most games: county caps at soccer and cricket and bowls, among other things, to say nothing of mixed hockey, where he sustained one of his few serious injuries, and playing the Hussars at polo in South Africa – four mounted Hussars against six cricketers on foot, and the cricketers won, and there was a hundred pounds on the match) – when, as I say, nothing more active was required of him, he would take long walks over the Quantock Hills accompanied by one of his friends. After the friend had reached a fair state of exhaustion, and civilization was miles away, Sam would ask: 'What would you say to a bottle of sparkling Somerset ale?' This usually produced an unkind reply, at which Sam would go to a hedge, or a burrow, or a hollow tree, and produce the bottles. He had these caches dotted all over the Quantocks.

His latter years in Somerset must have been among his happiest, though the steady onset of arthritis crippled that magnificent physique, a heavy burden for him he rarely showed. He went on playing local cricket as long as he could.

When he could no longer bowl over-arm, he bowled lobs. Once he took ten wickets in an innings with them, and was delighted with a headline in a local paper, presumably not the work of an eye-witness, 'S. M. J. Woods returns to form'. He had a lot of fun with what he called his 'Farmers' Eleven'. 'One day,' he says, 'I had three farmers, all about 6 feet 3 inches, playing for me. Just before the game started three white ducks crossed the wicket. I remarked to them it was a bad omen. They didn't understand why until, I having put them in 1, 2 and 3, they all got bowled first ball. I had the ducks killed and placed one in each of their bags. As they didn't have cricket bags but hand bags, I hope they found them that evening or next morning. I never inquired.' Such matches would end with dinner and a sing-song. Woods was always much in demand to sing at village concerts. He had been a singer since his Cambridge days, when on one occasion he caused a sensation by getting the words mixed up in the ballad of 'The Soldier's Grave', with the result that the dove settled, not on the green sward, but on the speckled bellied cook. How he came to make the particular mistake I cannot imagine, but Mr G. L. Jessop vouches for the story. He was a cornet player as well. When he was a boy in Australia he and two of his brothers all learnt to play. 'We practised in the stables about three hundred yards away from the house, and after about three months we were all playing "Killarney". One night father said, "Now, boys, I hear you can play a tune. Take the boat and row out half a mile and the one who plays it best will have a sovereign." I won it. Perhaps I played loudest.' But his zeal for the arts did not extend to literature. It is said, no doubt with some exaggeration, that he was well on in life when someone persuaded him to read a novel for the first time. It was *Oliver Twist*. He was enchanted with it, and thereafter always carried his copy about with him.

He was a great patriot, as men from the empire who settle in this country often are. Although well over-age, he managed to serve in the First World War, and although he never got into

I W.G.

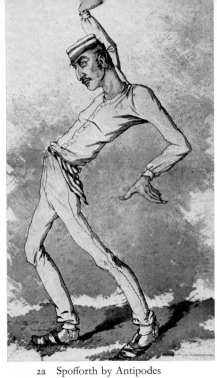

2a Spofforth by Antipodes

2c Spofforth by Spy

2b Woods by Stuff

2d Spooner by Chevallier-Taylor

action he had a spell at Khartoum and some hair-raising experiences on a shooting expedition up the Nile. A few years before that he had met some German naval officers at Weymouth. The Germans, after drinking to 'The day we fight England' were rash enough to observe that 'There is one thing the English cannot do: drink'. 'To cut a long story short,' says Sam, 'about four-thirty in the morning it took the landlord, the boots, a policeman and myself to get these gentlemen into their boat safely.'

Yes, he loved England, and he loved life. He died too young, reminding one irresistibly of Neville Cardus's comment that such men ought never to grow old, but go on playing the game they adorn until they are sick and tired of it. Above all, he loved the West Country, and I never see the line of the Quantocks without thinking of him. There, surely, along with the bottles of beer, his heart lies buried. He says, in one of those telling phrases which simple men can often hit off so much better than the professional writers: 'I have been in some parts of the world, but better scenery I have never seen. . . . From the top one can look across the Bristol Channel valley, and on the other side you see the Brendon Hills, Exmoor, and the lovely Minehead valley. In each valley we grow the best wheat and barley in the world; and in each valley live the best sportsmen in the west.'

from PLAYFAIR CRICKET MONTHLY *August 1964*

C. B. Fry

DENZIL BATCHELOR

If there is anyone on earth so benighted as to need a pen-picture of C. B. Fry, I suppose we could best present him with an impressionist sketch of an eagle in a monocle. He looks like an eagle. More often than not he behaves like an eagle. I some-times find myself fancying that he sports his monocle to make him look more like an eagle than the bird itself has any chance of looking. More imperious, more loftily aloof. Such is the outer likeness of the man – and it is plenty deceiving.

But then everything about the great Charles Burgess Fry is deceptive: his public reputation most of all. If you ask the best-informed man you know to tell you all about C. B. Fry, you must submit to be assured that this magnifico was once upon a time Captain of England at cricket, an international Association football full back, and a Rugby footballer who would have played for Oxford and in an English trial but for an injury a few weeks before the Varsity match. He will add that in his spare time Fry held the world's long jump record and repre-sented Oxford in the high jump and the 100 yards sprint. You will not be able to interrupt him before he starts theorizing about this athletic genius being a made and not a natural cricketer, and about having learned his batsmanship from associating with Ranjitsinhji and from practising strokes in front of his bedroom mirror.

Well, the list of athletic achievements is accurate, if not quite exhaustive. It doesn't mention that, at over sixty-five, he thought he would try his hand at golf and persuaded a local professional near Southampton to teach him; until, after a couple of rounds, the pro got discouraged at being outdriven at every hole and resigned his job. It doesn't mention, either, that at the same age Fry shot clay pigeons for the first time, and broke the heart of his local county champion.

But even so, the picture drawn by the well-informed friend is seriously inaccurate and sadly out of perspective. It depicts the subject as – heaven help us! – no better than a playboy. It doesn't mention any of the things Fry prides himself on having done in his *Life Worth Living*. It doesn't mention his deep classical scholarship. Did he not beat Lord Birkenhead in an open competition at Wadham, and achieve the most brilliant of Firsts in Honours Mods before he turned his attention to more serious affairs?

It doesn't mention his life-work. For the past forty years, with the help of his late wife – that great lady who was the model for one of G. F. Watts' most famous pictures – he has run a naval training ship at Hamble, Southampton. *Mercury* is one of the most famous and successful training ships in Britain, and has taught thousands of boys from public schools, modest homes, and slums, the craft that has stood them in good stead on lower and upper decks and qualified them for the bridge of tramps, merchant liners, or His Majesty's men-of-war. On the sporting side, that training ship produced Reggie Sinfield. In the first Test Match, when Bradman's men were last over here [in 1938], Reggie bowled the mighty Don hook, line and sinker. I had the luck to be sitting next to Charles at the time, and have not forgotten the look on his face.

But even the training ship has been only a part of that very full life. Fry is a great journalist. He was the first of the famous sportsmen to sign his name to his work in the *Daily Express*, in its very early days. Later, for many years, he edited his own magazine, in which all-round periodical all the experts from E. V. Lucas to P. G. Wodehouse, from Ralph Hodgson to Santos Dumont, used to write on their own subjects – or, if the editor could prevail upon them, on each others'.

Then there was Charles Fry's connexion with the League of Nations. He represented the Native States at Geneva for

several years, and made such a success of the job that an
Albanian delegate, a bishop with a beard like W.G.'s, called on
him one morning, drank several glasses of whisky, and in
perfect solemnity offered him the crown of his country, then,
as so often, going begging.

There are other sides to Fry as well. He is a bit of a dab at
astronomy and a bobby-dazzler on the Higher Mathematics.
He has the harmless hobby of translating hymns into Greek
poetry, or Latin verse into Greek verse. He is exceedingly
proud of the number of poets he has among his friends; but
even prouder of the fact that he recently had a poem (only in
English, it is true) in *The Times*.

With all his achievements, there are gorgeous gaps which are
quite as entertaining as the peaks. He once asked me, to satisfy
some listener to his performance on the Brains Trust, to give
him a list of the one hundred best books in English. Having
time on my hands – I was in the War Office just then – I compiled a very obvious, conventional list. He told me he had read
one of my hundred – *Pickwick Papers*. He had not enjoyed it. I
suspect he has read fewer Shakespeare plays than you would
need for the London Matriculation, though I once heard him
discuss with deep knowledge a sixteenth-century authority on
the philosophy of government whom Shakespeare may perhaps have been parodying in Polonius. (When it was sceptically
pointed out that only two copies of this author's work were
known to exist in England, Fry at once replied scornfully: 'Of
course. I read the one in the Bodleian'.

There are, it will be seen, plenty of achievements, but the
man at the back of them, behind the monocle, beneath the
laurel wreath, is more interesting even than his deeds. His
salient quality, as I see it, is his loyalty. If he likes you, he never
forgets you, and will not allow anyone else to forget or under-
estimate you either. I know more than one young writer who
has been beckoned out of obscurity into the limelight because
Fry (whom it will take all the King's horses to persuade to
write another book) has written enough letters to fill a volume

advancing their merits to all the editors he knows, and many more he does not know.

It is always possible that he might not like you. Here, however, you will be lucky, for you will never suspect as much. Fry is the only man of my acquaintance whom I have never heard say a biting, cruel thing about anybody. I have, of course, known him to denounce the whole world, cry down civilization and everyone in it, but never an unkind word against Tom Smith or Harry Jones. The nearest I have got to hearing him sound unenthusiastic is when he talks, with a slight drawl in his voice, about, say, some sot of a hack poetaster as 'a parsley-crowned Olympian only partly nurtured on the bubbly of the Pierean spring'. With the eyeglass up as he says it, I can vouch for that comment as a mild mark of disapproval.

A man like that might have won any of the glittering prizes; but life was too much of a lark for him to bother. Ambitions were too easily fulfilled: the only one of his known to me which remains unsatisfied is his wish to crash Hollywood as an English gentleman of the Grand Old School. His old friend Aubrey Smith had better look out. After all, Fry is only seventy-four years young, full of beans and rearing to go.

I believe myself this film ambition is conceived to help him escape from being labelled as a cricketer, for search the records as leniently as you can, it is the inescapable fact that Fry once upon a time played a certain amount of cricket. It is all very well pointing out that just as Mr Trygve Lie was once a well-known high jumper, so Charles Fry was once a Deputy Delegate to the League of Nations. Cricket, like cheerfulness, will keep breaking in, and we had better accept the fact and make the best we can of it.

The best, as I see it, is that Fry, every schoolboy's hero in his day, had every schoolboy hero's fortune when it came to captaining teams in matches of the first importance. He is not generally spoken of as the immortal captain of his day. That niche is reserved for Archie MacLaren, who captained England in four series of Test Matches, and lost all of them. Charles Fry, captain of Oxford against Cambridge, the Gentlemen at Lord's, and England against both Australia and South Africa, never lost one of these matches.

In the light of this record his own theories of captaincy are worth recalling. Assuming that cricketers know their own side's merits and the general strength and weakness of their opponents, and, roughly speaking, make good use of this knowledge, he believes that great sides are apt to produce great captains, and not the other way about. Success is the yardstick by which you must judge your great captain, and, with this in his hand, Fry generally lights on F. S. Jackson and Bradman when casting around in his mind for great leaders within the ambit of his experience.

'Jacker' clearly impressed him. There was a coolness and apparent casualness of execution which commanded his admiration. If things were going wrong and the enemy were slowly amassing a mountainous score, 'Jacker' would twirl his moustache, mutter, 'How about a change?' and toss the ball to the first idle bowler his eye happened to fall upon. And down would go a wicket. I think Fry admired the twirling of that cavalier moustache as much as anything else in 'Jacker's' strategy. It was the outward and visible sign of the Grand Manner which lent a grace and a gloss to the physical fine art.

It is strange that the art of captaincy should never really launch Fry on a flood of aphorisms. I fancy it is because he feels it is a matter of instinct, and you can't implant a gift of this description in a man with a surgical operation. Batting is another story – so is bowling. You may forget as many of C. B. Fry's centuries as you like; you may greet him, as he prefers to be greeted by strangers, with the assurance that you saw him once before; in a match in 1902 making 0 in the first innings and 2 in the second; but if you value his respect, you will not forget that he was once a formidable fast bowler. He was good enough to have taken five wickets in an innings against the Players at the Oval, and I believe he would be continuing as a fast bowler yet if Jim Phillips had not no-balled him for throwing. That, Fry darkly believes, was because Jim Phillips, an ambitious Australian who liked to be noticed conning a learned textbook on mining engineering, was anxious to earn a reputation as a strong-armed umpire. Fry did not throw, and to prove it he once upon a time had his arm strapped in a splint with the shirt-sleeves buttoned over it. In these conditions he proposed to bowl for Sussex and lure Jim Phillips to make a fool of himself by 'calling' him when the crowd was at its largest – to witness the stripping of his sleeve and the simultaneous exposure of the unbroken splint and the umpire. But Billy Murdoch got cold feet, and would not permit the exhibition.

from THE GAME GOES ON *1947*

K. S. Ranjitsinhji

K. S. DULEEPSINHJI

One of my greatest disappointments is that I never saw him play.

Owing him a greater debt than cricket owes to Ranji, I can say that he brought happiness to all who were near him. (All his nephews and nieces were educated by him and we all owe everything to him, whether one of us is today a maharaja or the secretary of a club). His palace in Jamnagar and his houses in England and Ireland were also our homes, and many Jamnagar boys brought up by him in England received the same allowances as we did, and Jamnagar House at Staines was their home. He was kind and generous to a fault, but at the same time strict; he could always forgive his greatest enemy and said that life was more pleasing if one only looked at the better side of a man's character.

He had an interest in nearly everything in life. But it was cricket which was his greatest hobby and passion. He could have been good at tennis, but he knew he could only play one of the two games as the season for both is the same.

I tried often to get him to talk about his own cricket, but failed. I never heard him say that he had done this or that. He would never talk about himself, but would change the subject, and talk about Fry, MacLaren and others of his time. The only innings of his he spoke about to me was a 'duck' in a Gentlemen *v.* Players match. He said he received nine balls and played a good shot off each of them, but in each case brilliant fielding prevented what should have been a boundary. He was brilliantly caught off the ninth ball, which he said, he had played correctly.

Not many people realize that Ranji left a greater imprint on cricket than anybody else. Before him, there were players here and there who had played back as a pure and simple defensive stroke, but on the whole, it was a forward game played then. It was Ranji who made the back-stroke an attacking stroke. The idea of batting up to then was that the ball must travel back more or less in the same direction from which it came to the bat. He changed this by helping the ball in the same direction, more or less, by slightly deflecting it. This was the great difference between him and others before him. He used the forward stroke for attack and back play for both attack and defence.

These are the two great changes he gave to the period which is known as the 'Golden Age of Cricket'. I think it might have been called so because attack and defence were then used in the right proportions.

If my uncle had not lost one eye, I might at least have seen him play in his later days. On one occasion, Dr Heasman, an old Sussex cricketer and a great friend of our family, and I went to dine with some friends in Eastbourne. There a well-known judge told us a story of the greatest self-control he had ever heard of. He began by telling how, at a shoot, the host was accidentally shot by the man in the next butt, and how he quickly went to a butt where a doctor friend was shooting and told him what had happened. They walked five miles before they reached their ponies and during the walk the only remark the host made was 'I am sorry for the man who shot me'. He knew all along the walk that one eye had gone for good. While the judge was telling this story, Dr Heasman kept looking at me and when the tale was told, he said, 'I am the doctor of that story and Duleep is the nephew of the host'. I know that, as soon as his eye was out and he was well enough to shoot again, uncle invited the man who had accidentally caused the terrible damage.

There is no doubt that any success I have enjoyed at cricket is largely due to my uncle. He coached me on a few occasions

2*

when I was a small boy and then did not see me till I was seventeen. At the end of that school match at Lord's, he said to me, 'God has given you a gift He gives to few. If you want to play cricket I will give you every help you need, but you will have to remember that when you are playing, you are not playing for yourself but for your country. Thousands of English people will be watching you play and millions reading the papers. To them you will be representing India.' He also added, 'I don't want you to do anything you will be ashamed of later and do harm to your country. Remember that God has given you a gift which you can use for the benefit of India.'

We agreed that I should play till I was thirty and then return to India for whatever work he gave me. Well, man proposes and God disposes, and before I was thirty I had to stop playing, and a year later uncle died while I was lying in a sanatorium in Switzerland. His last message to me was, 'You must look after yourself as I shall not always be here to do so.'

I think the first time I really made Uncle Ranji happy was when I got my blue. He had gone to Paris and from there came a cable of about twenty pages with all the advice, encouragement and congratulations in the world; also a fat cheque. So many Indians had failed to get a blue that Ranji had begun to give up hope of another ever achieving the distinction, and it must have been a pleasant surprise when opening a paper in Paris he found that after a gap of thirty-two years the second Indian had got a blue, and his nephew at that.

Uncle had a lot of humour, and he once sent me a telegram asking me to give up cricket and take to tennis and challenge Betty Nuttall, the then female star. On another occasion, he sent me a cable from a ship asking, 'What was the matter with the other eight?' I had made 92 against the Australians. Another time, when a Cambridge paper headlined my being fined for not having a light to my cycle, he telegraphed, 'Don't we get enough publicity without your having to get this kind?'

Ranji was not easily satisfied, and on only three occasions said or wrote 'Well played'. The first was when I got my blue.

The second when after a year in a sanatorium, I was fighting to get back my form. The third was my first Test at Lord's.

Ranji was the most unselfish man in the world. His character was as beautiful as his batting must have been. I believe that a man's character may be seen in his batting. He radiated happiness and laughter around him. My friends in England, if they see this little contribution, will smile . . . for they have heard me always talk about 'Uncle this' and 'Uncle that'. I dare say that every nephew can tell his friends the sort of stories I have told about my uncle. But how many nephews can boast of such a man as 'My Uncle Ranji'?

from DULEEP: THE MAN AND HIS GAME *1963*

R. H. *Spooner*

NEVILLE CARDUS

R. H. Spooner was one of the most beautiful of stroke-players cricket has ever known. *Wisden* in 1905 wrote of him: 'In point of style there are few batsmen of the present day to compare with him. Not even L. C. H. Palairet himself is better worth looking at. Style in batting is not thought so much of now as it was years ago, but it certainly makes for enjoyment. . . .' Today it is seldom that style is mentioned at all in connection with any cricketer; and perhaps only the Rev. David Sheppard of the contemporaries would survive comparison for ease and handsomeness of stroke were he batting with Spooner at the other end. A certain muscularity or crabbed effort occasionally dims the lustre of P. B. H. May at the wicket.

Spooner of course played in a period when no bowler worth his salt dreamed of pitching the ball defensively on or outside the leg stump, to a field set around the batsman's hind parts. Some few years ago Spooner, then a septuagenarian, was watching a match at Lord's. 'Against this sort of bowling I would have been no good,' he said, 'it is impossible to drive past cover to bowling aimed at the leg stump and swinging mostly outside.' I reminded him that he had scored often through George Hirst's leg trap, from fast left-handed in-swingers. But, he argued, in those days not many bowlers exploited swing – for the simple reason that only one ball was used in the longest innings. 'The seam could soon be flattened,' Spooner added, 'and they were not sewn so pronouncedly, not as big, as they are now.'

Spooner learned to bat against an attack directed mostly to the offside, or on the wicket. Bowlers of his day would apologize to their captains if they sent a ball down the leg side. For Ranjitsinhji's glance, no leg trap was set. Bowlers encouraged him to indulge the stroke; it was, they thought, risky, and the only conceivable way of getting him out – possibly l.b.w. Merely defensive leg stuff, common enough today, bowled to a close leg-side field, might have stopped 'Ranji' from performing his famous glance, but it wouldn't have got him out. Likewise, the same inglorious kind of attack must surely have frustrated Spooner's incomparable cover drive, but it wouldn't have got him out either. And even today not all bowling is inswing or defensive leg theory. Against the average attack of 1959 Spooner would, I am sure, have scored ample runs, good to watch.

It has been argued that Spooner was a fast wicket batsman, dependent on the ball that came on to his bat unambiguously. As a fact, Spooner was one of the first cricketers to find the answer to the 'googly'. . . . In 1912 at Lord's Spooner scored 119 for England *v.* South Africa, and the attack included Faulkner, Pegler, and Schwarz, each a master of leg and 'googly' spin. He was at the wicket three hours and, according to *Wisden*, the great feature of his innings was his 'forcing back play'. There is a notion nowadays that the 'stylists' of old all pushed forward, left elbow up, trusting to a straight ball. Spooner's elegance, his apparently effortless curves and thrusts deceived many a lazy fieldsman, some of whom suffered painfully bruised palms at the end of a century by Spooner.

He could drive the fastest bowling straight; I once saw Hitch of Surrey – as fast as Statham, to say the least – twice leap in the air in one over to save his shins from returned straight drives by Spooner, made off the back foot, the power generated from a lovely shoulder propulsion, and wrists flexible as fine steel. If he ever was guilty of a crude stroke I never saw it – and I saw him play over a period of many years. He always embodied the ideal public school batsman, slender, youthful, good looking in a sharp-featured way, and a tuft of hair sticking up at the back of his head was imitated by hundreds of hero-worshipping Lancashire boys of round about 1905-12. He opened the Lancashire innings with A. C. MacLaren; and J. T. Tyldesley came in first wicket down. No county's innings has begun with so superb a mingling as that of grace, majesty, and brilliance.

At Liverpool in 1903 MacLaren and Spooner scored 368 for Lancashire's first wicket against Gloucestershire; the rate of scoring was 80 an hour at least. Against Yorkshire at Old Trafford in 1910 Spooner amassed 200 not out, but amassed is a vile word to use about batsmanship that changed Old Trafford's turf into textures of silk or gold.

He was one of the most remarkable of all cricketers while still a boy at Marlborough. He ranks with such youthful geniuses as A. G. Steel, R. A. H. Mitchell, C. L. Townsend, J. N. Crawford, Peter May – all of whom could in their teens have worn the England colours – Crawford in fact did win them before he was twenty. In 1899 Spooner, not yet nineteen, made his first appearance for Lancashire at Lord's *v*. Middlesex. He scored 44, b Trott, and 83, c Ford b Trott. Before the match started, J. T. Tyldesley, kindest of professional players, took the youngster aside and warned him against Trott's slow ball. 'He hides it artfully, so watch out.'

Spooner went in first, and was round about 20 when Tyldesley came in, first wicket down and Tyldesley succumbed to Trott at once, clean bowled, deceived by the slow ball. Next innings Tyldesley again spoke warningly of Trott to Spooner. 'You did well yesterday, sonny, but don't take Albert Trott for granted. Look out again for his slow one.' And next innings, while the boy was getting his 83, Tyldesley was clean bowled by Trott for none, deceived once more by the 'slow one' he had twice warned the novice against.

Not the half is told about Spooner by a record of the runs he scored in his career or by his average. As well might we add up all the notes written down by Mozart and leave it at that. He did not play regularly through many seasons; he couldn't afford to do so. After his tremendously promising debut for Lan-

cashire he served in the Boer War. In his period only Test
matches against Australia really counted; and only South
Africa made pretensions to the levels occupied by England
and Australia. We must remember, too, in assessing Spooner's
achievements, that every one of the few Test matches he was
able to play in was limited to three days.

In his first innings for England, in his twenty-fifth year, at
Old Trafford, in 1905, he scored 52, then in the succeeding
game at the Oval, Cotter bowled him first innings for 0, with
a ball so fast that he hardly saw it in a bad light against the
Pavilion; next innings he dazzled the Oval with 79 in not
much more than an hour and a quarter. His next Test matches
were England *v*. Australia in 1909 at Manchester and the Oval,
where his contributions in runs amounted to 25, 58, 13, and 3.
In the Triangular games of 1912 he played six innings totalling
251, average 31.37, including a century against South Africa.

In 1920 he was invited by the M.C.C. to captain the England
team for Australia but was unable, because of need to earn his
living, to accept. Needless to say, he was an adornment to
every Gentlemen *v*. Players match in which he took part. His
114 in this engagement at Lord's in 1906 was talked of for years
by every connoisseur who saw it. 'Spooner played one of the
finest innings of his life,' stated *Wisden* (writing for posterity),
'Better batting was not seen at Lord's all the season. Powerful
on-driving and very skilful play on the leg side were the
features of his innings.'

Spooner was one of the cricketers who, when I was a boy,
made me fall in love with the game. I think of him now with
gratitude. The delight of his cricket went into my mind to stay
there, with all the delights life has given me. He was, at cover-
point, as lovely a sight as when he was doing honour to the
good willow of his bat.

from THE GUARDIAN *3–10–1961*

S. F. Barnes

IAN PEEBLES

On August 21, 1930 the rain fell drearily on the Oval. It was a depressing scene for the England side and its supporters as our position was that, with Jack Hobbs out for the last time in a Test Match, we still wanted 266 to avoid an innings defeat by Australia. Not a very promising start to the day, but as things turned out it proved to be one of the great ones of my life.

It did so because Lady Warner, with whom I was sitting at the time, suddenly had an inspiration. I was staying with Sir Pelham and Lady Warner for the match, and when it looked like 'no play to-day' we naturally started to think of cinemas. She was looking through the paper when her eye fell on the score of M.C.C. *v*. Wales at Lord's and paused.

'Never mind about the cinema,' she said. 'Come up to Lord's, and I will introduce you to Syd Barnes.'

In the game of cricket it has always been customary to accord more adulation to batsmen than to bowlers. It is also intriguing, as in most things in life, to speculate on the greatest ever, acknowledging, of course, that any verdict must be founded on pure supposition. There are at least half a dozen batsmen who have been protagonists for this title – Grace, Trumper, Bradman, Ranji, Macartney, and Hobbs, to name such a number.

In the case of bowlers there is no such dissension. I am willing to bet if you made a census of competent opinion on who is the greatest bowler of the last century, over ninety per cent would unhesitatingly reply, 'Barnes'. As late as 1929, when he had reached the age of fifty-seven, the South African team, having suffered enjoyably at his hands, were agreed he was still the best in England.

Barnes was a pioneer, just as W.G. and Bosanquet, with the difference that, although he must have attracted many imitators, he has not yet found a successor. He started his career as a fast bowler of beautiful action if no other outstanding merit, but characteristically he very soon discovered exactly what he wanted to achieve and started working towards it.

With what curiosity must he regard the modern school, whose almost universal tendency is to make the ball come *in* to the batsman. For him the wheel must have turned full circle. When he started, as a fast bowler for Derbyshire, all were aware that the most dangerous ball was that which went away from the bat, yet the prevailing cult was the break-back, erroneously called 'body spin', in the case of the fast bowler and the off-break in the medium-paced classes. The left-hander and the slow leg-break bowler alone made the ball break away, and, the out-swinger being a very occasional phenomenon, no bowler of pace made the ball run towards the slips.

Barnes, having pondered these factors, came to the conclusion that this could only be achieved at any real speed by bowling the leg-break in the same manner as the off-break; that is without the rotation of the bent wrist. Endowed with every physical requirement, he set about delivering the leg-break at quick-medium pace with the wrist straight and the palm of the hand towards the batsman. The advantages of this mode are obvious, but Barnes spent some years experimenting before, as he says, it came to him quite suddenly. It was rather as though he had penetrated the sound barrier, as from then on he encountered no further difficulties, the question then resolving itself into one of refinement and application.

This technique must not be confused with that of the modern cutter, which is to flip the fingers over the surface of the ball and impart enough spin to give the ball a little bias in advantageous conditions. Barnes gripped the ball firmly between first and third fingers and *spun* it. Possibly cutters have produced as good a delivery on occasions, but for consistent effect on all surfaces his method has never been equalled. The leg-break was the keystone of the attack, but it was, of course, combined with every refinement of flight, change of pace, life, and accuracy.

There came at a later date the swerver, who in given conditions could produce somewhat similar results. The swerver should never be under-rated, as in his greatness, exemplified by Maurice Tate, he could produce the unplayable ball and that with disconcerting frequency. In the 1930s there were many very capable exponents, but now it seems that the out-swerver has largely disappeared, and the in-swing and off-break bowlers are all-powerful.

Even the best swerver, however, is dependent on a number of elements beyond his control, such as the state of the ball, the humidity of the atmosphere, and the greenness of the pitch. He cannot therefore produce his effects so consistently as the man who achieves them purely by his own manipulations. Barnes's spin was equally potent with an old ball in any weather.

It is natural that one who could achieve such power from a theoretical start would exploit it with an unusual intelligence. Aubrey Faulkner, who presented as sound a defence as any batsman, had an illustrative tale of the craft and resource that lay behind those superb mechanics. Like his team mates Aubrey had a pretty rough passage with Barnes on the wet wickets of 1912, but at the Oval Test Match he became entrenched. At the end of an hour he had made no more than 10, but, as the Army says, 'time spent in reconnaissance is seldom wasted', and he reckoned he had seen the whole bag of tricks. Great was his astonishment when he received a rank long-hop. Greater was his consternation when he picked up the bat to give full rein to his favourite hook and saw his middle stump shoot out of the ground. It had been a long-hop all right, but just about twice as quick as anything before it.

It was apropos of this period of Barnes's career that I heard the sincerest compliment a rival genius could accord him. Many years ago a dinner party took place at Oxford. The hosts were Pat Kingsley, who captained the Varsity side that year, the Nawab of Pataudi, and myself. The guests were Charlie Macartney, Bert Oldfield, and Clarrie Grimmett. In that company it could hardly have been otherwise than an enthralling evening, and as it wore on the talk, surprisingly enough, turned to cricket and thence to Syd Barnes. He was at that time, to me, a legendary figure whom I had never seen nor met, and I asked Charlie Macartney just how good he was. The 'Governor General' wrinkled his brow and paused in careful thought before replying without trace of affectation.

He said, 'I'll tell you how good he was. In 1912 as I went out to bat I told the chaps I was going to hit this Barnes for six.' He paused again to give full weight to the point before adding, 'I had to wait until I was 68 before I did.'

We arrived to find Barnes sitting by himself gazing reflectively at the wet green turf at Lord's. Perhaps over the years he saw Victor Trumper look round the field for a gap in the covers. Perhaps he was brooding on Charlie Macartney's audacity. On seeing Lady Warner he smiled in friendly fashion and, when I was introduced, greeted me cordially. Lady Warner, apart from being a notable authority on cricket, is a lady of great wisdom, so having provided a cricket ball, she sent us off to the long bar.

The next hour I remember as one of the most entertaining I have ever spent. It was to be expected that one who had raised a fascinating craft to the level of a real art would be worth hearing on his subject. As he talked he demonstrated, wrapping the ball in that wonderfully powerful supple hand, snapping it out and manipulating it like a juggler. At the end of a wonderfully lucid exposition I knew, as any bonehead would, exactly what I wanted to bowl and just how it was done. Even with all the 'know-how' so completely and thoroughly revealed, the execution was, of course, a very different matter. So different that no one else has so far succeeded in implementing it.

The morning had passed very rapidly, and it was soon time to return to the Oval for lunch. No doubt I was much elated and talked a great deal about the meeting, and no doubt was a good deal barracked, by the rest of the team. At any rate the news got around, and this led to a rather annoying sequel, as some enterprising journalist got hold of the story, and the next day in his paper there appeared an article headed 'Barnes tells young bowler how to get Bradman out'. As the writer had no idea of what we had discussed, he made it up as he went along and the whole impression was that Barnes had spoken very handsomely of his own powers. Now he is a man who does not welcome publicity and is certainly not one to boast, so that he was somewhat displeased.

The first intimation I had of this unwelcome account of our interview was when he rang Sir Pelham up next morning in some irritation. As no one else had been present, he could only conclude that the material of the article had been based on my account given to the writer. However, Sir Pelham assured him that this was not so, and opined that the author had merely concocted the story on the information that I had been to Lord's. Barnes readily accepted this explanation, and was very gracious, considering the false position into which his kindness had led him. I was mortified at this unhappy ending to a meeting I had so greatly appreciated but Sir Pelham said that all was well and I had been completely absolved.

It was eight years later that we met again, on the exact spot where we had parted on that rainy morning. I re-introduced myself and prevailed upon him to come and have a drink at the box I had been lucky enough to draw for the particular match in progress, which happened to be England *v.* Australia. He was representing a West Country newspaper, and during the course of conversation I discovered he had made no plans for the week-end. I asked him how he would like to attend a real cricket match in which I was playing on the Sunday, explaining that it happened to be between the firm by which I was employed and the Bar Tenders Guild. He said he would be delighted, and forthwith volunteered to umpire.

The following day we had a very good lunch before we started, followed by a number of speeches, the best of which was delivered by our umpire. We fielded first, and the play, if not up to Test Match standards, was keen and whole-hearted. Barnes not only was an object-lesson in the discharge of his duties but a model for any guest artist, for it is not always easy for the celebrity in such circumstances to avoid the pitfalls of condescension or flippancy. He afforded the players the very real courtesy of receiving their efforts as a serious matter demanding his undivided attention. No recruit to the first-class list ever exercised greater care than he did on that occasion.

When between the fall of wickets he was able to relax, I seized the golden opportunity and, pressing the ball into his hand, got the wicket-keeper to stand guard at the farther end. He was then sixty-seven years old, arrayed in umpire's coat and Homburg hat, without a spike in his shoes. He ran two or three springy paces, and his sleeve brushed the brim of his hat as his arm came over in a beautiful smooth arc, ending in a supple flip of the wrist. It was the only time I ever saw him bowl, but I had a glimpse of the bowler's promised land.

We have met again at Manchester in the last two seasons, and although I shall not again see him bowl, half an hour's conversation with a cricket ball to hand is worth any day's play to me. Our last meeting was in the young professional's room at Old Trafford, and as the master talked, the young hopefuls of Lancashire ceased to watch the match and gazed at the subtle play of those still dominating fingers. I urged them to make the most of it, saying they were seeing something they would probably never again meet in their chosen profession. They will indeed be fortunate if they ever see another Syd Barnes – on either side.

P.S. I have but one fear in publishing these remarks. As I have said, the subject is not a man who seeks or welcomes publicity, and I may well receive a severe reprimand. If I do it will be in the most perfect copperplate that any cricketer has ever written, at least in our time.

from TALKING OF CRICKET *1955*

P. F. Warner

A. A. THOMSON

The 'sacred turf' to him was no hackneyed phrase; it was hallowed ground. He called Lord's the cathedral of cricket and he meant it. He knew every blade of grass there and he was never happy if away from St John's Wood for long. If ever, in later years, he was taken out for a drive in the summer, the journey, whatever its projected destination, would somehow finish up at Lord's. On one of the rare occasions when he was prevailed on to tear himself away he was taken by friends to admire the beauties, architectural and sacred, of a charming little French church. Standing by the font, he suddenly turned and stepped out firmly towards the chancel. Then he stopped.

'Just as I thought,' he said with his pleasant smile. 'Twenty-two yards exactly.'

His books, of which he wrote nearly a score, were, like his cricket, an integral part of himself. He did not attain the glittering prose of a Cardus any more than in batting he would have claimed the artistic perfection of a Trumper or a Hobbs, but it is a poor cricket library from which one of Warner's major works is missing. Like his batting, his style is graceful without ornament and dignified without heaviness; it succeeds perfectly in painting on a broad canvas the cricket scene of his choice. His history of *Lord's* and his autobiography *Long Innings* are minor classics of their kind; so also are *Gentlemen v. Players*, a monument of cricket scholarship on a series that will never be played again, and an especial favourite of mine, *How We Recovered the Ashes*, the modestly penned record of his victorious tour of 1903-4. Like all Warner's books it tells a story clearly with kindly humour and quietly shrewd judgment.

It also shows, indirectly and subconsciously, how to lead a side to victory in a contest of giants.

His character was that of a gentleman in the ideal sense of the word. (If the term seems an anachronism in the present age, so much the worse for the present age.) He and his old friend George Herbert Hirst, who died in 1954, might have stood as models for the perfect Gentleman and Player – the gentleman who was a fine player and the player who was a true gentleman. The old phrase, and indeed the existence of the old amateur, have been abolished, and social changes have probably made this inevitable, but the ideals enshrined in the older words remain.

Warner was courteous, urbane, incapable of an unsporting action; above all, *gentle* (again in the old-fashioned sense), even though he could hit a ball as hard as any but a few and even though he captained both Middlesex and England with resource and resolution. He played the game keenly, but within its rules; and not merely within its rules, but within its essential courtesies. I remember his saying in his old age: 'People keep on telling me about the rudeness and ill-manners of the younger generation, but I've never met anything of the sort.' Of course he had not. His own natural courtesy drew courtesy. Something in his nature called out the best in those who played for and against him, both as players and persons. This did not mean that the clash of the conflict was blunted. There were many matches when his strength and sagacity turned the scale. He loved the ardour, not the dust, of battle.

Cricket is a word for which too many and too high off-field claims are made by elderly schoolmasters and after-dinner orators; yet despite the sentimentalities of its friends and the gibes of its detractors, it evokes something that holds the respect and affection of inarticulate English folk; it embraces the English country scene, English individuality and English laughter; and it embodies that ideal of honour and the rule of law which we call fair play. These are delicate, almost private, matters and are best not paraded, but once in a while comes a man in whom all these traits are nobly blended. There have been greater performers (though he was a very fine performer indeed) but no one has in his person more truly symbolized cricket; its pageantry, its dignity and decency, its sense of 'civilization under the sun' than that very perfect gentle knight, Pelham Francis Warner.

from THE GREAT CAPTAINS *1965*

L. S. Constantine

LEARIE CONSTANTINE

It is generally accepted that cricket is a hard taskmaster, and it was always difficult in the early 1900s for someone in my father's position to play cricket regularly. There was more concentration on the job and little concentration on sport. There was no living to be made from cricket. So in that sense I was more fortunate than my father.

He visited England in 1900 with the West Indies side and was again invited to go in 1906, but he could not see his way to make the trip. Whereas in 1900 he had one child, in 1906 there were four, Leonora, myself, Osmund and Rodney. On the morning the boat was sailing, he left Maraval and went to Port-of-Spain. He would have liked to join the boys but he could not afford it. So ostensibly he went into town to have a few drinks with them and finally to see them off.

West Indies cricket organization was not then what it is now. He arrived in town too early for the players who were sailing that day. He felt lonely and isolated. At the bottom of Frederick Street a Mr Michael Philip Maillard, merchant, a great supporter of cricket and an admirer of the Constantine family, stood in the front of his business premises. He saw my father and called him in to say good-bye to him. But my father informed him that he was not going. 'Not going? Impossible!' said Mr Maillard. My father explained the position and Mr Maillard told him that he had got to go. There was no question. My father protested that he had made no provisions, no preparations at all, and the answer came, 'Never mind that, you have to go.'

Mr Maillard sent for his carriage and one of his fastest horses, and into the carriage jumped my father, and off to Maraval they raced. Meanwhile Mr Maillard did a bit of shopping, and by the time my father returned a trunk was packed, a sum of money was collected to cover the family's and my father's needs, and so my father was ready to sail.

Off to the jetty they went, but the boat which carried passengers to the sailing ship two or three miles off-shore had gone, and the ship had sailed. Chartering a fast launch they set out in chase, and before the steamer had got out of the Bocas into the open sea they caught up with it, a rope ladder was lowered, and my father joined the others on board.

My father was up against these difficulties all his cricketing life, but it is no exaggeration to say that he was one of the first to be selected to represent Trinidad and West Indies Cricket from 1895 until World War I. But when in 1923 West Indies sent a team to England he had the satisfaction of watching me leave on the steamer possibly to take on where he had left off.

In 1900 my father was a wicket-keeper batsman. When he returned in 1906, he was a bowler-batsman, and could keep wicket if required. He was a dead sure catch anywhere, and when he took the field he was a dominating figure and a personality in his own right. In private life he was modest and retiring. He hated cheating, and he used to say to us, if you know you touched the ball caught by the wicket-keeper, walk out, don't wait for a decision. The umpire's job is hard enough without you adding to it. . . .

My father's principle, as he taught me, was to get the ball away. He made strokes which I have never seen other batsmen attempt, never mind make. The hook to fine-leg was the most outstanding of these. He made the stroke in the West Indies and in England, and it was always admired and commented on. Off the fastest bowlers he would move the right foot over to the off-side and hit across the line to square-leg; but more often than not he would move the right foot back a little, stoop forward, put his head behind the line of the ball and flick the ball over his left shoulder to the fine-leg boundary, using the right wrist. His late cut had to be seen to be believed. He often made it so late that the wicket-keeper standing up was in danger of having the edge of the bat hit his wrist or his glove. Back on his wicket he played the ball anywhere there was a vacancy. Always looking for the open spaces, I, like him, found quite a lot of room in the air. But no one could ever have called him reckless. Yet one day – a Saturday – when we were living on the estate a good quarter of a mile from the main road, the dogs began to whimper as was usual when my father was coming home. It was about four o'clock, and of course cricket could not have been over. We ran down the track to see what had happened, and our father appeared with a bandaged head. 'What happened?' asked my mother in a voice which could not conceal her concern. My father's answer was as natural as it was final – 'I missed one'.

That was the spirit in which he taught us to play the game. And when one of us was injured, my mother's remark was invariable: 'He who serves the sword shall perish by the sword'.

from THE CHANGING FACE OF CRICKET *1966*

Victor Trumper

THOMAS MOULT

Victor Trumper died on June 28, 1915, and even in the midst of the greatest war the world has ever known the newspapers found space to record at great length the genius of this marvellous batsman. 'Death of a great Cricketer', and 'Death of Victor Trumper' were on all the London placards instead of the sequence of war sensations.

It is very doubtful if there has ever been a greater batsman than Trumper, and his wonderful deeds would have been even greater but for indifferent health, which, in the end, cut short his life.

No one ever played so naturally, and he was as modest as he was magnificent. To this day in Australia, he is regarded as the highest ideal of batsmanship. He was, I think, the most fascinating batsman I have ever seen. He had grace, ease, style, and power, and a quickness of foot both in jumping out and in getting back to a ball that can surely never be surpassed.

He had every known stroke, and one or two of his own, and when set on a good wicket it seemed impossible to place the field for him. He was somewhat slightly built, but his sense of timing was so perfect that he hit the ball with tremendous power. Most bowlers are agreed that he was the most difficult batsman to keep quiet. I have heard a great bowler remark, 'I could, in the ordinary way, keep most people from scoring quickly, but I always felt rather helpless against Trumper, for he was so quick, and he had so many strokes'.

Whenever I think of him, my mind goes back to December 1903, and to the Sydney Cricket Ground. England had a lead of 292 runs on the first innings, and three Australians were out for something like 100 runs. The position was rather desperate from an Australian point of view, when Trumper's lithe and graceful figure appeared, accompanied by the tremendous cheering that can come from an Australian crowd. Here was their idol, their hero; here was the man who, with all his magnificent greatness, was always charming and pleasant and modest, and here was one who was going to put things right – and he did. He played gloriously, was undefeated at the end of the innings, and Australia nearly won the match.

In the heyday of his power, Trumper had as partner R. A. Duff, a brilliant attacking batsman, and when these two were seen coming out to open the innings for New South Wales or for Australia, the crowd used to rub their hands and say, 'Here they come, Trumper and Duff', as, in later years, they paid the same tribute to Hobbs and Rhodes.

Trumper's best season in England was 1902, *a very wet summer*, and his play in that year is one of the monuments of cricket. He scored 2,570 runs and made eleven centuries. The state of the wicket made little difference to him, and his brilliant batting stirred cricketing England. His unrivalled skill and resource will never be forgotten. Before that, in his first Test Match at Lord's, in 1899, he had scored 135 not out, and, as Mr Altham says in his splendid book *The History of Cricket*, 'Before he had batted for half an hour, it was obvious that a new star of unsurpassed brilliance and charm had joined the cluster of the Southern course.'

It may be interesting to recall that the first googly B. J. T. Bosanquet sent down to Trumper clean bowled him. The occasion was the match between Lord Hawke's XI and New South Wales, at Sydney, in March 1903. Trumper and Duff had gone in first in the New South Wales second innings and in thirty-five minutes had scored 72 runs by batting, every stroke of which I remember vividly to this day. Bosanquet went on to bowl, and his first ball pitched a good length just outside the off stump. Trumper thought it was a leg-break, and proceeded to cut it, late, as he hoped, for four, but it came back and down went his off stump. Subsequently, he used to 'murder' Bosan-quet, but it is worth recording that the first 'googly' ever bowled in Australia bowled out the man who, in spite of all the deeds of Don Bradman, many Australians still regard as the finest batsman their country has ever produced.

Trumper was also a magnificent deep field with a fine return, and he could throw a cricket ball over 100 yards. When he died the whole of Australia mourned him, and at his funeral the streets of Sydney were lined five and six deep. He was carried to his grave by eleven Australian players. No cricketer was ever more popular, and he deserved it, for he preserved the modesty of true greatness and was the beau-ideal of a cricketer.

from BAT AND BALL *1935*

J. W. H. T. Douglas

CHARLES BRAY

On the evening of December 19, 1930, the s.s. *Oberoon* bound for London from Finland was steaming down the Kattegat in thick fog. The ship's siren was bleating its mournful note. Another ship, the *Arcturus*, was due to pass. To break the monotony of the voyage, several of the passengers in the smoke-room decided to go up on deck to try and see the *Arcturus* as it went by. They had just got to starboard rail when they saw the green starboard light of the other ship coming straight for them. With a tremendous crash the *Oberoon* was struck amidships. In a few minutes it had sunk carrying with it the former England and Essex captain, J. W. H. T. Douglas and his father. One survivor subsequently declared he saw Douglas trying to persuade his father not to go below. Apparently he was unsuccessful. Neither was ever seen again.

That was the tragic end of a great English cricketer and a great English gentleman. There have been better players. There have been many with a more impressive Test record but I doubt whether cricket has ever seen a greater fighter, a greater enthusiast or one who epitomized so well the British bulldog-spirit. He played hard. He played to win. He was a strict disciplinarian. He had guts. If you didn't like your cricket played that way you couldn't appreciate the man who became known all over the cricket world as 'Johnny Won't Hit Today' Douglas.

He was about five feet ten, powerfully built with shoulders and arms of immense strength. His features were regular and on classical lines. His eyes wide apart and deep-set. His eyebrows shaggy. A mass of black hair, always meticulously parted in the centre, was never untidy. There was strength of character in

3a Fry

3c Ranji

3b Warner

3d Douglas

4a   S. F. Barnes

4b   Trumper

4c   Macartney

his every movement. In the way he looked at you from under his eyebrows, in the square jaw and the firm straight mouth. Even before he left Felsted he had made his mark in the ring. In 1905 he won the Amateur Championship as a middleweight and three years later took the Olympic Middleweight Championship in an historic fight with 'Snowy' Baker. It was his boxing, I'm sure, which gave him such agility in his bowling and the records prove beyond any doubt that though one of the greatest all-rounders of his era, his bowling was much the stronger half.

He was born at Clapton in Essex on September 3, 1882. He died as I have already related on December 19, 1930. While at school he was coached by a notable hitter of his day – the Cambridge blue, T. N. Perkins. It is strange that such a forceful hitter of the ball should have produced such a dour defensive batsman but there were reasons. Johnny Douglas for all his success at cricket and association football – he played for the Corinthians and the Casuals and won an A.F.A. international cap – was not a born ball-games player. He had not that innate spark so pronounced in the great, like Jack Hobbs, Don Bradman, Wally Hammond, Denis Compton or Len Hutton. If ever there was a copybook-made player he was John Douglas. His father was crazy about the game. The son adored the father. He knew that nothing would give his father greater pleasure than for him, the elder son, to succeed in the world of sport.

Possessed of courage and determination to a marked degree – the personification of the bulldog – this youngster, well endowed physically but with little natural gift for either sport, forced his way to the top both in boxing and in cricket. He was aided, of course, by having a well-to-do parent – a successful hardwood importer – who was prepared to finance his son through the most troublesome years until John himself could play his part in the family business.

Nobody could have had a more disastrous start to his first-class cricket career. Largely I suspect through the influence of

3

his father, John was invited to play for Essex when he was only eighteen years of age in 1901. His first match was against Yorkshire and in the Yorkshire team was George Hirst then at his prime. The little 'Tyke' was far too clever for the Essex 'babe'. He got Douglas in both innings for nought, the dreaded 'pair' which many cricketers escape all their playing life, was Douglas's dismal début. It was not surprising that he played in only three games in that season and none in the next. At this stage he was not even considered as a bowler and his batting was stiff and devoid of scoring shots of any marked merit.

His disastrous début only increased young John's determination to improve. He worked hard and long. He practised for hours and hours. Maybe that was why he became such a stickler for pre-match practice in later years. How well I remember my first match for Essex. Douglas was captain and I had been forewarned on certain things. Number one was that every player, amateur or professional, was not expected but was ordered to appear at pre-match practice each day three-quarters of an hour before the start of play.

It was at Leicester. I was changed and ready even before the skipper. Some of the professionals were already at the nets when we arrived. Douglas immediately told me to go into one net and said to Stan Nichols: 'He's the new boy. I'm sending him in first so slip yourself at him.' I was too busy trying to cope with thunderbolts from Nichols and deliveries almost as difficult from Douglas, to note that Jack Russell was not out at practice. 'Where's Russell?' the skipper asked. 'He's a little tired and stiff, skipper,' replied Jack O'Connor. 'Tired . . . stiff . . . what nonsense!' fumed Johnny. 'Go and tell him that I expect him to be out here within five minutes.'

Jack went off to do his bidding. Russell appeared well within five minutes. He had made a hundred the previous day. That was Douglas. If you didn't like it that way he was a bad captain. Yet I still cannot find anyone who played under him who didn't prefer it that way with the possible exception of H. M. Morris, who later was to succeed Douglas as the Essex captain.

I have two other memories of my début. I had come straight from club cricket – no minor county cricket to bridge the gap. As I left the dressing-room Douglas said: 'These cocks have two fast bowlers. One [Alan Shipman] runs a mile, waves his arms all over the place and isn't fast. The other [Alec Skelding] takes a few paces, has got grey hair, wears spectacles and is bloody quick. Watch out for him.' I should mention that not having a county cap or even a second eleven county cap I was wearing a very pretty one which could have been mistaken for the Quidnuncs but was in actual fact the North and South of the Thames Licensed Victuallers!

As I stepped on to the field with Jim Cutmore I heard for the first time the stentorian tones of Alec Skelding bellowing to all and sundry: 'Eee, look what we've got. One of those beggars with fancy hats. Give me the ball, skip.' I made, if my memory does not deceive me, 27, which I thought was shocking, but which John Douglas considered a good enough début to warrant a bottle of vintage port with dinner that night.

After I had been introduced to the excellent wine – he was a connoisseur of port, incidentally, and laid quite a lot down each year himself – he asked us what we would like to do. His consideration for his players at all times was meticulous. One of the other amateurs more daring than myself, suggested we might go to the Palais de Danse. So we went. John had a look round the joint and then picked a girl for each of us. 'How about that one over there for you, Charles?' She looked good to me. Over he went. Spoke to her for a moment or two and beckoned me to him. He did the same for the others. All of a sudden there was a tremendous commotion at the door. Like a flash John had us all shepherded in a corner. 'Stay where you are. I'll go and see what's happened.' He came back after a few minutes chortling with glee. 'Some bloke has knocked another down the flight of stone stairs because he thought he had pinched his girl.'

We didn't stay very long after that. Douglas did not believe that a captain's responsibility ended after playing hours. He would never dream of going to bed on arrival in a town for an away match without going round to the professionals' hotel to find out whether their accommodation was satisfactory. If it wasn't, he was apt to create merry hell with the hotel. Each morning he did the rounds of the amateurs' bedrooms. He sat on your bed, asked how you had slept and whether you were feeling O.K. Then off he would go with 'I'll see you at breakfast'.

In 1903 Douglas played in eleven matches for Essex, but was still anything but a good player. It was not until 1905 that he made a distinct advance and then it was more as a bowler than a batsman. He finished the season top of the Essex bowling averages, his 31 wickets costing just over 26 runs apiece. Moreover he had a bit of his own back on Yorkshire. He took 5 of their wickets in 8 balls, a feat that must have given him special pleasure with the memory of those two ducks still fresh in mind.

In 1905 he did the first of three hat-tricks and it was against Yorkshire at Leyton. He also achieved the feat for the M.C.C. against New South Wales in 1920–1 and for Essex against Sussex at Leyton in 1923.

By the time he was twenty-five, John Douglas was being talked about as one of the most promising all-rounders in the country. He made a thousand runs for Essex for the first time in 1908. But 1911 was probably his 'golden year'. It began with his election as captain against, I must add, considerable opposition. John Douglas senior no doubt pulled the strings. Charles McGahey had been assistant secretary and captain since 1906. The other Essex 'twin', Percy Perrin, was not only a fine cricketer, experienced and very senior to the young Douglas, but had the time, inclination and financial stability to play as much cricket as he liked.

He was the obvious successor to McGahey. The Committee, however, after no little discussion and lobbying, invited the twenty-eight year old John Douglas to take over the captaincy. Perrin had many supporters in the county and the decision was not received with general acclamation by any means. The tall dour Perrin resented being passed over. For some time he refused to play under Douglas. Wiser counsels, however, prevailed. Perrin relented and became John's warmest and closest friend. If the Essex Committee needed justification for their choice of captaincy Douglas gave it to them straight away. He had a personal triumph playing for the Gentlemen at Lord's. He made 72 and 22 not out and took 7 wickets. He was established as an all-rounder of exceptional ability and when Plum Warner was invited to be captain of the England team to tour Australia in the winter of 1911–12 he was delighted to find the selectors had given him J. W. H. T. Douglas in his team. It was a pretty formidable England side as the Australians were to discover. The party which left England under the managership of Mr T. Pawley was P. F. Warner (capt.), J. W. H. T. Douglas, F. R. Foster, W. Rhodes, S. F. Barnes, J. B. Hobbs, G. Gunn, H. Strudwick, S. P. Kinneir, J. Iremonger, J. Vine, F. E. Woolley, C. P. Mead, E. J. Smith, J. W. Hearne and J. W. Hitch.

The team went off to a flying start, beating South Australia by an innings and 194 runs. But their jubilation was short-lived. On the rail journey to Melbourne, Plum Warner, the captain, who had been far from well for months, broke down completely, was ordered to hospital and did not put his pads on again throughout the tour. A new captain had to be appointed. Plum named Douglas as his successor and this is what he wrote of him in his book *Long Innings*: 'He did not have the side in hand by the time of the first Test Match – he made the mistake of not giving the new ball to Barnes – subsequently he did splendidly. Douglas was a man of character. He possessed courage and determination to a marked degree and was always the essence of physical fitness. He inspired the side with remarkable zeal and strenuous endeavour and thoroughly deserved the great triumph which was to be his, England winning the rubber by four matches to one after losing the first Test at Sydney.'

To bring the Ashes home was a remarkable achievement

considering the side had lost one of its best batsmen and captain
in the first week. Douglas's personal performance had not been
outstanding. His Test averages were: batting 14.57, having
made only 102 in 7 innings – bowling: 15 wickets at a cost of
23.66 apeice.

Even so it was surprising that he was chosen to play in only
one Test in 1912, the third against Australia in the Triangular
Tournament. When the M.C.C. came to pick a team to go to
South Africa in the winter of 1913-14 Johnny Douglas was
chosen captain. He had a very powerful side, including Hobbs,
Rhodes, Woolley and Hearne at their prime, and, for bowlers,
apart from himself, S. F. Barnes, A. E. Relf, M. W. Booth and,
of course, the Rhodes-Woolley-Hearne trio. This time Douglas
did much better. His batting average was 38 and his bowling
23.90 for 10 wickets. The outstanding bowler, I need hardly
mention, was Barnes who took 49 wickets and the runs were
hogged by Jack Hobbs (443), Phil Mead (378), and Wilf
Rhodes (289). England won the rubber easily.

So for the second time running 'Bull-dog' Douglas returned
home from an overseas tour victorious. His stock was very
high. It went even higher that home season when he stole the
Gentlemen and Players match at Lord's. First he stopped a
collapse. Then he took 9 wickets for 105 in the Players first
innings and in the second with F. R. Foster launched such a
terrific onslaught that Hobbs, Tarrant, Hearne, Mead, Gunn
and Woolley were all back in the pavilion for 28 runs. It was
Douglas's match, one of the greatest victories the Gentlemen
achieved in the whole series.

He did the 'double' for the first time in this season. He was
to do it again in 1919, 1920, 1921 and 1923. It is impossible to
give an accurate estimate as to how much the 1914-18 War
affected Douglas's cricket career. He was within days of being
thirty-two when it broke out. By the time he was playing again
he was thirty-six. As he was appointed captain of the England
team which went to Australia in the winter of 1920-1 and he
did the double for the first three seasons after the war, it is

quite obvious that the four years he lost would have seen him at his peak and his reign as the best amateur all-rounder in the country would have been that much longer.

He was commissioned in the Bedfordshire Regiment and rose to the rank of Lieutenant-Colonel. Back in cricket after the war he had four highly successful seasons, but his reputation as a winning captain took an awful hammering. First he went to Australia in 1920-1 and proceeded to lose all five Tests. Yet his own effort was his best. He was second in the batting averages, but his eight wickets cost plenty against the phenomenal batting strength of Australia for whom no fewer than five had a higher batting average than Jack Hobbs's 50.50 which was England's best.

Just look at them: Charlie Macartney 260 runs, average 86.66; Warwick Armstrong 464, average 66.33; Jack Gregory 442, average 73.66; Herbie Collins 557, average 61.88; C. E. Pellew 319, average 53.16. There was also a left-hander called Warren Bardsley and Charlie Kelleway to contend with. No wonder wickets were expensive. No wonder the series was lost! Douglas retained the England captaincy for the first two Tests against the Australians in England the following summer. Both were lost. Seven in a row was too much for the selectors. Heads had to roll. The captain's went first. Lionel Tennyson was made skipper, but Douglas retained his place in the side and gave loyal support to the new captain who lost his first Test, but managed to draw the last two.

Douglas had one more Test against Australia. At Melbourne in 1925 under Arthur Gilligan's captaincy. That was his last. Maurice Tate had arrived. He was a similar type of bowler to Douglas, probably better because he made the ball leave the batsmen. In any case at forty-two Douglas was getting old for Test cricket. There was a noticeable lack of zip off the pitch in 1925. He was unable to maintain those long accurate spells which were such a feature of his attack. He still had the lovely free springy run-up and the powerful follow-through.

He still bowled every ball as if he expected to get a wicket

with it and scowled if he didn't. He still strode back to his mark
as if he resented the time wasted in getting there (modern
bowlers please note), and rubbed the ball vigorously on his
forearm not on his trousers or shirt. He maintained the grease
from his skin helped to retain the shine. In 1926 he had an
operation for appendicitis and was unable to bowl at all. The
skill was going before the operation. After it, it had gone. The
decline which began in 1925 continued slowly but surely and
by the end of the 1928 season there were strong rumours that
the Essex captain of eighteen seasons was to be sacked.

Johnny had held office for eighteen years. He was something
more than captain. He was virtually a dictator. Selection Committees made suggestions. Douglas decided. I learned that very
early. I had never any expectation, intention, or desire to play
first-class cricket. It hadn't entered my head. It was a fact,
however, that I had had a phenomenal season for Southend
when I was approached by a member of the County-week
committe to know if I were invited to play for Essex in the
Southend week would I be able to do so. They thought a 'local
lad' in the side would help the 'gate'.

I said I would be only too pleased so long as they wouldn't
hold it against me if I wasn't the success they expected. Nothing
happened for some time. Then the committee man came to me
and very apologetically pointed out that they had strongly
recommended my inclusion in the team for the week but
Johnny Douglas wouldn't hear of it. 'If he wants to play for the
County and you think he's good enough, let him come and play
a couple of tough games *after* the festival week' was his attitude.
'Of course you'll decline,' said the committee man. 'Certainly
not,' I replied. 'If Douglas will have me, I'd be delighted to play
when and where he decides.' So I went to Leicester and then to
Liverpool to play against Lancashire.

As I left the team on Liverpool station – they were going on
to their next match, and I was returning to London having had
my quota – Johnny took me by the arm, led me away from the
others. 'If you care to get in touch with me next April,' he said,

'and come down and practise every day, I think I can make something of you. Don't forget.' I got in touch with him. I practised like mad and was in the side for the first match against the West Indies and stayed in it, but not without much heart-searching and anxiety. A string of small scores and I was asking the skipper to drop me. His reply was typical: 'You're trying your hardest, aren't you? Yes! Well that's all I want from you. When I think you are not good enough I'll tell you.'

We were about to start the second innings of a match with Middlesex at Leyton. Waiting until the last possible moment he suddenly told me to go in first with, 'I don't want to see you until tea-time'. I made a hundred – my first, and the first is always the biggest thrill. John didn't come near me for a while. Of all the congratulations the ones I wanted most of all, the ones that meant more than all the others put together, would come from him. He waited until I was alone in the dressing-room. Then he came in, put his hands on my shoulders, looked at me with his piercing eyes from under those shaggy eyebrows and said, 'You see, I still had faith in you when you had lost faith in yourself. Well played,' and turned and walked out of the room.

During the winter of 1928 the rumour that the committee was going to insist on a new captain not only persisted but hardened. Douglas was asked to resign. He refused. He refused, he told me, because he strongly objected to the committee's choice of his successor. He considered H. M. Morris would not make an efficient captain, was not a good enough player for the job. Subsequent events proved Douglas to be correct. I saw a lot of him during those troublesome days. He fought the committee with all the tenacity, energy and guts he possessed. This was one fight, however, he could not win. He was superseded. Morris was elected captain and a very embittered Douglas retired from first-class cricket, with, I suspect, a broken heart.

He lived for cricket. He knew that one day he would have to stop playing, but he consoled himself with the belief that he would be able to go on working for the county in some helpful

3*

capacity. He didn't live long enough for the bitterness of the parting to be healed. You either liked and respected John Douglas or you loathed him. There was no half-way course. Yorkshire would have loved him. He played the game their way. No quarter given, none asked or expected. I remember a game being held up for fully five minutes while John and Vallance Jupp, the Northants captain, had a fearful argument in the middle of the pitch. John wanted the umpire to stand back so that he could see Jupp run all the way up to the wicket. Jupp ordered the umpire to stand up close to the stumps. He liked to run round behind the umpire's back. If the poor umpire didn't stand up Jupp refused to bowl and if he did John refused to take the strike. So it went on. Douglas won in the end!

For a man of such brusqueness and strength of character he had a ready wit, and he particularly loved stories against himself. In Australia, a wag turned his initials 'J.W.H.T.' into 'Johnny Won't Hit Today' which was so appropriate that it became known the world over. He used to tell with great gusto of the Aussie who yelled at him 'Put yourself on the other end, Johnny, then you can see your analysis!' He had been bowling for a long time without any success for a lot of runs.

After we had dropped a near record number of catches against Somerset, Johnny called a team conference and read the riot act. In future for high catches he would shout the name of the player who was to take it and woe betide anyone who disobeyed him. We didn't have any high catches in the next match, but in the following one there was a beauty. Rather belatedly John realized what was expected of him. 'O'Connor!' he yelled. Jack looked aghast, for it wasn't coming anywhere near him. Still he started off. 'No, Nichols!' yelled John. Nick looked just as startled but obediently tucked his head down and ran madly towards the ball. Too late John realized that it was in fact his catch so he made a desperate effort to get to it and might have caught it had not Nichols crashed into him at the crucial moment. 'You bloody fool!' he snarled, 'I'd have

caught it, if you hadn't bumped into me.' Then he realized
what had happened and roared with laughter.

On another occasion when the same system was supposed to
be in operation, a batsman tried to hit against the spin of
Harold Palmer's medium paced leg-breaks and skied the ball
straight back to the bowler. Harold was an excellent bowler—
the nearest thing I've seen to Bill O'Reilly – but he was not
renowned for his fielding, particularly his catching. Therefore
it was generally understood anyone who could get to a Palmer
catch did. But this time we all waited for the skipper to shout.
He was so busy looking at the ball that he forgot his own
instructions. At the very last moment Harold realized with
horror that nobody was going to take this beastly high catch.
He made a frantic effort which only succeeded in twisting his
legs rather in the manner of the famous Tishy, and the ball
landed with a terrific thud smack on Harold's head. He was
furious. John and the rest of us rocked with laughter.

One of the complaints about modern first-class cricket is the
absence of personalities. It is true they are now few and far
between whereas in Douglas's time there were many. He was
certainly one himself. I can well understand my old friend Bill
Ferguson, the famous baggage master, finding Douglas a
difficult captain to please. Fergie complained that Douglas not
only expected him to be baggage master and scorer but his
personal servant as well. What Fergie couldn't understand,
coming as he did from Australia, was that John was definitely
one of the old school, an aristocrat who treated servants well
but as servants, and I'm quite sure he looked upon the baggage
master as a servant of the team and particularly of the captain.

Yet there was a side of John Douglas which was not shown
to any but his intimate friends and sometimes not even to them.
A kindliness and understanding of personal problems. He was
most generous in helping any professional who got into difficulties financial or otherwise. He regarded them as part of his
household. There are others more fitting to judge his abilities
as a captain on the field. He was more brusque of manner than

might be expected or desired in a skipper. Yet there have been glowing tributes from amateurs and professionals who played under him.

Cricket would be the richer for more of his kind.

from CRICKET HEROES *1959*

Sir Jack Hobbs

E. W. SWANTON

There have been three men, as one surveys the history of cricket as a whole, whose genius and influence have transcended all others: W. G. Grace, Jack Hobbs, and Don Bradman. The last days of Hobbs overlapped the early triumphs of 'the Don'. Similarly W.G. was still playing when Hobbs started in 1905. Moreover at the age of fifty-six the Old Man's keenness could still lure him on to the field before the end of April, and it is to this fact that we owe the altogether appropriate coincidence that when Hobbs made his first appearance for Surrey, against the Gentlemen of England at the Oval, the opposing captain was W.G.

And we can well believe that the Doctor tugged away at his beard, and uttered a prophetic word or two in his squeaky tones as the young fellow, starting the Surrey innings with Hayward, made the highest score of the match, a matter of 88, got in two hours.

Like most of the truly great – it has been the same with Hutton and Compton, Hammond and Woolley – Hobbs proclaimed his promise beyond all argument more or less right away. He made 155 in his second match for Surrey, against Essex, he scored 1,300 in his first season, improved considerably on that in his second, and in his third was chosen for the Players, and finally won a place in the M.C.C. side to Australia. It was said of him already that there was no better professional batsman in England, bar Hayward and Johnny Tyldesley.

To Tom Hayward he has acknowledged the debt he owed, both for the first steps and the subsequent encouragement, and, most of all, no doubt, for the constant example of his batsman-ship at the other end. 'On whose superb method,' says *Wisden*, 'his own style of batting has obviously been modelled.' In the earlier days Hobbs's speciality, as also was Hayward's, was the on-side. It is hard for one who saw no pre-war play (save, according to a family report, a distant view of W. G. Grace from a perambulator) to judge how much scoring to leg-ward there was prior to 1914. Charles Fry, we know, forced strongly to the on.

Ranji was a master of the glance. Plum Warner was adept at persuading the ball off his legs down towards the Tavern. And to this illustrious school belonged Hobbs and Hayward. By swift degrees, of course Hobbs perfected all the strokes, and it was the completeness of his armoury which made him so very difficult to subdue.

It was the second of his five visits as a player to Australia, with Warner's second M.C.C. side, that brought him right to the top of the tree. In that series he actually averaged 82, and the following English summer, the wet and dreary one of the Triangular Tournament (1912), his 48 runs per innings was half as high again as the next man's. Looking through the scores one can appreciate the remark of Frank Woolley, made to the writer a good many years ago now: 'They can say what they like about him, but only those of us who saw Jack before 1914 knew him at his very best.'

However that may be he was, and remained, the world's premier batsman, by any basis of reckoning, until, when nearer fifty than forty, his gradual decline coincided with the advent of Bradman. On his last tour in Australia, as senior professional to A. P. F. Chapman, he had the thrill, twenty years after he had first gone out with M.C.C., of helping England to win four Tests in a row, and so retain the Ashes he had done so much to capture at the Oval in '26. And he said good-bye at Melbourne in the fifth Test with two superb innings of 142 and 65.

The top-most summits in the range were, as must always be the case with an English batsman, his innings against Australia.

But the South Africans suffered equally in their turn, and it was his performance against Faulkner and Vogler, the great googly bowlers, and the rest of the South African attack on the mat which completed the picture of his ubiquitous command. 'Of all batsmen,' writes H. S. Altham, 'he was the most versatile; the glazed wickets of Sydney and Adelaide, the matting of Johannesburg and Durban only enhanced his reputation.'

As for the West Indians, they were only just coming into Test cricket as Hobbs was fading out. He never had the fun and the exhilaration of playing in the islands, which no doubt he would have enjoyed as much as the West Indians would certainly have done; but the great fast bowlers, Francis, Constantine, and Griffith had a taste of the old gentleman's quality when in his only two Tests against them (in '28) he collected 53 and 159, scoring at something around forty an hour off his own bat.

The long span of Hobbs's career made it probable that he would corner most of the aggregate records. Thus none can match his number of runs – 61,237 – any more than they can compete with his 197 centuries. None except W.G. has scored so many runs in Gentlemen and Players, or come near his sixteen hundreds in the matches. No doubt he was lucky in his opening partners – compared, shall one say, with Hutton. Nevertheless his stands for the first wicket, 166 of a hundred or more, set an almost unassailable target. He and Hayward reached three figures 40 times, he and Andrew Sandham 66 times, he and Sutcliffe 26 times. He made at least three hundreds against every county in the Championship – and it was generally the top sides against whom he was the most dangerous.

His twelve hundreds against Australia compare with Hammond's nine, Sutcliffe's eight – and the five each of Hutton and Compton.

Even more conclusive may seem the consistency of his performances. He averaged .07 under fifty an innings in England over his whole time, stretching from 1905 to 1934. In Australia he averaged 51, in South Africa 68. The overall figure is 50.63.

In Tests alone it was six runs higher, at 56.94. Series after series
went by without his dropping below 50.

If one summer marked his peak it was, perhaps, 1925,
wherein at the age of forty-two he scored three thousand runs,
including sixteen hundreds, with an average of 70, and with
two hundreds in the match, against Somerset at Taunton, in
which he first equalled and then exceeded the 126 hundreds
made by W.G. Many who read this will recall the national
fervour – in those more decorous reporting days – accompany-
ing the chase for W.G.'s record, and will remember how, for a
week or two, innings of 50 and upwards were greeted with
placards announcing HOBBS FAILS AGAIN. In a less publicity-
conscious age the Oval Idol – or, in the next paragraph, the
Surrey crack – was a national figure in a sense that no sportsman had aspired to since the Doctor himself.

It has been written of him often enough that he was the
bridge between old batting and the new. He was brought up in
the Golden Era, when only Hayward and Johnny Tyldesley
could compete for batting places in the England XI with Fry
and the Jam Sahib, A. C. MacLaren, F. S. Jackson, R. H.
Spooner, G. L. Jessop and R. E. Foster. It was the age of
elegance, and the best professionals absorbed, and were caught
up in, the classical style based on the swing of the bat from the
shoulders, driving, and the off-side strokes.

There were strong back players, of course, notably Fry; and
more and more men came to practise the art of working the ball
to the on. Hobbs, as I say, was quickly identified with this
school. Then, when he was still climbing to the top, came the
revolution in technique that was made necessary by the arrival
of the googly and the advance of the wrist-spinners.

About the same time the fast bowlers, following the example
of Hirst, were exploring the possibilities of swing. They varied
the grip, so that the seam was held parallel with the fingers to
help it to 'move' in the air, as well as at right-angles with them,
which was the acknowledged way of producing the break-
back. Although these fetishes were not achieved without some

loss in direction and length they posed fresh batting problems. It became the more necessary to watch the ball as nearly as possible on to the bat: hence a greater dependence on back play, and a more frequent use of the pads as a second line, with the right foot brought back and across, to cover the off-stump.

In a wireless talk, given on Hobbs's seventieth birthday, Neville Cardus explained how he 'was the first batsman really to master the new bowling. Hobbs combined with the classic freedom of forward play and full swing of the bat the necessary adaption to defeat the googly and late swerve; that is to say, he also demonstrated the use of the delayed defensive stroke, legs and pads over the wicket, with the handle of the bat held loosely, so that if the ball "got through" the spin would be killed and rendered as null and void as if it had collided with a sandbag'.

It was an adaption, but it was anything but a surrender. Hobbs could hit as well as anyone past extra-cover, and if anyone, observing his open stance, might doubt whether he could do so they had only to study his secondary position when poised to drive, with wrists cocked and left elbow and shoulder pointing squarely at mid-off.

But enough of technique. In the last resort the difference between talent and mastery is a matter of character. Hobbs brought to his cricket an ascetic self-discipline which in tight corners expressed itself perfectly in his play. He was a man of conspicuous personal modesty; but his pride in his position as – in every sense – England's No. 1 gave to his batting an aura of serenity equally communicable to his opponents and to his fellows. None ever saw Hobbs rattled, or in a hurry. And if he was anxious it never showed.

There was a quiet dignity about him which had its roots in mutual respect; for others as for himself. He had the natural good manners of a Christian and a sportsman, and the esteem in which, in his day, his profession came to be held owed much to the man who for the best part of a quarter of a century was its undisputed leader.

from CRICKET HEROES *1959*

C. G. Macartney

NEVILLE CARDUS

If cricketers were long-playing records, and I were asked to select eight to keep me company on a desert island ('that is, assuming you possess a gramophone'), I should unhesitatingly choose Victor Trumper, C. G. Macartney, Denis Compton, George Gunn, Frank Woolley, Cecil Parkin, Keith Miller and R. H. Spooner (I could, of course, name at least eight others). Macartney would be included almost first choice. His batting was a constant thrill and delight. Even the most attractive players occasionally disappoint and bore us on days when they are 'out of touch'. Macartney was never uninteresting; when he had to suffer one of those dull fallible moods which come inexplicably over the greatest, he got out. On one occasion, as he told me, he really did play an innings boring to himself. In the Test Match *v.* England at Old Trafford in 1926, he scored 109 in rather more than three hours. Fred Root bowled his leg-trap inswingers. 'Wasting time,' said Macartney; 'Rootie couldn't get me out, and I wasn't such a fool as to get myself out. So I watched the ball go past me . . . If it hadn't been a Test match I'd certainly have given my wicket away. I've no time for negative stuff.' He certainly hadn't; on or off the cricket field he was one of the most positive temperaments I have ever known, quick in all his reactions, alert always in mind and body.

He was square-shouldered and square chinned, of medium height, with forearms so strong that the power in them could be felt at a glance. His eyes were keen as a bird's. At the wicket, after he had taken guard, he would raise his bat high over his head, stretching himself. This action expressed, more eloquently than any spoken words, 'Now then – we're all ready. So here goes.' His confidence knew no bounds. But he was not at all boastful. One morning, the day of a Test match, he joined me at breakfast in the hotel. Macartney looked out of the window. The sun was shining full glory. He slapped his hands. 'Lovely day,' he said. 'By cripes, I feel sorry for any poor cove who has to bowl at me today.' No, he wasn't boasting at all. He was sincerely saying that he was sympathizing (in advance) for sweating and frustrated and wasted human hopes and energy.

He hated a maiden over bowled at him. 'When a batsman's in form he can get a single whenever he likes.' His quickness of footwork has never been excelled. 'If you get in position to the ball – to *any* ball – it's hard to miss it.' In style he was a sort of Bradman *de luxe*, Bradman plus wit and genius for improvization. When Bradman was scoring at his fastest, his cricket seemed pre-organized, so to say, every stroke planned and perfectly executed accordingly. Macartney's batting gave the impression that it was perpetually creative throughout an innings, with several strokes for the same kind of ball. He was, like Sir Donald, a 'killer', ruthless in attack. But his style and presence told us that he was vastly enjoying himself, especially when, at the last split second, he changed an incipient off-drive into a late cut. Bradman's bat was like a broadsword, Macartney's like a rapier. But this 'rapier' metaphor won't quite do as a means of describing Macartney at the wicket. His drives had as much power as they had steely brilliance. It will be truer to his character and his cricket to say that he made his runs with broadsword and rapier alternatively. He batted with an extraordinary mingling of brain and impulse. He was fond of saying that a batsman should be able by rapidity of thought to know exactly at what point of its flight and momentum the curve of an outswinger should be 'sort of bisected'.

He scored a century before lunch for Australia at Leeds in July 1926, after A. W. Carr, England's captain, had won the toss on a soft slow pitch and put Australia in first (Charles

Parker, best slow left-hand bowler extant at the time, was left
out of the match and given the job of 'drinks waiter'). And
Carr missed catching Macartney when Macartney was only
two. A. W. Carr had good reason to remember Macartney, and
of what he was capable in the way of assault and battery. For in
1921, at Trent Bridge, Macartney scored 345 against Nottinghamshire in just under four hours. And when he had made nine
George Gunn missed him in the slips ('They should have
started a collection for me,' said George.). This was one of the
most dazzling exhibitions of strokeplay ever witnessed.
Macartney simply trifled with a Notts attack consisting of
Fred Barratt, Richmond, Staples, Jack Gunn, with reserves of
Lee, Whysall, Hardstaff and Carr himself. At one period of the
afternoon the Notts field was a shambles, running here, there
and everywhere at the crack of Macartney's bat. Carr then decided to 'make a move'. He changed his bowlers round. 'I did
it just to let the high hats on the pavilion know that I hadn't
lost grip on the situation. Nothing in it, of course – just a
gesture.' And Carr also decided to bowl the over needed for a
change of ends. 'I thought it would look well in the score-
sheet – "A. W. Carr, 1 over, 1 maiden, no runs, no wicket,
because I was going to bowl wide, so that Charlie wouldn't be
able to get at them".'

Wisden preserves what happened to Carr's one and only
over:—1-0-24-0. Macartney drove a ball clean out of Trent
Bridge on that day of blinding sun and blinding batsmanship.

In 1912 England, Australia and South Africa played each
other in this country – the 'Triangular Tests'. At Lord's,
Australia batted first *v.* England. S. F. Barnes and Frank
Foster opened England's attack, with Rhodes, Hearne and
Dean to follow. Macartney, in first wicket down, was putting
on his pads when a colleague, looking through the window
down the wicket from the pavilion end, said, 'Cripes, Charlie,
Barnes looks pretty hot stuff today – cripes, that one went
away like 'ell and missed the off-stump by inches!' Macartney
said nothing, but when he went out to bat, so I was told by a

reliable witness, 'he was livid with rage'. Macartney scored 99, with thirteen fours, one from Barnes second bounce into the Mound Stand. 'The finest innings seen at Lord's during the season,' records *Wisden*.

At the beginning of Warwick Armstrong's all-conquering invasion of our cricket fields in 1921, the Australians' first match was at Leicester. On a lovely day Leicestershire were shot out for 136 – McDonald 8 for 41. Then, when Australia went in, Leicestershire's fast bowler, W. E. Benskin, immediately clean bowled Herbert Collins, amidst scenes of great local patriotism. I was sitting on the pavilion as Macartney, going out to bat, passed the defeated Collins, coming in. 'I'll attend to that cove,' said Macartney to Collins – meaning that he would attend to Benskin. He scored 50 in half an hour and 177 in all. I have seldom witnessed cricket as daring, as electric, as rapidly changeful as Macartney's that day. Cuts like the headsman's axe on the block, cuts from the middle stump, swinging drives glorious in rhythm, leg-glances so late that the wicket-keeper had to gape. Like an artist, Macartney sometimes tired of going through all his known and proven technical repertory; he would perform strokes hard to classify, yet every one of them sent the imagination and the aesthetic senses dancing.

Old Australians maintain that Macartney as a stroke player approached closer than any other batsman to Victor Trumper . . . But I think there was a difference of style between them. Trumper was lithe, elegant, youthful. Macartney's batting, for all its glamour, was more obviously aggressive and bloodthirsty than Victor's, who always scored with a kind of courtliness. Trumper really did 'play' with the bowlers; he enchanted them. Macartney pulverized them and put them to flight. In Test matches Macartney scored 2,132 runs, average 41.80.

He is known today as a great batsman. People forget that as a slow-medium left-arm bowler (he batted right, of course), he was one of the best of his day. At Birmingham, in 1909, he clean bowled MacLaren, and Fry and trapped Hobbs, all for a total of 5 runs on the scoreboard. I can't recall a bigger, a more illustrious haul with three balls, not consecutive, but delivered in an over or two:

A. C. MacLaren, b Macartney 5
J. B. Hobbs, lbw b Macartney 0
C. B. Fry, b Macartney   0

This score-sheet is perpetually astounding. At Leeds, in the same rubber of 1909, Macartney took 11 wickets for 85 in one and the same Test match; his victims included MacLaren (twice), Tyldesley (twice), Hobbs, Sharp, Hirst and Rhodes. He was always 'in the game'. As a fieldsman on the off-side, he was quick and accurate, with a vehement throw-in. I liked him as a man. When he talked to you, he looked at you straight. His eyes had a twinkle. But he could be dour and severely critical of all non-triers and dilettanti. J. M. Barrie made a close friend of him. Barrie once said to me, 'I'd like to think that I have ever written a play as technically good and as stimulating to imagination as an innings by Macartney.' I wrote to Barrie on an occasion when I had been annoyed by a production of a Barrie play in which certain cuts had been made. Barrie replied, 'I expect the explanation is that the author is a little like Macartney and tires of always making the same strokes.' One morning, at Lord's, Maurice Tate in his first over or so, sent a superb ball at Macartney – it swerved and came off the pitch with quite nuclear velocity. Macartney went back on his right foot and punched the ball, with all his highly tempered fore-arms, to the off boundary. At lunch I saw Macartney and said, 'Good Lord, that was a blinding ball Maurice bowled at you first thing this morning.' 'It was, by cripes,' said Macartney, 'it was doing everything, so I said to myself "Charles, one of us is for it". So it had to be Maurice.'

In Australia Macartney was called 'the Governor-General'. But it was in this country that he found and sustained his finest ability. At first he was chosen for Test cricket as a useful all-rounder. During his first visit to England he went in to bat among the 'tail enders'. In 1909, his batting performances against England on English turf were quite modest: 148 runs in 9 innings. When he came to England a second time, in 1912, he made runs so brilliantly and so masterfully in a wet season of 'sticky' wickets that he really did seem to be wearing the mantle of Victor Trumper. From May 9 to May 22 he scored 127 *v.* Northamptonshire, 208 *v.* Essex, 123 *v.* Surrey and 74 *v.* M.C.C. The same summer of 1912 he scored 142 and 121 against Sussex in one and the same match. In each of these innings he batted not more than two and a half hours. For Australia in 1926, at Lord's, Leeds and Manchester, he passed a century on each occasion. Yet at the end of this season and rubber he told me he was disappointed with himself. It was at the Oval in 1926 that England, captained by A. P. F. Chapman, won back the 'Ashes.' When Australia went in a second time with 415 runs needed for victory in a deciding match, the wicket was not entirely trustworthy. There was moisture in it and Larwood made the ball rear menacingly at a great pace. Macartney, in first wicket down, dazzled everybody by a series of rapid strokes. He was marvellously caught in the slips by George Geary off Larwood for 15. 'I never in my life hit a ball harder – smack in the middle, one of my delayed square-cuts. A miraculous catch'. 'But,' I said, 'you were not expecting to win the match?' 'Perhaps not,' he replied, 'but I was determined the England bowlers should pay for it.' He was always of an independent mind, quietly but confidently aggressive. 'Any batsman worth his salt,' he often said, 'should let the bowlers understand at once that he is the boss here today.' Conceit? I once asked him, 'How would you compare yourself with Victor Trumper?' Without hesitation came the answer: 'I'd always have been proud to carry his bag.' The parfit – but not very gentle – knight!

from PLAYFAIR CRICKET MONTHLY *February 1961*

C. P. Mead

JOHN ARLOTT

Charles Philip Mead – 'Philip' – must be reckoned among the greatest of left-hand batsmen. Indeed, in some eyes, he is the greatest of them all. Less attractive to watch, certainly, than Frank Woolley, he had a defence which must challenge comparison with that of any player – left-handed or right. His consistency was amazing. In a side whose batting would have been no more than indifferent without him, he was often obliged to carry the innings on his shoulders. Yet he emerges from any examination of the cricket of his times as more nearly approaching the impossible batting standard of infallibility than any other player except Jack Hobbs.

His total of 48,892 runs (average 48.84) for Hampshire is the greatest number of runs ever made by any batsman for any county, and even on the highest level of Test cricket, his average against Australia, in, rather surprisingly, only seven Tests – is 51.87.

He was born in Surrey – at Battersea – and when he was only ten he scored the first century ever made in South London league cricket. He played for West against East in the London Schoolboys' match and, in 1902, when he was fifteen, he joined the Surrey ground staff as a slow left-arm bowler. He was dismissed, along with a number of other second-eleven players, from the Oval in August 1903. He went down to Southampton for a trial in the following week and when, a few days later, Surrey offered to re-engage him, he had already signed a two-year contract with Hampshire.

While he was qualifying for the county by residence, Mead played against the 1905 Australian team: he took two wickets for 56 in the touring side's total of 620 and, in his first innings for Hampshire, scored 41 not out against Cotter at his fastest. In 1906 he became qualified: in his first county match – ironically enough, against Surrey, at the Oval – he went in first and failed – with nought and three. In the next match, against Yorkshire, at Southampton, he batted at No. 4, the position he was to hold all his career, and scored 66 and 109 in a losing side. Although he did not maintain that standard, he made 1,000 runs in the same season and settled down to become the county's major run-scorer for almost thirty years.

Mead was rarely a spectacular batsman: like Hobbs, his strokes had an air of inevitability. He was unforgettable. When two Hampshire wickets had fallen – which frequently happened quickly – you would see Mead come out with his unmistakable, self-reliant, rather rolling walk; he was above average height, with wide hips, thick legs, long arms and powerful drooping shoulders. He held his bat in lean wiry hands and, after he had taken guard, he would look round the field and then go through the ritual which he performed before every ball he received. First, with his bat pointing straight upwards, he would put his hand to his cap and, looking towards square-leg, give the peak four little tugs: then he grounded his bat, tapped it four times on the ground and took four small shuffling steps to it. However impatient the bowler might become, Mead never departed from this sequence of mannerisms and, if anyone attempted to bowl to him before he had gone completely through it, he would pull away from the stumps, stop him, and begin all over again.

His batting was all but complete. His build militated against an impression of grace, but he had the essential mark of the class player in seeming always to have time to spare in playing his stroke. He was a natural batsman: his bat seemed to be an extension of his arms. As all the bowlers of his time said, Mead's bat always seemed extra wide. The fastest bowling left him quite undisturbed, and he would stolidly accept blows on the body from deliveries he deemed it injudicious to play with the bat. Against spin bowling, he played with unfailing sympathy for the turn of the ball. With the exception of the true late cut, he had all the strokes, and he played them shrewdly. Some thought him slow, but his pace was always steady. He treated all bowling with the exact degree of respect it merited, taking no liberties with the good ball, while he was unfailingly severe on anything loose. Although *Wisden* refers to his 'powers as a hitter', he never seemed to exert himself. He used a lot of left hand in his strokes which he placed with remarkable precision and to which he imparted the pace of innately perfect timing.

Forget, if you wish, his great hitting innings of 233 in the Scarborough Festival of 1929; and let it be admitted that he would hang on grimly and frugally rather than get out when the dice were loaded heavily against the bat. Look at *Wisden*, however, and you will find that figures do not confirm the allegation that Mead was a slow batsman. You will find such rates as 180 in three and a half hours, 213 in four and a quarter hours, 110 in two and a quarter hours. He did not seem to be hurrying, yet in most of his big scores, he probably struck at an average rate of 40 runs an hour. It looked slow. An old member of Southampton once said to a group of us, which included some of the present day players, 'Of course, Mead was very slow: I once watched him stonewall all day against Notts for 280.'

Sometimes, when a bowler was bowling outside the off stump to a packed off-side field, Mead would walk across and glance him down past the leg stump, and for many years he seemed able to take a single – especially on the leg side – at will.

His favourite stroke was the cover drive which he played massively; and he was extremely strong when he pushed his left foot across and hit behind point: indeed, at times, his power in that stroke compelled the placing of two third men on the boundary to him.

Philip Mead had an unfailing hunger for runs; he would go tirelessly from one innings to another, never seeming to relax his concentration, moving steadily as a train through his second hundred or his first. Any bat which happened to be in the dressing-room would do for him to pick up and use to make a hundred: it was *runs*, not batting, which absorbed him. Often he did not go to the nets for weeks on end. 'You lead in May, but I'll catch you in June' he used to say. He took his practice in the middle. The exactitude of his skill was never more clearly revealed than when he played pace bowling on a 'green' wicket. He would turn his bat, at the last moment, away from a ball which 'angled' off the pitch, allowing it to miss his stumps with bare inches.

In his early years with Hampshire, he was regarded as a useful change-bowler, but he bowled less and less as the years went by, though, to his amusement, he was sixth in the first-class averages in 1928, with 14 wickets at 17.5. At slip he had so good a pair of hands that only seven men in the records of cricket have taken more catches than his 650-odd.

In all his first-class cricket he scored 55,060 runs at an average of 47.57. Though Hobbs, Hendren and Woolley scored more runs, we may note, without challenging their eminence, that they played in stronger batting sides and made more overseas tours: indeed, Woolley's average is seven runs an innings lower than Mead's. Mead scored 153 centuries – thirteen of them over 200 – and made 1,000 runs in each of twenty-seven seasons – more than 2,000 in eleven of them, over 3,000 in two. Twice he scored 1,000 runs in a month; four times he made ten centuries in a season and three times two centuries in a match. On four occasions he scored centuries in each of three consecutive innings, and during 1923 he played a sequence of eight innings of over 50. In two seasons – 1913 and 1921 – he was top of the first-class batting averages; in three he came second; in four more, third.

Statistics, however, cannot clearly show how, year after year, this monumentally competent player carried the Hampshire batting on his shoulders. Philip Mead was a cricketer's cricketer. Not only bowlers, but also his fellow batsmen, respected his skill to a considerable degree. It was Bill Bowes who told me that, constantly bowling to him the ball which leaves the left-hander's bat late in its course, he became convinced beyond all possible doubt that, even though such a ball started on the line of his stumps, Mead could pull out of his stroke and let it pass through later and more closely to the stumps than any other batsman against whom he had ever bowled. Indeed, the bowlers of a generation found Mead a much harder batsman to bowl at than the more felicitous Woolley.

Even in his late years, he rarely fell to really fast bowlers and he was, too, such a master of the turning ball that Alec Kennedy once said to me, 'Philip made 153 centuries – and at least seventy-five of them were made on turning wickets; I used to think sometimes that he would sooner play when the ball was turning than on a plumb wicket.' A number of the bowlers of his time recall how, merging the first few strides of the run into his stroke, he would reach another fifty or hundred – Hampshire paid £1 talent money for every fifty scored – and chuckle. 'That's another ton of coal for the winter.' It meant more than that to him, however; he was a born maker of runs.

Early in the war of 1939-45, I played in a match at Ringwood in aid of the Red Cross. To my amazement, Philip Mead was playing. On a terrifyingly rough wicket, he made the highest score of a bowler's day with consummate ease and assurance. He was not out when the tenth wicket fell and had never looked like being out to any one of the four county bowlers, twenty years his junior, who strove keenly for his wicket. No one would have dreamt, watching that innings played by a man of fifty-five, that he had already lost the sight of one eye. 'Look at that old man,' a useful county batsman said to me, in a mixture of incredulity, admiration and envy, 'batting from memory, and batting better than I shall ever do.' A year later, Philip Mead was blind.

from HAMPSHIRE COUNTY CRICKET *1957*

F. E. Woolley

R. C. ROBERTSON-GLASGOW

Frank Woolley was easy to watch, difficult to bowl to, and impossible to write about. When you bowled to him there weren't enough fielders; when you wrote about him there weren't enough words. In describing a great innings by Woolley, and few of them were not great in artistry, you had to go careful with your adjectives and stack them in little rows, like pats of butter or razor-blades. In the first over of his innings, perhaps, there had been an exquisite off-drive, followed by a perfect cut, then an effortless leg-glide. In the second over the same sort of thing happened; and your superlatives had already gone. The best thing to do was to presume that your readers knew how Frank Woolley batted and use no adjectives at all.

I have never met a bowler who 'fancied himself' against Woolley, nor heard one who said, with conviction, 'Woolley doesn't like an off-break on the middle stump or a fast bumper on the leg stump.' I never heard Woolley confess that he preferred or disliked any bowler whatsoever. But then he is a very quiet man. I have a belief that he was particularly fond of them fast and short. They went that much more quickly to the boundary.

It has been said that he was not a good starter. Like other great batsmen, he would sometimes miss in the first minutes. But equally he could kill two bowlers in the first six overs of any match. His own innings might be only about 50 or so, but he had fathered the centuries that followed. Only a few years ago, when he was some forty-seven years old, I saw him 'murder' Voce and Butler, the Nottinghamshire bowlers, in the first overs of a match at Canterbury. They were pitching a

little, only a little, too short, and they extracted an exhibition of
cutting and hooking which was . . . but we have refused the
use of adjectives.

Merely from a personal aspect, I never knew so difficult a
target as Woolley. His great reach, and the power of his
pendulum, made a fool of length. Balls that you felt had a right
to tax him he would hit airily over your head. He was immensely discouraging. The only policy was to keep pitching
the ball up, and hope. He could never be properly described as
being 'set', since he did not go through the habitual processes
of becoming set. There was no visible growth of confidence or
evident strengthening of stroke. He jumped to his meridian. He
might hit the first ball of the match, a good ball too, if left to
itself, crack to the boundary over mid-on; then, when he had
made 60 or more, he might snick a short one past slip in a
sudden freak of fallibility, a whim of humanity.

Sometimes he is compared with other famous left-handers,
such as the late F. G. J. Ford. But these comparisons seem to
be concerned only with attack. It is often forgotten, I think, that
Woolley's defence was as sure and correct as that of Mead or
Bardsley. Of its kind it was just as wonderful to see, on a sticky
wicket, as was his attack. It had a corresponding ease and grace,
without toil or trouble. For this reason I think that Woolley
will rank as the greatest of all left-handers so far seen in the
game. None has made so many runs while giving so much delight.

For many years Woolley was a great part of the Canterbury
Festival. Myself, I preferred to watch him or play against him
on some ground not in Kent. Praise and pride in home-grown
skill are natural and right; but at Canterbury, in the later years,
these had degenerated into a blind adulation that applauded
his strokes with a very tiresome lack of discrimination. They
had made a 'raree' show of a great batsman.

. . . I have tried to avoid metaphor and rhapsody; but there
was all summer in a stroke by Woolley, and he batted as it is
sometimes shown in dreams.

from CRICKET PRINTS *1943*

A. A. Mailey

DENZIL BATCHELOR

Behind the Aztec mask the hazel eyes sparkle like a beech-hanger in midsummer sunshine. Arthur Mailey was amused. You could not expect his gnarled leather face to show it any more than you could expect to wring a smile out of a hickory trunk, but his eyes flashed gayer for a moment than any obvious mask of comedy punctually assumed by the hardest-working actor at the rumour of a joke. What had amused Arthur was that his protégé, young Cecil Pepper, having diligently bowled his leg-breaks for three and a half sweltering hours at the nets in Sydney, had at last taken a wicket – at the next net but one. 'All you want now, Cecil,' murmured Arthur judgmatically, 'is a slight adjustment of direction, and you've got a very good ball in that one.'

There is no longer a flicker of the hazel eyes. You see, in Arthur's opinion the one way of certainly rubbing the gloss off a joke is to laugh at it. Once you labour a point by making it, all the point of the point is gone. Just suggest that it may be there – that will do well enough.

I remember Arthur's car trip from Sydney to Melbourne with G. O. Allen at the wheel on the way to the Test Match in 1936. The car broke down in the bush, and a garage hand in a one-horse town was recruited to put it right. When he'd finished he mopped his brow and asked, 'Going to the Test?' Gubby Allen seemed struck by the idea. 'Not a bad notion, Arthur. What do you say – shall we have a look in at it, as we'll have to be there anyway?'

I asked whether no one had told the garage hand that he'd been repairing G. O. Allen's car. It would have made his day.

'It would have ruined mine,' Arthur replied, appalled at the bad taste of showing up a fellow Australian's inability to recognize a Test Match captain by instinct.

The highlight of Arthur's humour, in my experience of him, glittered on a sultry summer afternoon at Port Hacking, where, ten years ago, friends were giving me a week-end party of farewell. Arthur had sailed over on that shambles of a yacht he loved so dearly – I say sailed over, but I imagine he must have been towed by someone. In broiling weather, our resistance weakened by a Pickwickian lunch, we waddled out to play rounders according to the whim of Charles Moses, General Manager of the Australian Broadcasting Commission, and an athlete in international class at half a dozen sports. Charles is of the type that lusts after results in all contests. He could not bear to break off a rubber of bridge for a shipwreck. Arthur is at the opposite pole. If all needle matches could break off at the moment of climax he'd be perfectly satisfied to go to sleep in the corner of a hayfield.

Our rounders began. We played four a side, and we played two innings a match, and we played five matches to a rubber. That was Charles's Five-Year Plan for our afternoon. With two games apiece, the final tie was embarked on by seven saturated, resistless bits of string and Charles Moses.

Suddenly Charles himself tapped the ball – the only ball in two hundred square miles – to where Arthur was fielding, and scudded off on an insane short run. Arthur was on the ball like a flash – Charles was not five yards from him and more than that from his base. No one could miss this six-foot, sixteen-stone target at such a range. Arthur hurled the ball. It missed Charles. To be exact, it whizzed fifty feet above his head and pitched a hundred yards away, deep in impenetrable bush. Arthur snapped his fingers in hopeless grief. 'Missed!' he had the audacity to mutter in fierce self-reproach. Six of us found strength to laugh rebelliously, for Charles's fury was only less worth watching than the frozen features of the man who could

5a Hobbs (Oldfield keeping wicket)

5b Mead

5c L. S. Constantine

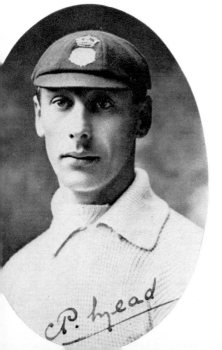

6a   McDonald

6b   Woolley

6c   Mailey

6d   Hendren

nominate the blade of grass on which he would pitch at the far wicket.

You will have gathered that I see Arthur as an iconoclastic figure. Memory reveals another glimpse of the same touching quality. Seven of us are at a bar in Melbourne, one foot on the brass rail that runs the length of the counter, one foot on the strip of coconut matting behind. We buy each other whiskies. One after another, each buys his round, until at last we come to Arthur on the end of the row. 'Six whiskies are quite as many as any man needs,' he murmurs, raising his green pork-pie hat politely, and going out into the night.

Goodness knows how or why this youth of Northern Irish stock should have sought self-expression in cricket. He had none of the early advantages, possession of which seems almost certain to deprive any Australian cricketer of a place in the sun that shines on the first-class game. His parents were working-class folk, and the best part of little Arthur's education was acquired after he had finished some very primitive schooling not nearly grand enough to fit him for one of those Civil Service file-passing jobs which one Australian in six occupies with the tenacity of a limpet. His instincts for the beautiful and the witty filled in the gaps in later life, as much of which as possible he spent standing and staring with a vacuous concentration which would have satisfied W. H. Davies. Today he probably knows enough about music to make him fit company for Neville Cardus, and he knows it because harmony and melody happen to soothe his ever-calm soul.

Outside his cricketing skill, he soon developed two gifts. He became either the best or the second best cartoonist in Australia. (The point is not hotly debated, for his rival is his best friend, Jim Bancks, creator of the Australian urchin, Ginger Meggs, who is Everyboy and whose adventures are syndicated in comic strips in this country and in the States.) Secondly, Arthur could write about the game he dominated. He eschewed embroideries, but he could read tactics from a distance and gently interpret their subtleties, and though many

4

frivolous people prefer gaudier writers, I fancy that the cricketers themselves (and especially the captains) read Mailey, if they are foolish enough to read at all.

But, of course, these bread-winning gifts were chiefly developed after he had left the cricket field. There was a time, aeons ago, of course, when he actually played the game himself.

I often wonder how easy a man this serious humorist must have been to incorporate into a team. You see, it is downright impossible to instil into him a proper solemnity with regard to the game. At the back of his mind there is always the belief that cricket is a lark. Worse still – or is it worse? – I think he believes life ought to be a lark. That people ought to enjoy it: to write poems because they are happy, to work as little as possible if work turns out boring, to dance from sheer light-heartedness; above all, to mess about with yachts designed by Heath Robinson in lands where it seems always afternoon. Square this sort of philosophy, if you can, with the grim combativeness considered proper to Test cricket.

All too often the members of the Australian Board of Control are to their international players what witch-doctors are to their tribes. Not being fighting men themselves, they demand reverence from those who are; and when these broths of boys see no particular occasion for it, they lose no time in taking disciplinary action. It can have caused little surprise when, as soon as his presence in the Australian team was no longer necessary, the Australian authorities found Arthur too cavalier, too independent, to play games within their jurisdiction. The impertinent fellow had actually contributed to a newspaper. It clearly stamped him as unfit to associate with lily-white amateurs whose names over their sporting goods shops assured them of a livelihood. The first-class game knew Arthur Mailey no more.

from THE GAME GOES ON *1947*

C. H. Parkin

C. S. MARRIOTT

At one time the most extraordinary bowler I had ever seen was C. H. Parkin. It is true that eventually he limited his efforts mainly to bowling big off-breaks round the wicket to a leg-trap but it is not for that comparatively dull, stereotyped form of attack that I like to remember him. What I recall with enjoyment in his earlier seasons was his astonishing versatility, of a rich abundance such as I have seen equalled by only one other English bowler – P. G. H. Fender. There similarity ends: although Fender brought a keen sense of humour to the game and showed it, he never went in for clowning on the field or playing to the gallery. For Parkin was not only a brilliant natural cricketer but a born comedian. He had about him something spontaneous and infectious, an exuberant flair for the comic, which raised him at moments into the ageless tradition of laughter-makers from Shakespeare to Grock and Danny Kaye.

It was at Whitsun 1919, playing in my first Lancashire *v.* Yorkshire match at Old Trafford, that I had my first astonishing sight of him at close quarters. I was pretty keyed up in any case; I do not know how many people were packed into the ground, certainly well over thirty thousand, and the atmosphere was electric – the nearest thing to that of a Test Match I have known. When Yorkshire went in, Parkin embarked upon a performance I shall never forget. He took fourteen wickets in the match. He bowled every possible variety of ball from fast-medium away-swingers to the highest of slow full-tosses; he swung it both ways, he spun it like a top, producing out of the hat leg-break off-break, top-spinner and googly, with an occasional straight ball for good measure. If it had been possible to deliver it over-arm and make it reach the other end, I believe he would have bowled the counter-googly, which I have only seen done on a table playing twistygrab.

In Yorkshire's first innings he was comparatively serious, content with raising an occasional laugh and a general expectation of things to come. But when they batted the second time needing 294 to win, he flung off all restraint. Had it been possible, he would have bowled more than six different balls per over. In his continual startling variations of pace he actually gave the illusion, at the end of one over, of having brought his right hand over empty and served up a lob with his left. In another, he played the farcical trick already referred to, when he suddenly stopped dead three yards behind the bowling crease and delivered a high slow donkey-drop which, of all people, foxed out George Hirst, l.b.w. My word, the crowd rose to that one! They roared and yelled in great gales of laughter, egged on by Parkin with some clown's gesture. Eeeh, Our Cis were making a reet bit o' fun for us! He even did Learie Constantine's famous juggling turn when the next wicket fell, throwing the ball high over his head and catching it one-handed behind his back without looking. And once, when he bowled up into the sky a monstrous balloon designed to drop on the bails, like Spedegue's Dropper in Conan Doyle's story, Herbert Sutcliffe, sheet anchor of the Yorkshire innings, narrowly escaped being caught off the maker's name in awkwardly steering it clear of his wicket. When Parkin did get Sutcliffe caught off a vicious leg-break, that settled it: soon afterwards Yorkshire were all out for 153 runs and Our Cis had bagged eight of them for 53. What a performance! And for myself, after all the hilarious excitement was over, I felt a quiet contentment at having bowled out Roy Kilner in each innings.

I never again saw Parkin clown it quite so triumphantly, but he always cheered us up, players and spectators alike. I never actually saw him bowl left-handed, but would not have put it past him to do that too, maybe in a club match, and take a wicket, with some queer ball of his own invention. Potentially he was a fast-scoring bat with some brilliant shots, but he rarely took it seriously enough to stay in for long, generally aiming at some colossal hit for six, and delighting the crowd whether it came off or not. One of his pantomime turns was to try to put the bowler off, by darting down the pitch and back, perhaps a couple of times, as he ran up to bowl; at the same time waggling his bat, elbows, hips and knees, and then having an almighty wallop at the ball. The fact that he was able to get away with this one at all showed, I think, what a flair he had for such things: it needed a rare blend of born comedian and brilliant all-round cricketer. The first time he tried it on me was the first time we found ourselves playing on opposite sides; in the Gentlemen v. Players match at Lord's in July 1921. In this game Parkin took none of the wickets, most of which were shared by Frank Woolley and Durston, but he did astonish everyone by making the second highest score for the Players (45) with some extremely brilliant shots. I was bowling from the Nursery End, keeping a completely accurate length, and I could see Parkin getting more and more impatient; I knew he was bursting to hit me into the Finchley Road. Suddenly, darting out to meet me as I ran up, he started this waggling stuff, but he was not quite there, and at the last moment pushed out a dead bat, much to the amusement of the crowd. Next ball I knew it was coming. Again he darted out, and this time really let fly. I had banged the ball down a yard shorter with all the top spin on it that I could summon, with the result that the whole force of the tremendous blow went upwards, and it rocketed straight above his head to a giddy height. I followed up the pitch, George Wood majestically emerged from behind the stumps offering an enormous pair of wicket-keeping gloves, but a voice which I suddenly recognized as my own yelled 'mine' . . . and I found myself staring up at the ball, now on its way down and swinging round and round in hideous circles. What happened I scarcely knew, but to my infinite relief I suddenly found that I had caught it somewhere at the back of my left shoulder. Our Cis, who had been watching my fearful contortions with great amusement, gently smacked my bottom with his bat, said 'Well bowled' and marched beaming off to the pavilion amid roars of applause and laughter.

from THE COMPLETE LEG-BREAK BOWLER *1968*

E. Hendren

BRIAN JOHNSTON

He sat there in the sun, busy scoring at a table surrounded by a crowd of schoolboys – a small squat figure in shirt-sleeves smoking a pipe, his brown trilby hat half hiding a rather pug-like face. It was a lovely July day and I had gone along to Leyton to broadcast the Essex *v*. Middlesex match. The opportunity arose to take time off from the commentary box to go and sit beside this rare character – Elias 'Patsy' Hendren – back once again with his old county as their scorer after several years spent coaching at the nets at Harrow and at Hove.

'Oh dear, oh dear,' he said. 'I'm scoring many more runs every season than ever I did as a player.' And so it went on for the next half hour or so. In between jotting down in the book forty or so very typical Denis Compton runs, Patsy told a succession of stories linked by an occasional chuckle and his favourite interjection of 'Oh dear, oh dear'. I went back to the commentary box refreshed, as many others have been, after a talk with cricket's greatest and most lovable clown. For Patsy was the man who brought a smile into every crisis – even into Test cricket.

When batting he seemed to be in permanent conversation with the wicket-keeper judging by the laughter of those lucky enough to be fielding close to the stumps. His twinkling feet as he sprinted for his usual first short single, his posterior sticking out in a cheeky sort of way as he crouched at short-leg, his pretence at picking up a ball which he was chasing – when still ten yards short – these were the incidents and the interludes the spectators could enjoy. There always seemed to be something happening when Patsy was on the field and those on the boundary edge were often treated to a volley of back-chat in his earlier days when he ranked as England's finest out-fieldsman.

Unlike many comedians Patsy never went too far – or hardly ever, anyway. Perhaps his skipper, Walter Robins, once thought he had done so during a Middlesex-Derbyshire match at Lord's. 'Robbie' had developed the habit of advancing yards down the pitch to the slow bowlers and if he happened to miss the ball, continuing straight to the pavilion without looking round. On this occasion it was a very muddy day and T. B. Mitchell was bowling leg-breaks from the pavilion end and Patsy was the non-striker. As usual 'Robbie' advanced up the wicket, missed, and started to walk towards the pavilion without a glance round. Quick as lightning Patsy called out: 'Look out, he's missed it.' Robins stopped in his tracks, turned round and flung himself full length on the muddy pitch to just get his bat inside the crease.

The crowd roared and he got up feeling pretty well pleased with his effort as he brushed the mud off his shirt and trousers. Then he looked up and saw to his horror that the wicket was broken. Wicket-keeper Harry Elliott was tossing the ball from hand to hand and immersed in earnest conversation with the slip fieldsmen. No wonder Patsy kept well clear of his captain for several days after this incident.

I first heard the name of Hendren when I was a new boy at my preparatory school in 1921. I was going to play cricket in the nets with my eldest brother and he chucked a bat at me and said: 'Go in and bat – you're Hendren'. From that day until Patsy retired seventeen years later he was unashamedly my hero. I used to pinch the morning paper before the rest of the family could get to it, spread it on the floor and lie on my stomach, anxiously scanning the cricket columns to see how Hendren and Middlesex had done. Patsy very seldom let me down. Admittedly there were some early disappointments in Test matches, but he soon overcame this trait and in 1934, at the age of forty-five, Hendren made a wonderful come-back by hitting a sparkling century against Australia in the Manchester Test. Four years later he retired, having made 170 centuries – more, even, than his great friend, Jack Hearne.

He had scored more runs than anyone else except Hobbs and Woolley and, like his young protégé, Denis Compton, he also hit a century in his last county match at Lord's. Incidentally he must have been one of the first Test cricketers ever to broadcast on sound radio for I still remember tuning in to the B.B.C. at the end of the 1926 Test at the Oval when England regained the 'Ashes' from Australia. The announcer ushered in Patsy something like, 'And here straight from the ground to describe the scene for us is Patsy Hendren.' I cannot remember all he said but the words he did utter that remained with me as a constant memory were: 'The Oval crowd was real glad and all was merry and bright.' How typical of Hendren that was.

He used every stroke in the game and most famous of all was his own very special hook. How he loved a fast bowler who pitched short. Did he not say to Alf Gover the first time Alf played for Surrey at Lord's: 'Don't pitch them short to me today, young man. I can't see 'em as well as I used to.' Naturally when Patsy faced him Gover started a series of short bumpers and was promptly hooked for boundary after boundary until Jack Hobbs suggested it might be better to pitch them up. 'But Mr Hendren said he didn't like them short,' wailed poor Alf.

As you can well imagine, Patsy made a wonderful companion on tours – the complete travelling jester – and it was from one of these journeys that many of his favourite stories stemmed. For instance what about the occasion in Australia when Patsy had a day off and went by car into the outback? Miles from anywhere he came upon a lovely cricket ground on a high plateau and, as the game was obviously just about to start, he drew up to watch. Immediately one of the players came up and, without recognizing Hendren, said that the fielding side were a man short – would he like to play? After a bit of persuasion Patsy agreed and was sent to field out in the bottom of the

4*

plateau way behind the bowler's arm. He couldn't see anything of the play but from time to time he fielded the ball and threw it back.

After about an hour and a half of doing this the ball came soaring over the top of the hill high in the air. It was just the sort of catch that Patsy made a speciality off. He got underneath it, safely hugged the ball to his body, and rushed up the hill holding it aloft and shouting, 'I caught it – I caught it.' He was greeted by a roar of laughter from the fieldsmen but a howl of anger from the small shed that did for a dressing room. 'You b . . . fool, you've caught *our* opening batsman. *We're* batting now.' Is it a true story? I wouldn't know, but if you can ever get Patsy to tell it to you you will readily believe it could well be. You might run into him shopping as I so often do in St John's Wood High Street. Yes, he lives only a stone's throw – or rather a cricket throw – from his beloved Lord's. Better still, try and get him behind a pint of beer in the famous Lord's Tavern. Then he's sure to start . . . 'Oh dear, oh dear,' and you'll love him all the more.

from CRICKET HEROES *1959*

Roy Kilner

NEVILLE CARDUS

It is sad for a cricketer to die in the fullness of life, but sadder
still when a cricketer passes away at the spring of the year.
Players of the game will everywhere be sad indeed at the news
of Roy Kilner's death in the month of April [at the age of
thirty-seven], just as the call of a new season [1928] is gladdening
their ears.

To say that Roy Kilner was a popular cricketer is not half
enough. It would be a poor sort of man who could not make
himself a popular figure with a cricket crowd, for he lives
through his summers against the background of the most
beloved game of all. It was not only as a clever cricketer that
Roy Kilner was liked; the crowd saw more than the successful
professional batsman and bowler. They understood that within
this rotund and happy shape there resided a deal of honest
Yorkshire county. The North Country's humours, its breadth,
directness, roughness, and kindliness, were visible wherever
Roy Kilner walked. He stood for a rich and substantial part of
this England of ours. In Roy Kilner, the average man of the
Yorkshire crowd could behold his own self. It is hard to believe
we shall never again look upon Roy, with his cap cocked
jauntily on his head, a little askew; his wide, bland face; his
compact circumference, beautifully rounded at the back; his
little pert run to the bowling crease; his flick at the offside ball
with an impudent bat – have all these lovable and very human
sights gone for ever from a Yorkshire cricket field? It is hard to
believe, indeed; it is like being told that some genial Yorkshire
breeze has died and will never again blow over the faces of
men and refresh them.

In recent years the Yorkshire eleven has been a machine, almost inhumanly working for victory, day after day, grimly inevitably. You could never fit Roy Kilner into that great machine. He was, of course, as fine a match-winner as anybody else in his eleven, but he was never disciplined by an iron collectivism out of his own original senses. He was constantly a jolly Cavalier amongst a lot of dour Ironsides. Many a time I have seen Roy, in a Lancashire and Yorkshire match, flashing his bat dangerously at McDonald's fastest off-side bowling. And at the other end of the wicket I have seen Wilfred Rhodes, or Emmott Robinson, regarding Roy's laughing countenance with the utmost disapproval. Often have I wondered what Emmott was thinking (deep in his heart) about Kilner's behaviour. 'Look at the man! A tryin' to cut! And Ah've told him till Ah'm tired that the cut never were a business stroke. Hey, Roy! Will t' *never* get any sense?'

With Roy Kilner, as with every true cricketer, the style was the man himself. The rare blend of shrewdness and gusto, of humour and the fighter's spirit, which came out in his batting and bowling – all these qualities were to be felt during a moment's contact with him, in the briefest conversation. Your Yorkshireman is always proud of the stuff of nature out of which he has been put together. Roy Kilner was always himself, whether he happened to be in Yorkshire, in Middlesex, or in Bombay. He had charm, the most delightful ways about him – but there was not a hint of self-conscious manners, acquired second-hand. He was not ashamed of his Yorkshire speech, and what a rich, friendly flavour it had in his mouth! To hear Roy speak of a Lancashire and Yorkshire match was indeed to be warmed with his own county's humour. 'Ay,' he would say, 'it's a reight match, Lancasheer and Yorksheer. Tha knows, t' two teams turns up on Bank Holiday, and we all meets in t' dressin' room, and we all says "Good mornin'" to one another. And then we never speaks again for three days!' A year or two ago I was discussing with Roy the present condition of our county cricket – the absurdly perfect pitches, the huge scoring in Australia, the slow batting, the poor bowling. But Roy was against any alteration in the rules or procedure of the game. 'T' game's all reight,' said he. 'It's crowd that's wrong – it wants educating up to t' game. Listen to me – when I were a young lad I goes up to London and there I sees a play by Shakespeare. And by gum! it did make me tired and weary wi' yawning. When I gets home I says to mi father, "No more Shakespeare for me!" But mi father, he says, "Now look 'ere, Roy, lad; tha's just talking folly. Shakespeare's good enough for me, and 'e's good enough for thee. Tha wants *educating* up to him, that's what tha wants".' And Roy closed his delicious homily in these words, uttered most gravely and sagely: 'And it's same wi' t' crowd and county cricket. They wants educatin' up to it!' To tell this story is to feel one's heart running over with affection for Kilner; to hear it, to read of it, will surely draw cricketers closer and closer to the man's humanity. Men of humour never ought to die anywhere or anyhow. And cricketers of the North Country, broad and full of fellow feeling, ought every one of them to live on and play the game until they are sick and tired of it.

from THE SUMMER GAME *1929*

'Ted' McDonald

NEVILLE CARDUS

A fruitful argument could be started by putting the question, 'Who was the greatest of fast bowlers?' But naturally there's no possibility that anybody could answer it and receive unanimous agreement, no matter how convincing the statistics regarding performances. By the history book Tom Richardson would need some beating. In our own time Lindwall's claim to a foremost place is difficult to challenge. Much depends on material environment, the general standards of play, and so on.

If we change the question and ask, 'Who was the most beautiful fast bowler to see in action?' I personally have a quick and positive reply – E. A. McDonald, the Australian, who first came to England in 1921 with Warwick Armstrong's conquerors, then qualified for Lancashire. He was lithe and apparently boneless, yet strongly sinewed, suggesting that he was really taller than his actual inches. His face, swarthy and handsome, announced at once that he was Australian. He ran to bowl in a slightly curving track, not too long. Len Braund, who often stood umpire for McDonald, told me that it was hard to hear McDonald coming to the attack. 'Not until he was almost at the crease did you sort of *feel* he was there.' After McDonald had bowled thirty overs in an innings – which many times he did – there were no rough footmarks, no drastic disturbances of the earth's surface to be found on the pitch. He might well have bowled on a cat's paws. At the point just before delivery he curved his wrist – I used to call it the poise of the cobra's head before the venom was released. There was little effort in his action. The energy was finely concentrated.

His pace was really fast; Statham at his most dangerous is not faster. But the main asset in McDonald's attack was a late out-swing while the ball was new, and a breakback when it was getting worn. Then, as George Gunn would say, 'Mac can make the ball come up to the wrists late from a good length on the best wickets.' When he 'bounced them' McDonald was truly a menace to skull, thorax and breastbone. George Gunn, greatest of all players of fast bowling, had no doubt that McDonald was the best of all he had faced. George was the cause of a burst of temper from 'Mac', and 'Mac' seldom lost his temper. He was by temperament immovable; in an earthquake he wouldn't have turned a hair.

At Old Trafford, one evening after rain on hard bony ground, Larwood let the ball fly alarmingly. One or two Lancashire caps, sporting the red rose, were removed. Next morning McDonald went into the dressing-room of the Nottinghamshire men and told them to ring up the Royal Infirmary and order a 'few' stretchers. He then proceeded, as soon as he got on the concrete Old Trafford turf of those days, to bombard Nottinghamshire with the most terrifying 'bouncers' I have ever seen. The new ball might have been a red-hot explosive. But George Gunn walked out to this fearsome attack. He upper-cut a 'flier' into the Ladies' Pavilion, over third-man's head, standing on his tip-toes to do so. Whereat McDonald said, 'George, do that again and I'll knock your block off.' And George replied, 'Why, Ted, you couldn't knock the skin off a rice pudding.'

When 'Ted' played his first full season for Lancashire in 1925 he took 205 wickets, average 18.67 in all matches (182 at 18.37 runs each for the county); and he bowled 1,249 overs. Nowadays we look upon Shackleton, medium-pace, as a marvel of perpetual motion; each summer he wheels down 1,500 overs or thereabouts. McDonald was thirty-three years old in 1925. He was the spearhead of Lancashire's attack until 1931, and for the county he took more than 1,000 wickets, most of them the wickets of the top batsmen. Sometimes, after he had broken the back of a formidable batting side, he would ask for his sweater and stand at mid-on, flat on his feet, chewing a blade of grass. If a hit went past him involving a long hurried run, he would motion to the nearest fielder to him that it was *his* job. On a sweltering Saturday at Trent Bridge he bowled for hours. In the last over of the day, a Nottinghamshire henchman, name of Flint, smote him for two fours and from the last ball of the day hooked him for six to square-leg. 'Mac' didn't even look at this violent stroke. He turned his back on it, grabbed his sweater from the umpire, and walked from the field.

On Monday the first ball from him went past Flint's nose at about 95 miles an hour; the second sent the off-stump hurtling yards. Again, 'Mac' didn't even look at what was happening to Flint. This was the 'Buccaneer' gesture of this great bowler and, most times, quiet and friendly man. But he was sometimes unpredictable. Even as a bowler he could have his terribly and inexplicably erratic days, when he would actually galvanize his lovely action awkwardly as he hurled down 'bouncers'. He was subject to these strange eruptions and nobody knew why. He also harboured a private pride in his ability to spin an off-break at a slow-medium pace from round the wicket. At Dover, in 1926, Lancashire declared, leaving Kent the whole of the closing day in which to score 426, not an impossible task to perform on a very fast ground not too large of circumference, with Woolley, Chapman, Hardinge and the Bryans there to score brilliantly. Indeed Kent, with only five wickets down, were within 65 of victory at tea. While Woolley played gloriously McDonald bowled his supposedly spinning off-breaks at him. At the tea interval I asked Leonard Green, Lancashire's captain, what was the grand idea? 'Go and ask "Mac" yourself,' said Green. I spoke to 'Mac', pointing out that Lancashire's skipper would get into trouble at Old Trafford if Lancashire were to lose after a declaration. 'I'm surprised,' said McDonald, 'that you of all men should prefer to see brute-force bowling instead of art.' Anyhow, after tea, McDonald bowled as fast and as beautifully as at any time in his life. He did the 'hat-trick', and Lancashire caught the boat train to London, winners by 33 runs at the pinch.

It was against Kent, at Old Trafford in 1928, that McDonald touched the heights. Lancashire needed to win this match to keep in the running as county champions. As a preparation for it, McDonald was given a three-day rest. Kent, in first, scored 277, Woolley 151. Lancashire retaliated with 478–5 declared, 40 minutes before lunch on a golden day, with the wicket a batsman's dream of heaven. Surely a drawn match, we all said, more or less philosophically. McDonald's first ball pitched short, flew over the heads of Hardinge and Duckworth, and crashed thunderously against the sight-screen. This was a sign of McDonald's intentions. He took 8 wickets for 53, 15 in the match for 154. Seldom, if ever, have I seen fast bowling as finely tempered, as finely speared as this. The whole body of McDonald that day moved like visible rhythm; it was energy concentrated into sinister grace. But, even now, McDonald went round the wicket, slow-medium, to Woolley – a rare compliment to the batsman 'Mac' liked most to bowl at, excepting Jack Hobbs.

In 1921 he was the rapier to the bludgeon of Jack Gregory, who charged along the earth seeming to shake it, visible strength in contrast to the nearly invisible silent flow of McDonald's destructive force – which the music of his action so alluringly concealed. Batsmen saw their stumps sent somersaulting by McDonald almost before they had picked up their pretty white willow blades. In the Test match at Lord's in 1921, McDonald took 5 for 32 in England's second innings. I could swear that I can see to this day, in my mind's eye, the ball by which McDonald bowled 'Patsy' Hendren. Very fast from the sinuous wrist, a late apparent swing leg to off, then after pitching, a break-back knocking the leg-stump yards. He took part in only two Test series against England, first in 1920–21 v. J. W. H. T. Douglas's team, when his bowling figures were 6 wickets for 392 runs; then, in England in 1921, and now he established his class with 27 wickets in the rubber at 24.74 each.

He wasn't as consistently accurate a fast bowler as, say, Lindwall, Larwood or Statham. Towards the end of his career he certainly lost much of his control and wonderful physical balance and elasticity. He must be estimated now at his best – which he delighted us with in the summers of 1926 to 1928, summers in which consecutively Lancashire headed the Championship table. I have known Old Trafford crowded on a Monday morning, thousands there already, to watch McDonald bowling. Kennington Oval's gates were thronged on any afternoon if McDonald was to be seen matching his pace against Hobbs. One of the lasting joys of all that I have lived through at cricket is a memory of McDonald and Larwood in opposition and splendid contrast at Trent Bridge, whenever Lancashire were playing Nottinghamshire there. McDonald was as gentle a character as ever caused acute apprehension in a batsman. Nothing really disturbed his rather 'couldn't-care-less' philosophy. A newcomer to the Lancashire XI missed three catches from 'Mac', all before lunch. During the interval he thought it would be wise to apologize. But 'Mac' simply shrugged his shoulders, saying, 'Ah, that's all right, son, a fast bowler should knock stumps out of the ground.'

He was killed, aged forty-five, after a car accident. His own car swerved and, turning over, landed down a bank. McDonald miraculously escaped unhurt, then was fatally knocked down by a passing car as he was giving details of his own accident. A bitter irony – which, somehow, would have tickled his own relish of the way things, as he used to say, 'turned out'. He was the living image of the beach-combing Australian in his moments of relaxation. And, bowling at his best, he was as beautiful and thrilling a sight as any lover of cricket could wish to see, not only at Old Trafford, Lord's or Trent Bridge, but in the Elysian fields.

from PLAYFAIR CRICKET MONTHLY *March 1964*

M. W. Tate

JOHN ARLOTT

Maurice Tate had no place in Douglas Jardine's master-plan to win the 1932-33 series against Woodfull's team in Australia – but he could still bowl. Joining the party late in the tour, he played his first match against New South Wales. He was not given the new ball first, Allen and Voce had that privilege: Tate took it when they had worn off the finest of the shine and then he took the wickets of four of the first five batsmen – Wendell Bill, Bradman, Kippax and McCabe – and his final figures were four for 53. He was not picked for a Test, but became one of the players who cheerfully called themselves 'The Ground Staff' and who made the most of the tour, playing cricket chiefly in minor matches; in fact Tate bowled in only ten first-class innings in Australia although he played against New Zealand in one of the minor representative Tests of the tour.

So Australian batsmen had never again to face their greatest opponent of the 'twenties in a Test. The measure of Tate's greatness lies not solely in 83 Australian Test wickets at 30 runs apiece but in the fact that, in the time, partly, of Bradman, and plumb wickets, more than a quarter of his 1,175 overs were maidens – 184 of them eight-ball maidens. And, most convincing of all, of those 83 wickets, *sixty-two* were the wickets of appreciable Australian batsmen. Only 21 were minor batsmen – and my estimate rates Tate's friendly opponent Bertie Oldfield, whom he dismissed nine times, as a minor batsman. He took Bradman's wicket five out of the thirteen times it fell in Tests in which both played.

Sussex, with their new weight of batting, their varied

bowlers and their keen fielding were, under Duleepsinhji,
R. S. G. Scott and Alan Melville, serious challengers for the
County Championship in the 'thirties. Maurice Tate, still their
greatest attacking force, wore the mantle of senior pro with an
air of boyish embarrassment but backed by the knowledge of a
man who has lived the game. His figure grew a little thicker
and when Jim Cornford came, to bowl with an action which
looked like a mirror held to the younger Maurice Tate in
action, there was a strange Alice in Wonderland air about the
Sussex outcricket. Perhaps, too, his pace decreased along the
'thirties, but those strong fingers could still cut a ball with such
buzzing ferocity that you were amazed it did not flick out a
divot when it pitched. He knew his batsmen like a book, from
which he read with profit, and his length never faltered. The
new ball still swung obediently for him, and would still, from
time to time, perform those unique antics which it reserved for
emanation from the hand of Maurice Tate. He was still portent-
ously and unendingly truistic from the shelter of his hand, and
would still swing his bat and drink his pint broadly. Perhaps
there was less than the old battle in his manner, for no longer
could he have the delight of tearing his heart out against the
greatest batsmen in the greatest arena – that of a Test match.
But he never gave of less than his best – and that was always
good – cricket was still his life. And little boys and many of
their seniors, not only at Brighton but up and down England,
went to watch Sussex to see Maurice Tate once again. For he
had a place in the hearts of many cricket followers, if only because they remembered when he was all the England attack and
we looked to him for miracles, and he always did his best to
satisfy us and, sometimes nay, often, *produced* miracles, to the
surprise of his opponents and to our delight. When the sea-fret
was on the pitch at Hove, the best batsmen in England still
respected 'Chub' Tate and, for all their respect, he could still,
from time to time, beat them when they were concentrating on
not being beaten.

Then, one day in the summer of 1937 he was ordered to

report to the committee room on the Hove ground. 'Of course, you realize you are past cricket' were difficult words for those sun-and-weather-reddened ears to recognize. He was dropped for the next match and then recalled, and he played until the end of the season because the side was less good without him. Then, at the end of the 1937 season, Maurice Tate left the Sussex County Cricket Club. He does not go back there now to watch the cricket because he still does not quite accept those words nor understand why they were spoken to him.

Between the day of 1912 which he still remembers, when he took the Sussex baggage to Northampton as the county's eleventh player, and the late summer day of 1937 which he cannot forget, when he ceased to be a Sussex cricket pro, Maurice Tate performed many labours at cricket, and touched many of them with a light which those who watched did not fail to mark and remember. He played in thirty-nine Test Matches: he played ten times for the Players against the Gentlemen: three times he took two hundred wickets and scored a thousand runs in an English season and in five other years he had a thousand runs and a hundred wickets, and he once, and uniquely, performed that same double on an Indian tour. He and Rhodes are the only English cricketers with a hundred wickets and a thousand runs to their credit in Tests. He scored 23 centuries in his twenty-two thousand runs and his batting average, first to last, was over twenty-five runs an innings. Two hundred and forty-two catches went into those large hands, one of them, in that final Test at the Oval in 1926 so fast that the catching hand is merely a blur on the snap-exposure of the press camera. Figures do little enough credit to his batting, for they cannot tell of its power and gaiety and how it often saved a game and how we warmed to the sight of him lurching into the wicket at a friendly roll, wriggling his pads comfortable, his bat cocked from a grip close to the handle and with a word to the fieldsman and the umpire on the way. And figures can tell us less than ever of his bowling. He missed four good cricketing years to busy himself about his small corner of a war, but he found time, between the year when he was seventeen and the year when he was forty-two, to bowl more than fifty thousand overs in five countries of the world, and he took 2,786 wickets at an average cost of 18.18 runs each in a day of plumb wickets and great batsmen. And he once took sixty-five Test wickets in a year. But do not worry about the figures, for statistics, particularly cricket statistics, can be wrong.

Go, rather, to the old-hand county cricketer of the 'twenties. Ask him about 'Chub' Tate – *young* 'Chub' – for 'Chub' was his father's title too. The name always evokes response. You can almost imagine the shrewd fingers of memory testing the quality of Tate's cricket in recollection. 'There was a bowler for you.' He will tell you that the batsmen were lucky – *all* of them – if 'Chub' didn't get them when they first came in: how often he beat them and how often and how narrowly he missed their stumps – how often he hit them. He will tell you how you could never be sure, however well set you were, that he would not bowl you all over the shop when you were playing a strict defensive stroke. He will tell you, too, in his own fashion, how watching Maurice Tate bowl was a fine thing, how it set a thrill inside the chest like fine music when he ran so smoothly and so mightily to bowl, and the ball swung to the pitch and left it an angry devil which snarled at the knuckles or spat at the edge of the bat. He will tell you 'Chub' was the unluckiest of all great bowlers. And he will tell you that he could roll out a fine round oath when the slips dropped a catch, or the ball flew for the tenth time only a coat of varnish from the bails, or when the cautious pad kept his thunderous breakback out of the stumps. But, he will add, he had usually a grin, and always as many words as you wanted. He will tell you that 'Chub' was a great bowler, and a good chap.

from MAURICE TATE *1953*

D. R. Jardine

R. C. ROBERTSON-GLASGOW

It was no joke for a bowler when D. R. Jardine came in at number five for Surrey on a perfect Oval wicket – Hobbs, Sandham, Ducat, Shepherd, Jardine. He used to say: 'The position is peculiar. Either you hustle to a sticky wicket with your pads crooked, or else you go in when there are already so many runs on the board that it doesn't matter whether you make nothing or a hundred.'

Jardine stopped playing first-class cricket at the age of thirty-three; that is, in his prime. He had never played regularly. By then he had been twice to Australia. Twice running he had headed the batting averages. He had captained England abroad and at home, and had played a classic century against the fierceness of Constantine and Martindale at Old Trafford in 1933. But when summer 1934 came round, and the Australians were here again, he was in the Press Box. Rightly or wrongly, he had differed with the Marylebone oligarchy; and he was lost to English cricket when he was much needed. I remember a spectator at Leeds, where Bradman batted on and on, calling up to the Press Box: 'We want you out there, Jardine.' And, upon my word, we did. For the captain was gone, Larwood was injured and out of it. English cricket was at its lowest ebb since the disasters of 1920 and 1921.

Few great batsmen can have matured so early. At the age of fourteen he looked like a County batsman in miniature, and I am sure that at seventeen he could have walked from the Winchester eleven into a Test side and done reasonably well. Among amateurs of his time he was the supreme example of orthodoxy, but what placed him above the others was the

strength of his back-play, which equalled that of the best professionals. His skill was to a great degree inherited, his father,
M. R. Jardine, having made a century for Oxford *v.* Cambridge
and played many fine innings for Middlesex. To this was added
natural intelligence and coaching of the very finest order, first
at Horris Hill, where he enjoyed the influence and precept of
the famous Evans family, then at Winchester, where his skill
was polished by such notable cricketers as E. Rockley Wilson
and H. S. Altham.

His own model and hero was C. B. Fry; and in many ways
Jardine resembled him; in the method of his back-stroke – the
right leg well over, the left away from the stumps, the stance
boldly upright; in concentration, and in the powerful will to
improve; and in a certain combativeness of character, which
not only made him a most stubborn fighter in a crisis but led
him into first place in one of cricket's most perplexing controversies.

But the time to see Jardine batting was in a care-free net on a
summer evening in the Oxford Parks; and many of these we
had together. Here he would show every stroke in the game,
all played with grace and power, and with an abandon which
he hardly ever allowed himself in a set match. And that was the
one weakness in all this strength, that the stringency of an
occasion was reflected in a corresponding restriction of his art,
which was in itself so effortless and fluent. Something of iron
in his temperament would not let him play free and full in the
greater matches. It is said that the best innings he played in
Australia was one of 140, in 1928, against New South Wales.
Bradman has told me that it was one of the finest displays of
stroke-play that he has ever seen. But, in general, as the task
grew greater, the strokes grew fewer. He remained a terrific
problem for the bowler to solve; but my point is that he had it
in him to kill a bowler, yet was so often content to wage a long
battle on fairly level terms.

As a captain I should rank him very high. He was thorough
and observant. His preparations and his study of individual

methods were exhaustive. None knew more exactly what he meant to do nor could express his thoughts more pointedly if some plan misfired. He took far more pains than many knew to weigh the abilities and inclinations of his own team. He had the true Scottish dislike of waste in material or words; but his cursing, at its best, was Elizabethan in scope and variety. His wit could be both deep and broad, as when, after batting for many slow hours in a Test in Australia, he apologized to an Australian for playing 'Like an old spinster defending her honour.'

So much for Jardine as a cricketer. Old acquaintance may perhaps allow me the liberty of remarking that, if he has sometimes been a fierce enemy, he has also been a wonderful friend.

from CRICKET PRINTS *1943*

Maurice Leyland

NEVILLE CARDUS

Maurice Leyland was a born Yorkshireman and cricketer from the vintage soil that reared George Hirst, Schofield Haigh, and Roy Kilner. He could be as dour and canny as Emmott Robinson himself but, also, he always saw the humour of it all, even in a Yorkshire *v.* Lancashire match of the 1930s when, especially at Old Trafford, an engagement was seldom brought to a finish on the flawless pitches built and prepared there. 'No fours afore loonch – on principle, lads!'

It was for Yorkshire, against Lancashire, at Old Trafford, in the August Bank Holiday match of 1924, that Maurice first gave us a taste of his skill, character and Yorkshire relish while scoring a century from a Lancashire attack consisting, to begin with, of McDonald, Cecil Parkin and Dick Tyldesley. On this occasion, rain and sunshine caused the ball to fly about; and McDonald was at his fastest . . . Leyland that day actually drove McDonald 'on the rise', skimming hits to long-off. He would drive from a grip high up the bat's handle, firm of foot. In fact, so swift was his judgment, so rapid his footwork, that he could get himself into position a split-second before the ball pitched. The stroke itself was performed with only the swing of the arms in motion; the rest of his body was still, but beautifully in rhythmic poise. After the ball had been propelled to the boundary Maurice would shade his eyes with one hand, as though gazing into the distance, to be quite sure of the stroke's destination.

He took guard wide of the block, and was of that now almost extinct breed of batsmen of whom it was difficult to distinguish between offensive and defensive methods in their technique. At the first hint of a good ball, one keeping low, Maurice's right hand went down quickly and suspiciously to the bottom of the handle. 'You know,' he once said to me, 'bowlers are a decent lot of folk, takin' 'em on the whole – but you can't always trust 'em.' He was a rich Yorkshire character, even before he was a great cricketer for his county and for England. It was, indeed, his sterling character and personality that made his cricket great. He belonged to a period of individual identity and performance, a period in which 30,000 people would go to watch Yorkshire *v.* Lancashire – finish to the match or no finish – just to see north-country character in action: Rhodes pitting all his experience and craft to keep Harry Makepeace quiet, and Harry wouldn't readily have ventured a four (before lunch) if the ball had been placed before him on a plate, with parsley round it.

Leyland always mingled humour with his Yorkshire distrust of apparently smiling fortune. He was a member of G. O. Allen's unlucky England team playing in Australia in 1936-7. The first two Test matches were won by England, before Christmas. On Christmas Eve, standing outside Usher's Hotel with Maurice, in the declining heat of the evening, I said that England were now right on top and we really ought to do this particular Christmas 'proud'. Maurice sucked his pipe. 'Aye,' he admitted, 'we are two up and only three to play.' (All Tests in Australia were played to a finish then.) 'But,' he added, 'we've not finished with the "Don" yet, so Ah'm sayin' nowt just yet.' Bradman had so far, in this rubber, scored 38, 0, 0, 82. He proceeded, in the next three games, to score 13, 270, 26, 212, and 169. England lost them all. At Melbourne, the rubber's turning point, Leyland was 111 not out when England's last wicket fell in defeat by 365 runs. Towards the innings' end, somebody nearly ran Leyland out as close of play approached. Leyland chastised his eager partner: 'Hey, lad, what's the hurry? We can't get *all* these runs tonight.'

He was nurtured in a hard Yorkshire school, during a time when cricket in Yorkshire was jealously and proudly guarded. The Yorkshire tradition of clannishness no doubt remains; but

I fancy that cricket in the county is generally thought of today as one game among others. At any rate, if Yorkshire should suffer defeat on an afternoon on which England were winning the World Cup at soccer, I don't think there would be any obvious sign that Leeds, Sheffield and Bradford were going into mourning. Leyland first played for Yorkshire when a Test match between England and Australia was not, in the north of England, the more important and agonizing event. The Lancashire *v.* Yorkshire engagement was the thing! The crowds packed Headingley, Sheffield, Bradford and Old Trafford to see the cricketers they were proud of, cricketers who, by their personal characteristics, somehow sublimated the county blood, soil, accent and living image. During a certain Lancashire and Yorkshire match, a man in the crowd applauded impartially, handclaps for a boundary by Sutcliffe, handclaps when a Lancashire bowler took a Yorkshire wicket. This was too much for the adjacent spectators, one of whom asked the impartial enthusiast, 'Tha seems to be enjoyin' thissel all time. Wheer dast tha coom from?' 'Oh,' replied the impartial one, 'I'm from Sussex.' 'Oh, art tha,' was the Yorkshire response, 'Well – tha can keep the clapper shut. This match 'as got nowt to do with thi.' In such a dedicated school was Leyland brought up. At Sydney, he was obliged severely to stonewall on a hot afternoon, with England in trouble. 'The Hill' barracked him raucously. 'Listen to 'em,' said Maurice, 'why – they should hear crowd at Sheffield. Compared to them, this Sydney lot is as harmonious as Huddersfield Choral Society.'

I first got to know him on the tour of G. O. Allen's England team in Australia, 1936-7. . . . He was the spirit-enlivening presence of the party. His face was boyish, and he wasn't tall. When he spoke to you he looked straight at you, even as he looked straight at the fastest bowler. His shoulders sloped, but his beam was broad. Never has there lived a more naturally courageous cricketer. In fact, the word courageous is too rhetorical to fit him. He simply faced facts – propitious ones or uncomfortable ones. His confidence was a 'natural-born' part

of him. At Brisbane, on the morning of the first Test match
of the rubber of 1936-7, a group of us stood outside the Belle
Vue Hotel, waiting for transport to take us to the ground.
Maurice was present, also 'Bill' O'Reilly, the greatest spinner
of the period. Maurice spoke to him. 'Well, Bill, destiny of
rubber is in lap of gods. But Ah can tell thi one thing already,
for certain. Ah've got thi taped – and tha knows it.' This wasn't
a boast; it was said with the most disarming geniality. Maurice
then proceeded, with the rest of us to the Brisbane (Wool-
loongabba) ground, and proceeded to score 126, against
O'Reilly and Co.

He first played for England in Australia at Melbourne in
March 1929, the fifth game of the rubber. He was not given a
chance in the preceding four. He scored 137 and, second
innings, 53 not out. Back in England, 1929 v. South Africa, his
innings worked out at 3, 73 and 102 (same match), 45, 0, 55,
and 16. In those years it was not easy even for Maurice
Leyland to hold a place in the England XI. He was left out of
the first and second games of the rubber v. Australia, here in
1930. Not until 1934 could he regard himself as an 'automatic
choice'. Then, in Australia, he announced his quality and
indispensability once and for all with Test match successive
innings of 6, 18, 109, 153, 16, 49 not out, 110 and 17. 'Once
and for all'? – not exactly. He didn't play for England in the
1938 rubber until the fifth Test at Kennington Oval v.
Australia. This was the occasion of England's colossal total
of 903–7 (declared), Hutton 364. The total was piled-up with
a deliberate slowness. Leyland batted nearly six and a half
hours for 187. After his innings ended – run out – I chided him.
'You, of all men, Maurice, going steady with the score at
300–1.' 'Hey, Mr Cardus,' he retaliated (with a wink), 'you
must bear in mind that Ah'm playin' for mi place in England
XI' – *he*, who for years, had been England's steering wheel in
many stormy seas.

Wise and lovable by nature, Maurice was any cricket team's
godsend. He could settle an argument with one humorous

honest saying. An argument broke out about fast bowling and
'bouncers', several famous players hot (and evasive) in dispu-
tation. Then spoke Maurice, 'Fact is, none of us likes fast
bowlin' – but some of us don't let on.'

In his career he scored 33,660 runs, average 40.50, 2,764 in
Test matches, average 46.06, with seven hundreds *v.* Australia,
two *v.* South Africa ('playin' for mi place tha knows'). In all,
his hundreds amounted to 80. But statistics about Maurice
Leyland tell only of the half of him. He was, I repeat, a Yorkshireman made from the original type, image, humour. His
passing, at an early age these days, is grievous. I count him
among the most endearing of all the various men I have ever
known.

from PLAYFAIR CRICKET MONTHLY *February 1967*

E. A. Paynter

RAY ROBINSON

Eddie Paynter must be the most bashful record-breaker England ever had. He seemed to me like a stowaway, found hidden among the Test team's baggage and put to working his passage in the hope of a pardon.

Paynter is one of the meek who inherit the earth around the popping-crease. Playing for England in Australia in 1932, the little Lancashire left-hander crept in to bat as if he were not sure of his reception – not certain that he was entitled to take his stand in such company.

Unable, despite a stoop, to conceal much of his person behind the bat, he unobtrusively settled himself with both feet pointing somewhere in the direction of mid-off, as if he were ready to sidle away into the slips if the bowler shouted too loud an appeal for leg-before-wicket. If an inattentive umpire neglected to ask him where he would like to take guard, it seemed doubtful whether Paynter would be bold enough to demand that aid to navigation. (Doubtless that was an illusion, and in reality he would speak up for his rights with accents like Gracie Fields' only an octave or so lower.)

You never heard anyone mention this shy century-stealer as E. A. Paynter. Nor was his surname used, alone, in the same tones as people spoke of Hobbs, Hitler and other men of moment. Usually he was called Eddie Paynter, which fitted him much better than Duggie Jardine or Bertie Sutcliffe would have suited those two cricket dignitaries.

Eddie Paynter hardly looked the part of a great Test batsman. It was not merely that he was small (5 ft. 5½ in. and 10 st. 5 lb.). Many pint-size men are perky and cocksure, some of them assertive, raspingly assertive. Anyway, the height of a Woolley or the tonnage of an Armstrong is not essential for dignified deportment, as Hassett's bearing proves. More likely, the lack of faith selectors had shown in Paynter over the years left no reason for jauntiness. He probably felt lucky to be where he was.

Much of his career reads like a hard-luck story. He was born in 1901 – on Guy Fawkes Day, though I doubt whether that has any real significance. As a boy he read all the cricket books he could get, apparently without giving much heed to the illustrations, because he never acquired style in his batting. Not long after he left school he lost the tops of the first and second fingers of his right hand in an accident. As he followed the Lancashire team's performances in newspaper reports he little imagined that he would play for his county, though his father, captain of Enfield Second XI, had that ambition for him.

Paynter was eighteen when Tom Lancaster, former Enfield professional, introduced him to the county club. Though Johnny Tyldesley's coaching put him wise to many tricks of the trade, he had to wait seven years for his first chance in the Lancashire XI. Playing for his living, he had to struggle for another three years before he was given a regular place in the team. He was in his thirtieth year before he scored his first hundred in first-class cricket – a decade beyond the age at which Clem Hill and Archie Jackson had made their mark in international matches.

When England's team to visit Australia in 1932-3 was selected, Paynter was not chosen. He scrambled in only when K. S. Duleepsinhji withdrew because of ill-health. When the matches began, Jardine and his co-selectors regarded Paynter as a spare-part batsman among the seventeen, for they played him in only half the matches before the first Test and usually his place in the batting order was No. 8, down among the bowlers.

The tour was half over before he worked his way into the Test eleven. Going in at No. 7 at Adelaide, he played a fighting three-hour knock for 77, helping to retrieve an innings which

7a Jardine

7c Tate

7b Parkin

7d Kilner

8a   Hammond

8b   Bradman
8c   Learie Constantine

8d   Headley

had begun with the loss of four wickets for 30. If Paynter thought Fortune was making amends at last he was mistaken. In the field a few hours later his luck, and his ankle, turned on him. He was helped off with a sprain, and in the second innings limped in at No. 9 with a substitute runner, to score 1 not out.

It was in the next Test, a month later, that the little man became a hero. The story runs that his throat was sore before play began but, hoping the trouble would pass, he could not bring himself to forfeit his place in the side. After a day's sizzling in the field under the Brisbane sun Paynter was sent to hospital, suffering from sunstroke or tonsilitis (or both) with a temperature of 102 degrees. Doctors ordered rest for several days.

On the third afternoon of play, when England's sixth wicket fell with the score 124 short of Australia's, the name PAYNTER was hoisted on the scoreboard, to the astonishment of the crowd. They thought it must be some mistake, because they knew Paynter was lying back on the pillows, probably with a thermometer under his tongue. But the incoming batsman was Paynter, sure enough, and as he walked slowly to the wicket the crowd burst into applause for his gameness. For an hour and a half in enervating heat he defied the bowlers. He even ran between wickets under his own power, though the Australian captain was willing to agree to a substitute runner. At the day's end he was 24 not out.

Paynter was driven back to hospital. I cannot vouch for the published report that his captain insisted that he must reappear next day to finish his innings. In any case, such a command would have been unnecessary; with his team still 69 in arrears, Paynter would have been there if he had to travel by ambulance. He batted two and a half hours more, and when he was caught off a weary stroke for 83 his side was 16 ahead. He fielded for two hours that afternoon. When at last he gave up the crowd cheered him off the field.

After four days, Paynter left hospital, where he was chiefly sustained by cold chicken and iced champagne – an enviable diet in the heat-wave. On the sixth day of play, when the

5

weather broke, rain was falling as he made the winning hit, a six, which decided both the match and the Test rubber.

Like the people of Lancashire, the Australian public showed appreciation of Paynter's pluck by subscribing to a testimonial. Eddie was a shrinking hero when the Australian cheque was presented. For moral support he brought Maurice Leyland and George Duckworth along with him. Or perhaps they brought him along. In England, when a speaker in the House of Commons mentioned his name it was a signal for cheers.

In two other instances of players leaving sick-beds to bat in Test matches neither fielded. After two days down with influenza Clem Hill scored 160 for Australia at Adelaide in 1908, though he almost collapsed at the wicket. At Manchester, in 1934, Arthur Chipperfield, suffering from a throat infection, left Monsall Fever Hospital against medical advice. In reply to England's 627, Australia's seventh wicket had fallen at 411 when Chipperfield tottered in. He scored 26, went back to hospital, and did not rejoin the team for a week. In the Test at the Oval, 1934, Bowes went to hospital on the third day for examination of an intestinal complaint. He was declared unfit to bat. England's innings closed without him, and he spent the night in hospital. Yet next day, though it pained him to run, he took five wickets for 55, then returned to hospital for treatment.

When Paynter headed the averages for the 1932-3 Tests, above Australian and English batsmen of the greatest renown, it might have been expected that at last he had made his place in England's eleven secure. Not a bit of it. He became a forgotten man. England played seven Test series without him, including two rubbers against Australia. The chief cause of England's loss of the 1936-7 rubber was that the flight and spin of O'Reilly and Fleetwood-Smith reduced several of the batsmen to stumblings and gropings. Yet Eddie Paynter – quick-footed, a left-hander, and a resolute batsman who had proved himself on Australian wickets – could do nothing except read about it in the *Manchester Guardian*.

But some notice had to be taken of the modest little man in

1937, when his deeds included a hundred before lunch and 322 in less than a full day against Sussex at Hove, highest score ever by a Lancashire professional. His chief comment on that Bradmanlike achievement was a wistful remark about wishing it had been at Manchester.

Wisden hung his portrait among its Five Cricketers of the Year. By then he was 36 – an age at which many cricketers run full-tilt only when they have no option, and grow canny about sudden stoops in the field, for fear of fibrositis. But out near the boundary no slackening was perceptible in Paynter's swallow-swoops on the ball, which he could throw with either hand. And he always ran each run as if it were his last, or as if he were 99. (He is the only Englishman who has been dismissed for 99 in a Test against Australia.)

Yet he only scraped into England's eleven for the first Test against Australia in 1938 when another batsman, fair-haired, free-driving Hardstaff of Notts, was hurt. In that game Paynter became the first Briton to score 200 off Australian bowling in a Test on English soil. On the Sunday a heap of congratulatory telegrams lay unopened in the team's hotel, for he had slipped away to his home village, Oswaldtwistle. With Compton at Trent Bridge and Hammond at Lord's he took part in record partnerships of 206 for the fifth wicket and 222 for the fourth.

In the next South African summer Paynter scored a hundred in each innings of a Test, a feat which only five other batsmen[1] had accomplished in 276 Tests played by England and the Empire countries. A few weeks later he made the record score, 243, for Anglo-African Tests and became the only Englishman who had scored a double-hundred against both Australia and South Africa. Though an injury kept him out of the fifth Test at Durban his aggregate, 653, set a record for either side in an Anglo-African rubber. Over two consecutive Test rubbers he had outscored the mighty Hammond.

[1] Bardsley (Aust.), Russell, Sutcliffe, Hammond (Eng.), Headley (West Indies) before World War II. Since then by Compton (Eng.), Morris, Bradman (Aust.), Melville, Mitchell (South Africa). Hazare (India).

Though lacking the polish which made strokes by cricket's stylists live in the memory, Paynter could cut and drive and place the ball where the fieldsmen weren't. For his size he packed a big punch. In one innings against West Griqualand he hit nine sixes. On a more solemn occasion, Yorkshire *v.* Lancashire, he irreverently landed five hits over the Bradford boundary. After the war he was still going so strongly as a Bradford League player that at the age of 45 he hit a six and a dozen fours in his twelfth League hundred.

His most exciting stroke was the hook. In playing it he went to town, whirling around with his left toe digging into the blockhole. In his long innings there was an occupational risk that his toe would excavate a crater big enough for him to fall in and be lost to view. His hook brought him countless runs, yet I always thought the best chance of trapping him into a catch was with a shortish, quick-lifting ball on the leg stump.

The real pillars of his batting, lifting it above his technical imperfections, were quick thinking and nimble feet. More than most English batsmen of his day he had both the footwork and the inclination to go forward to kill the spin of the Australian bowling, instead of depending on back-play and reluctant lunges from the crease.

But to take Eddie Paynter's methods to bits to find the secret of his success would be a fruitless piece of dissection. It would miss the soul of his play. No other player survived so many discouragements as he, but hope deferred never made his heart sick. His buoyancy of spirit was revealed in a report from a source usually reliable: after a heavy day in the field Lancashire's players had stepped wearily out of one train in the middle of the night and were awaiting another when Paynter threw a few handsprings along the near-deserted platform. If he had been given a *nom de guerre*, like 'Turner the Terror', it should have been 'Paynter the Persistent'.

from BETWEEN WICKETS *1946*

L. N. *Constantine*

C. L. R. JAMES

Even his countrymen know only the body and not the bones of Constantine's career. The rest of the world, England in particular, knows a great and original cricketer, a man of character, shrewd and genial; and, of late years, with a tendency ('rather a pity') to lay emphasis on racial discrimination. Circumstances placed me in a position to observe at its critical stages the development of one of the most remarkable personalities of the day. He belongs to that distinguished company of men who, through cricket, influenced the history of their time. Head and shoulders above all others is W. G. Grace. There are C. B. Fry, Ranjitsinhji, Lord Hawke, Sir Pelham Warner and Sir Donald Bradman. . . .

Constantine, of course, is a lucky man. But for the war, England would have seen Challenor, Tarilton, George John and W. St Hill in 1913 or 1914. History would have been made. His cricket career, therefore, began at the right time for him, in 1921, and came to an end just at the right time, in 1939. He was lucky, too, in his ancestry. Evans reports a speech of Constantine's brother Elias as follows: 'I'se only hopes, Godfrey, that you happens to be bowling when I'se comes out to bat. Then I shall show you'se how I'se can hit 'em.' Where Evans got that from God only knows. I have never heard *anyone* in the West Indies speak like that. Elias must have been pulling his leg. I knew Elias well. Another brother attended a secondary school where I taught him Latin and French, algebra and geometry. He played for the school team and was a magnificent boy batsman. Youth though he was, he put the length ball through the covers off his back foot in a manner that made me wonder at the injustice which allows one person to do without effort what others sweat in vain to achieve. He died young. . . .

Constantine, as I say, had ancestry. He came from a good family. His father was an overseer on an estate, often, though not always, a white man's preserve. The job, however, was modest. On it he raised a family of fine children, and at the same time managed to maintain his form as an international batsman for a quarter of a century. It was no easy task. In those days black men were usually bowlers. . . . Old Constantine[1] was an independent spirit. Cricket must have meant a great deal to him. Yet when some dispute broke out with the authorities he refused to play any more. One man who saw it told me how A. E. Harragin left the Queen's Park pavilion, walked over to where Constantine was sitting in the stands and persuaded him to come back. Few people in Trinidad, white or black, could refuse Bartie Harragin anything. He was an all-round athlete of rare powers, of singular honesty and charm. I would have accepted any cricket pronouncement of his at face value. (He was one of the very few white men in the island at the time who never seemed aware of the colour of the person he was speaking to.) Many years later a dispute between Old Cons, captaining Shannon, and the Queen's Park Club arose about an umpire. Old Cons did not want him. The Queen's Park captain refused to change him. 'Then you can have the match,' said Old Cons, and led his team out of the Oval. On the cricket field the Constantines of Shannon met all other men as equals.

From the time young Constantine knew himself he knew his father as the most loved and most famous cricketer in the island. His mother's brother, Victor Pascall, was the West Indies slow left-hander, a most charming person and a great popular favourite with all classes. We cannot overestimate the influence of all this on young Constantine. He was born to the purple, and in cricket circles never saw himself as inferior to anyone or dependent for anything on anyone.

[1] See above, page 58.

Constantine is not a pure Negro, if that term has any meaning. Any West Indian who took one glimpse at his father would know that somewhere in his ancestry, and not too far back, there was European blood. The Constantines, however, were black people. Off the cricket field the family prestige would not be worth very much. Constantine was of royal ancestry in cricket, but in ordinary life, though not a pauper, he was no prince. This contrast explains not all, but much.

I saw him for the first time about 1911, a thick-set, rather slow boy. He came to my father's school in St Ann's, Port of Spain, for a short while. A mob of boys used to play 'pass out' in the school-yard. He was already known as his father's son. What I distinctly recall is that in the scramble for the ball he rather stood aside and watched. I did not know that already his father was coaching him and this rough and tumble probably did not appeal to him. My father's school was a Government school, non-denominational. Learie is a Catholic and he soon left to go to a Catholic school.

I lost sight of him for some years until about the early twenties, when I was playing first-class cricket for Maple and he for Shannon. He bowled at me in a match, fast straight stuff to which one could play forward comfortably. He began to get wickets, make a few runs and, above all, take some catches. Even to my interested eye he was full of promise, but not more. Major Harragin, however, was captaining Trinidad in the evening of his cricketing days. He knew a cricketer when he saw one and he probably could see much of the father in the son. Practically on his own individual judgment he put Learie in the intercolonial tournament of 1921. But for the Major's sharp eye and authority it is most unlikely that he would have got in so early. Apart from a wonderful left-handed catch in the slips, he did nothing unusual. (In his only innings he tried a mighty swipe at, I believe, his first ball and was caught at deep point for nought.) Thus the heir-apparent to his father was god-fathered by the most respected and influential cricketers in the island. I have to stress this. From the very beginning he felt himself as good as anyone else. This was a West Indian black man, of the lower middle class, but a man conscious of status.

Now comes the second Constantine characteristic.

George John, always belligerent, announced that when he met the new star in the club competition he was going to send his wickets flying and all turned up to see. (Some people had been making provocative comparisons between John and Learie.) Constantine has described the innings more than once – sixty-seven in an hour, composed of classic defence and the most brilliant strokes against fast bowling of the highest class on a matting wicket in the Savannah. More remarkable than the innings was what followed. Nothing followed. Constantine never played another such innings until 1928 in England. In England or Australia such a display would have marked him down as a rare batsman. He would have been selected as such in big games, coached as such, advised as such, made to feel his responsibility as such. Not so in the West Indies of those days and not so for Constantine. The innings was talked about for a while, then forgotten. Constantine put it behind him and went his own carefree way.

The innings against John was an explosion. Now follows another. He goes to British Guiana with the intercolonial team, does nothing to speak of with bat or ball, but, placed by chance at cover-point, by the end of the day emerges as one of the most brilliant covers ever seen in the West Indies.

The princely career continues. H. B. G. Austin, like Major Harragin, knew a cricketer when he saw one, and Constantine was one of his earliest choices for the 1923 tour. Constantine is now sponsored by the man who has more than any other made West Indies cricket what it is. In England he makes useful runs, gets useful wickets and Sidney Pardon calls him an 'amazingly good' cover-point. Mr Pelham Warner arranges for him to be coached at Lord's. Hobbs tells him that he is yards faster to the ball than anyone he has ever seen; he gives him some hints on technique and finesse which Constantine stores

for future use. He is a success, but he has not set the Thames
on fire, and, what is more, he hasn't tried to.

He goes back to the West Indies. Although one of the first
choices and always doing astonishing things with bat, ball or
in the field, his actual performances in big cricket do not single
him out in any way. Except for his fielding at cover, where he
is now an admitted master. In fact in 1926 he was dropped from
the first All West Indies XI against the M.C.C. in Barbados.
No Trinidad selection committee would have dared to drop
him in Trinidad. Again it was H. B. G. Austin who took him to
British Guiana for the All West Indies side. Austin had just
fielded out in Barbados to nearly 600 runs, he wanted a cover-
point in the team and Constantine by this time had made
himself into a cover-point such as no one had ever seen before.
He now bowled very well, but he was not really fast. He might
make runs or not, more often not. One brief episode, however,
in 1926 remains clearly in my mind from the time I saw it to
this day.

Late one afternoon he walked in to bat to the bowling of
Hammond. Hammond bowled him a ball pitching a foot or so
outside the off-stump, breaking in. Constantine advanced his
left foot halfway to meet the ball and saw the break crowd in on
him. Doubling himself almost into two, to give himself space,
he cut the ball a little to the left of point for a four which no
one in the world, not even himself, could have stopped. He
tried it again next ball, but this time Hammond brought the
ball closer to the wicket. He could get only two and was
soon out.

What made us sit up and take notice was that he had never
in his life made such a stroke before – that came out afterwards
– and he had had no premeditated idea of making any such
stroke. I do not remember seeing it again. He went in, there
was the ball, and on the spur of the moment he responded.
Every few years one sees a stroke that remains in the mind, as a
single gesture of an actor in a long performance remains in the
mind. (It is not always great batsmen who make them: I have

5*

seen two at least made by Freddie Trueman.) This one brought
back vividly the innings against John. It stamped Constantine
as a batsman who could do anything that he wanted to do. But
after the Englishmen left he relapsed into his carefree batting.
We used to beg him to settle down and bat. He simply wouldn't
'settle down'. When the news of his scoring in 1928 began to
reach us we were startled enough, but nothing as startled as
when we saw his first innings on his return. He had indeed
settled down to bat, but in a manner peculiar to himself;
every other stroke seemed an improvization of the type that
had flashed before us in 1926. Nobody, not a single soul, had
ever seen Constantine bat in the West Indies as he batted in
England in 1928. This was the biggest explosion so far. He
took 100 wickets, made 1,000 runs and laid claim to being the
finest fieldsman yet known. He had changed. If the change had
taken place in England it had been well prepared in the
West Indies.

Constantine, the heir-apparent, the happy warrior, the darling of the crowd, prize pupil of the captain of the West Indies,
had revolted against the revolting contrast between his first-
class status as a cricketer and his third-class status as a man.
Contrary to all other West Indian cricketers, his development
was slow. An occasion presented itself and he added a cubit to
his stature. That is the cricketer. That is his character as a man.
The restraints imposed upon him by social conditions in the
West Indies had become intolerable and he decided to stand
them no longer.

from BEYOND A BOUNDARY *1963*

Walter Hammond

NEVILLE CARDUS

Walter Hammond was one of the truly great cricketers in the game's history. It would be hard to leave him out of any recorded England XI, though blasphemy might be committed if we altered a single name of the magnificent membership of the England XI which played at Birmingham in 1902; who of these could with justice and decency stand down even for Hammond – A. C. MacLaren, C. B. Fry, K. S. Ranjitsinhji, F. S. Jackson, Tyldesley, Lilley, Hirst, G. L. Jessop, Braund, Lockwood, Rhodes? Do I hear a whispered suggestion that Tyldesley was not greater than Hammond as a batsman and no bowler at all? But I cannot argue reasonably on behalf of J. T. Tyldesley. In his heyday he was the only English professional player who by batting alone could retain his position in the England team. I flatter Hammond by bringing his name into contact with Tyldesley's, even as I honour Tyldesley by the same verbal conjunction. Hammond indeed was the complete cricketer in his superb physique, which combined power and lissome movement; his batsmanship attained in time classic poise and the habit of long domination. He was a dangerous medium-paced bowler who, given the ambition, might have vied with George Lohmann in all round and elegant skill; for I doubt if even Lohmann was Hammond's superior as a slip fieldsman.

He looked the part too, even as Lohmann looked it. His shoulders were broad; the physical frame as a whole maybe at first hinted of top-heaviness somewhere, and there seemed a tendency of his legs, as he stood in the slips, to go together at the knees. At the first sight of a snick from the edge of the bat his energy apparently electrified the shape and substance of him; he became light and boneless, and down to the earth he would dive, all curves and balance, and he would catch a ghost of a 'chance' as if by instinct; quick though it moved, the body no doubt lagged behind the born gameplayer's intuitions. He could take a slip catch as the ball flashed rapidly away, wheeling on the ballet dancer's toes and not so much gripping or seizing the ball as bringing it back, so to say, with time to spare. Only A. P. F. Chapman of Hammond's contemporaries equalled Hammond at catching close to the wicket.

I first saw Hammond in 1923 playing against Lancashire at Gloucester; he was an unknown youth, and he batted low in the innings, amongst the tail-enders. He drove one four to the off, then got out; but I had seen enough. I wrote half a column in the *Manchester Guardian* about the boy and ventured a prophecy of greatness to come. It was easy to look into his future; there is no mistaking the thoroughbred. We needn't look for hours at quality. The scoreboard and the statisticians must wait for results; and mediocrity needs the proof of print and percentages before it is recognized even as mediocrity. Hammond was born to distinction on the cricket field; before he had been playing for Gloucestershire long most of us knew that here was one of the elect, the chosen few. But not everybody knew; in 1924 I argued with John Sharp of Lancashire, then on the England selection committee, that already Hammond was worth his colours. But Sharp thought he lacked discretion; 'He's a bit of a dasher,' he said. In fact, Hammond's career as a batsman can be divided into two periods, much as the career of Hobbs can be divided. First he was all swift aggression, even to the verge of recklessness. Then followed the illness which in 1926 nearly put an end to his cricket. And now he merged into maturity just as Test matches were changing in temper and attitude according to what I shall herewith call the Jardinian theory, the theory taught by the strongest-willed of all the captains of England Elevens, the theory of the survival not so much of the fittest but of the most durable. The great batsman for the purposes of Test matches, according to this theory, was he who stayed in for hours and compiled large quantities of runs, not necessarily by command and beautiful strokes but by the processes of attrition. Hammond remained to the end a batsman handsome to look at, a pedigree batsman, monumental and classic. But I shall continue to try to remember well the young Hammond who in 1927 when the Gloucestershire cause seemed lost beyond repair, hooked the pace of McDonald with a savage power I had seldom seen before and have never seen since. At this point I imagine the eyebrows of most of my more experienced readers are going up questionably – 'Hammond hooking? But Hammond didn't use the hook. If he had a weakness at all it was lack of resourceful strokes to leg. O'Reilly could keep him quiet by bowling on his leg stump.' On the morning of Friday, May 20, Gloucestershire, with two wickets down in their second innings, were only 44 ahead. The Lancashire professionals planned to get the match over quickly, so that they could go to the Manchester races. From the first over of the day, bowled by McDonald with the velocity and concentration of a man determined to get to Castle Irwell in time to back a certain winner at 5 to 1 against, Hammond drove five fours from five consecutive balls. The sixth ball would also have counted for four, but it was fielded on the boundary's edge at the sight-screen behind McDonald's arm. A straight drive from the first over of the most dangerous fast bowler of many decades! Hammond punished McDonald so contumaciously that short 'bumpers' soon began whizzing about Hammond's head. He hooked them time after time as ferociously as they were discharged at him. I watched this death-or-glory innings standing in the dusty earth near the Manchester end of the ground, near long leg. Several of Hammond's hooks crashed into the earth, sending gravel flying about us like shrapnel. In some three hours Hammond scored 187, with no chance, four sixes and twenty-four fours.

In August 1924 at the age of twenty-one he wrecked the

Middlesex attack on a dreadful wicket at Bristol. Gloucestershire in first, scored 31, then dismissed Middlesex for 74. In
Gloucestershire's second innings Hammond scored an unbeaten 174 out of 294 for 9 (declared), in four hours, winning
the match. It was cricket of this dauntless kind, with strokes
blinding to the eyesight, strokes of controlled power and
strokes of controlled imagination, all kaleidoscopic and thrilling to the romantic vision, which impelled me to a column
article I sent to the *Observer*, then edited by J. L. Garvin, who
also became convinced of young Hammond's genius. But we
couldn't convince yet the England selection committee that
here was the greatest England batsman since the high noon of
Hobbs. The philosophy of 'safety first' was at this time in full
swing and sway. By the by, when Hammond first got married,
Garvin wrote to me: 'For the next few months he'll probably
not do very much – but afterwards better than ever.'

Because of illness Hammond did not play for England until
1927. Then as one of Chapman's team – in Australia in 1928-29,
Jardine the vice-captain – he scored 905 runs in the rubber,
with an average of 113.12. He began modestly in the first Test
Match of the series, played at Brisbane: 44 and 28. Next at
Sydney he scored 251, followed by 200 and 32 (run out) at
Melbourne, followed by 119 not out and 177 at Adelaide (two
hundreds in the same game), followed by 38 and 16. The world
of cricket was staggered, not realizing of the wrath to come
from Bradman. So far in cricket's history no one human batsman had amassed runs in Test matches with this insatiable
appetite and with Hammond's austerity of purpose and disciplined technique. For he had now put childish things behind
him, at least while playing in Test matches. The glorious un-
certainty of cricket was a term no longer to be sensibly applied
to Test matches between England and Australia; the wickets
all this time were anaesthetic, somnolent couches stuffed with
runs. We must bear these wickets in mind as we make an estimate of the bowling of W. J. O'Reilly, who was doomed to go
to work on them and to toil on them for hours, if he could not

spin. In the circumstances his record and performances well bears comparison with that of the unparalleled Sydney Barnes. Hammond fitted himself into the new economy and the new ethic of sport; and he lost nothing of the grand manner while making the adjustment and the ordered concession to the mathematical and the mechanical. He cut out all but his safest strokes; he became patience on a pedestal of modern concrete; Phœbus Apollo had turned fasting friar. He reserved for matches of lesser importance flashes or flickers of his proper brilliance. His stately and pillared centuries and double-centuries were as classic as the Elgin marbles and about as mobile and substantial. With the ease of absolute mastery he batted maiden over after maiden over, his body bending to the ball almost solicitously, making strokes of cradled gentleness. For the Cause he clipped his own wings; but there is something majestical in wings in repose. He played henceforward mainly off the back foot. His terrific punches to the offside received their strength from a propulsion or a swift thrust of the body beginning at a bent right knee, then steely wrists directed the energy, so that none was wasted; it all ran like a current of power into the bat and through it into the ball.

At Lord's in 1938 his greatest Test match innings may be said to have added to the ground's lustre and history. When he went to the wicket England had lost Hutton, Barnett and Edrich to the alarming pace of McCormick, and not many more than twenty runs had been scored. Hammond at once took charge of the game and after due scrutiny and circumspection he hammered McCormick and Fleetwood-Smith and O'Reilly to shapeless helplessness, never seeming to hurry himself or use his strength combatively; no; he went a red-carpeted way to 240, his cover-drives thundering against the rails under the sign of Father Time. This innings announced that for Hammond ripeness was all that mattered now; the early and dazzling shooting-star had by some astronomical decree changed into the benign satisfying and fulfilled harvest moon. His batting at Lord's this day was marmoreal; an appeal against him for leg-before-wicket, a raucous appeal at that, sounded so incongruous that I was there and then strangely inspired to a satire, in the form of Meredithian parody:

Hammond leg-before-wicket
has anybody noticed that he has a leg?

Usually the leg of the modern batsman is ever before us, obscure it as you will, dressed degenerately in pads of breadth and length, inordinate unvaried length, sheer longinquity ageing the very heart of bowler on a view. Most cricketers have their legs, we have to admit. But what are they? Not the modulated instrument we mean – simply legs for leg-work, legs of an Emmott Robinson. Our cavalier's leg – our Hammond's – is the poetic leg, a valiance, a leg with brains in it, not to be traduced by the trick they ken of at Sheffield . . .

After Hammond put an end to his innings this day in June 1938, everybody stood up as he returned to the pavilion, stood up to render tribute to a cricketer who had ennobled Lord's. After the second war, Hammond again visited Australia, this time as captain. He suffered physical ailment and mental worry, so could not make a good end. But during the 'Victory' Test matches in England, not regarded as official, the original Hammond was seen, riding on the crest of his youth; or, to drop the metaphor, he attacked as of yore, the bat swinging free of care again, sure of aim, and, best of all, a source of enjoyment to himself as well as to all others. One of his more remarkable innings was played on an absurdly difficult wicket at Melbourne, during the 1936-7 rubber; the ball broke most known laws of geometry, trigonometry and suchlike. Now it shot along the earth like a stone thrown over ice; now from the same length would it rise upward at an acute angle threatening batsman's skull or thorax. On this turbulent pitch Hammond maintained his customary poise and calm; his innings of 32 came like oil in raging waters. He stayed in easefully for an hour and a half, never once obliged to hasten a stroke. The irony of it all was that all this mastery was really a service

to Australia; much more good would have come England's
way had Hammond driven and hooked, defying every tabu-
lated principle of science, and scored his runs in a quarter of
the time – so that Australia might have had to go to the wicket
and face the music. J. T. Tyldesley in 1903, also on a foul pitch
at Melbourne, made 63 out of England's total of 103, and by
brilliance and versatile if sometimes indiscreet strokes, won the
match, or at least brought victory within England's reach.

Hammond in his pomp occasionally suggested that he was
batting lazily, with not all his mind alert. When he at times
scored slowly on a perfect wicket he conveyed to us the impression that he was missing opportunities to get runs because
of some absence of mind or indolence of disposition. He once
said to me after he had made a large score on a comfortable
wicket, 'It's too easy.' He preferred a worn dust-heap at
Cheltenham, where he would put the most dangerous attack to
the sword, and where fielding in the slips he was Nijinsky and a
myriad-armed Indian god at one and the same animate time.
His career had its pungent ironies, apart from the disillusion-
ment of the curtain's fall. When he first met Fleetwood-Smith,
a googly bowler of rare and enchanting art, Hammond nearly
knocked him out of cricket for good and all. Then in 1937 at
Adelaide, when the rubber was at stake, Hammond and
Fleetwood-Smith came face to face; and we knew that the
decision rested with one or the other. On the closing morning,
England needed 244 to win, with 7 wickets in hand, Hammond
not out. It was the fourth match of the series, England had won
two, Australia one. All our eyes were riveted on Hammond as
he took the bowling of Fleetwood-Smith in a gleaming sunshine. To the third ball of the day Hammond played forward
and was clean bowled. Australia won, drawing equal in the
rubber; they also won the fifth. As Hammond's bails fell to the
ground, Fleetwood-Smith danced, walked on his knees, went
nearly off his head. And I heard Duckworth's voice behind me:
'We wouldn't have got Don out first thing in the morning with
rubber at stake.'

'Too easy.' He was an artist of variable moods. But he was greater than the statisticians suspect. Perhaps all of a beautiful batsman's innings should be of brief duration – as Edgar Allan Poe said all poetry should be short. At least no innings by a master and artist should seem longer than any ever played by Trumper, Woolley or John Tyldesley. There were more things in Hammond's cricket than are dreamed of in the scorebook's economy.

from CLOSE OF PLAY *1956*

Fast Bowlers 1921-46

RAY ROBINSON

Fast bowlers' rewards for hurling the ball swifter than full gale force (63 m.p.h.)[1] are unjustly inadequate. They tear into action reckless of sprained ankles, synovitis, hernia and lumbago, yet their bowling averages are no better, often worse, than those of men who amble up comfortably to bowl. No fast bowler has lasted long enough to be among the nine players who have taken 100 wickets in Tests between Australia and England.

Yet the most dramatic moments of the game belong to them. They allow batsmen only a split second to sight the ball and play a stroke. They send stumps cartwheeling, sometimes smash them. There is no moment in any sport more tense than the hush as a fast bowler rushes up to fling down the first ball in a Test, especially if it is at Melbourne with about 80,000 people holding their breath at once.

An attempt to grade fast bowlers in order of speed is likely to provoke even more disagreement than those tennis ranking lists in which players are told off by numbers. I would place those who have bowled for or against Australia since World War I in five groups:[2]

1. H. Larwood (England).
2. E. A. McDonald, J. M. Gregory (Australia).
3. L. N. Constantine (West Indies), E. L. McCormick (Aust.), K. Farnes, G. O. Allen, H. Howell (Eng.), R. J. Crisp (South Africa), H. H. Alexander (Aust.).
4. T. W. Wall, R. R. Lindwall, K. R. Miller, L. J. Nash, H. M.

[1] The estimate that Larwood bowled at 90 m.p.h. may be near the mark; the record for a baseball pitcher's throw is 98·6 m.p.h.

[2] *Published in 1946 – Ed.*

Thurlow (Aust.), J. W. Hitch, E. W. Clark, T. J. Durston (Eng.), H. C. Griffith, G. N. Francis (West Indies).

5. A. J. Bell (S. Africa), A. E. R. Gilligan, M. S. Nichols, W. Voce, W. E. Bowes, W. J. Edrich (Eng.), J. Cowie (N.Z.).

Harold Larwood was the greatest fast bowler, Ted McDonald the finest bowler of the men who could bowl fast. They were strikingly dissimilar – Larwood short (5 ft. 8½ in.), blue-eyed, with fair hair standing up from his forehead as if the wind had blown it back; McDonald tall (6 ft. 1 in.), dark-eyed, with black hair parted a little left of centre. In action they were superb. Either could have been a model for the sculpture of a 20th-century equivalent of the ancient Discus Thrower, but in an attitude suggesting greater mobility and enough heedlessness of the rules of discus-throwing to launch it overhead. They surpassed all others in rapid ease of approach and delivery, and in their interplay of arm and body-swing to bring the ball back off the pitch six inches or more in dehydrated Australian conditions – like a continuation of in-swing, only sharper.

Larwood's nickname 'Lol' could not have come from anything he did on the cricket field. His bowling style was more emphatic than McDonald's. He came bounding up with almost a military briskness in his fourteen strides, as if he had practised his approach to a quick march by a regimental band. At the climax his left foot came down with a positive stamp; he tilted his head aside so that his arm could swish over vertically for the downward snap of the wrist that put the fly in flier. His right boot dragged over the line but his foot placement was so sure that everybody was surprised when he tripped over the stumps and fell, smashing one stump, in Australia's second innings at Brisbane, 1933.

McDonald's approach looked more gliding. He ran 18 yards, and there was something ominous about the way he came up, his arm swinging with rhythmic menace, the wrist coiling like a cobra about to strike. Many a bruised rib testified to the venom put into quick-rising balls by the man with the lean, sun-tanned face. Mac never fired until the batsman could see the whites of his eyes. Though his fastest deliveries hardly equalled Larwood's in muzzle velocity, he smashed a shoulder off Ducat's bat in the Leeds Test, 1921. He broke two stumps in a match against Essex. MacLaren, who sized up cricketers with almost psychic discernment, said of him: 'The best fast bowler I have seen. Not the fastest, but the best.'

McDonald and Constantine were the cleverest bowlers I have seen at confusing batsmen with changes of pace. Mac's slow one was so well concealed that sometimes the victim finished his stroke before the ball arrived. Often it was a yorker. McDonald was so adaptable that if a wet foothold or a dead pitch made fast bowling hopeless he could jettison speed and send down medium-pace off-breaks as expertly as if he had bowled nothing else all his life. Skill in making the most of varying conditions was one reason why he was a greater bowler in England than Australia. Another was that continuous play tuned him up to a pitch of physical fitness he never attained in his own country. (He was known to open the season for Fitzroy without a single practice and bowl 15 overs on the first afternoon without a creak from muscles which had been out of use during the winter.)

When he measured arm-spreads with the Victorian all-rounder Arthur Liddicut (another man of 6 ft. 1 in.) Mac's span was six inches longer. From fingertip to fingertip it was 6 ft. 4 in., an inch more than the reach of Max Schmeling, 1936 world heavyweight champion, who was the same height. Double-jointed in the shoulders, McDonald could clasp his hands in front and, without unclasping them, pass them back over his head and down behind him until they rested on his hindquarters.

His action was smoother than Larwood's, and this helps to account for his superiority in stamina. Because of the 1914–18 war his first chance in Test cricket did not come until he was 29 – an age when most fast bowlers have passed their peak. Yet in the five Tests in England in 1921 he took 27 wickets –

still the record for a fast bowler of any country in a rubber on English soil. Whereas Larwood's Test captains always rested him after four or five overs, McDonald would have regarded it as a gesture of no-confidence if he had been taken off so soon. He was known to open with half a dozen overs against the wind and soon to reappear with the wind behind him. In one innings against England he bowled 18 overs for only 24 runs in 2¾ hours' play (12.30 to 4 p.m., with lunch intervening) and in 3½ hours sent down 136 balls in taking five wickets for 32, the fifth with a trimmer which sent a bail 50 yards.

No Australian bowler of any type since 1890 has taken as many wickets on a tour of England as McDonald's 150 in 1921. After he left Victoria for Lancashire and became a professional, McDonald took 205 wickets in the 1925 season, at the age of 33. In his six full seasons for the county he bowled 1,300 more overs and took 300 more wickets than Larwood, though he was twelve years older. At 38, McDonald bowled 1¼ hours unchanged for Lancashire against the Australians; he made the ball fly shoulder-high, posted five slip fieldsmen for Bradman and sent the leg stump careering for yards with a snorter. McDonald was 39 before a sudden fading in form ended a career in first-class cricket covering a 22-year span, for he first played for Tasmania in 1909. He was 45 when he was killed in a car accident in Lancashire. Of his 1,400 wickets (average 20) 315 were taken in 60 matches before he went to live in England.

With Gregory he formed the most overpowering double-edged speed attack that ever cut Test batsmen down. They opened the bowling together in 22 English and South African innings; in 18 innings one wicket or more fell before the score passed the thirties; only three opening partnerships reached 50 (highest 65) when they played a full part in the attack.[1] The

---

[1] On the last day of the fifth Test, 1921, when A. C. Russell and G. Brown scored 158 for England's first wicket, Gregory and McDonald bowled only nine overs between them. With the match petering out in a draw, batsmen did much of Australia's bowling.

first time they bowled together in a Test in England, at Nottingham, 1921, the Englishmen were bundled out for 112; given a couple of breathers when rain interrupted play, Gregory (19 overs, unchanged) and McDonald (15 overs) bowled all except three overs in the innings. It was primarily their tempestuous assault which enabled Australia to win that match in two days and to clinch the rubber by winning the next two Tests well inside the three-day time-limit. In that season the pair took 46 of the 71 wickets that fell to Australia's bowlers – a higher proportion (almost two-thirds) than was gained by any two fast bowlers in the English battery which unhinged the Australians in 1932-3 or in the West Indians' tornado which unroofed England's batting in 1934-5.

The terrible pair, especially Gregory, exploited the time-honoured right of fast bowlers to test batsmen's pluck with steep-rising balls. The equally time-honoured riposte for batsmen is to hook short-pitched fliers and make them so costly that the bowler has to desist. As no more than three fieldsmen were placed on the leg side, sometimes fewer, the batsmen's scope for hooking was not curtailed but the Englishmen suffered heavy casualties. At Nottingham Gregory knocked out and bowled out Ernest Tyldesley with one ball – it glanced from the batsman's head to the stumps – and the crowd hooted every ball he sent down in the next couple of hours. At the Oval Tyldesley attempted a hook and was struck on the jaw, this time by McDonald. In scoring 93 and 95 at Lord's, Woolley earned great admiration for skill and gameness; two bumpers from Gregory hit him on the ribs and left shoulder-blade early in his second innings.

Jack Morrison Gregory was the greatest cricket-field personality I have seen. If in his day there had been radio descriptions which swelled interest in the game soon after his retirement I believe he would have been the greatest drawcard in cricket history.[1] At his peak he was the world's best

---

[1] Total attendances (943,000) at the five Tests in 1936-7 were 256,000 greater than in 1924-5, Gregory's last full Test season in Australia.

all-rounder, a whirlwind bowler, entertaining left-hand bats-man, superb slipfielder, acrobat and juggler all rolled into one – a romping giant of 6 ft. 3½ in. and 14 stone, agile as a circus tumbler. He played bareheaded, no matter how hot the sun, and never took a sip from the drinks carried out on the field. (At dressing-room functions his glass never got mixed with others because he parked it on ledges nobody else could reach.)

Gregory was the most spectacular bowler of the lot. After a few walking steps he rushed at the batsman with ten bounds. The ninth was a kangaroo hop with the right foot; the hop and his final delivery stride each covered 8 ft. or 9 ft. His towering figure and fearsome expression – blue eyes bulging, teeth bared – were terrifying enough to scare the wits out of bats-men before he let fly with the ball. Hobbs said he found Gregory more dangerous than McDonald because of the way he made the most of his advantage in height. Of all speed bowlers taken by Oldfield he made the new ball swing most.

The most deadly burst by a fast bowler in a Test between the wars was Gregory's 3 for 0 in two overs at Nottingham, 1921. His 23 wickets in 1920-1 are still the record for an Australian fast bowler in a rubber in Australia. No fast bowler has since equalled his endurance feat of 491 balls in one Test at Mel-bourne – bowled in eight-ball overs at that. Though he flung his body about as he bounded up his feet came down about the same places each time, and he wore ten brown patches in the grass, as if an elephant had passed that way. Gregory lasted ten years in first-class cricket. Twisting and jarring damaged the cartilage of his right knee in 1921 and he had it removed in 1923. He was 33 when the knee gave out in the Brisbane Test, 1928, after he had bowled 41 overs. With 85 wickets (average 21) in 21 matches against England and three matches against South Africa he is the heaviest Test wicket-taker among right-hand fast bowlers of any country since World War I.

Larwood was half a foot shorter than Gregory but had a tall man's reach of arm, was strong in the back and made the ball lift just as abruptly. He entered Test cricket at 21, three years after he had changed his occupation from coal-mining to professional cricket. He was the most feared of England's bowlers from the first time he bowled in a Test in Australia, at Brisbane, 1928, when he took 6 for 32, his greatest haul in a Test innings. His ability to break the back of an innings with a surge of speed was proved in that match when he took 3 for 9 in his first five overs. Similar bursts were his 3 for 15 in five overs at Sydney, 1932, 3 for 14 in eight overs on the same ground in 1933, and 2 for 3 (Bradman and Ponsford) in two overs at Brisbane, 1933. In the 28 innings in which he bowled against Australia only two opening partnerships exceeded 100 and four others got past 50. In twenty Tests against Australia, South Africa and West Indies he took 78 wickets (average 28). With a ball that bowled G. F. Martin (Tasmania) at Launceston in 1929 he sent a bail 66 yards.

Watching Larwood in action it was difficult to imagine that anybody could ever have bowled faster, though old-timers were convinced that C. J. Kortright (Essex), J. J. Kotze (South Africa) and Ernest Jones (South Australia) had greater speed. I cannot credit that fast bowlers – unlike golfers, swimmers, runners, pole-vaulters and other agile members of the human race – have failed to advance with the times but have fallen back. Assuming that those who believe bowlers were quicker in the horse-tram days have been able to carry an accurate picture in their minds of the exact degree of pace necessary for a true comparison, it is more likely that the change in wickets is responsible for that impression. The way pitches have been prepared, steadily growing easier for batsmen, has denied fast bowlers some of the response they used to get from the earth.

Dull-paced wickets and modern, long-term batting skill reduced even Larwood to panting futility in Tests against the Australians. When he had played ten Tests against them his 31 wickets had cost 41 runs each and an excessive expenditure of energy – 88 balls for each wicket. In 1930 Sir Pelham Warner said the spearhead of England's attack, Larwood and Tate, had been blunted and asked: 'Had we a better fast bowler than

Larwood who had been very unsuccessful against the Australians since he bowled them out at Brisbane and – though not so inexpensively – at Sydney?'

Two years later Larwood reasserted himself in the most dramatic of all Test rubbers. His 162 wickets in the 1932 English season – 24 more than his previous best in 1928 – suggested that he was an even better bowler than before. But the paramount reason for the havoc he wreaked in Australia, dwarfing all other factors, was the adoption of the tactics which caused the bodyline row. Larwood took 33 wickets in the five Tests, an all-time record for a fast bowler in one rubber; their cost fell from 41 runs to 19 apiece, and the number of balls he bowled for each wicket dropped from 88 to 40. Just as he was the world's master of the nobler arts and crafts of fast bowling, Larwood exploited his anti-personnel stuff more intelligently and dangerously than the others. Getting batsmen to cock up catches off rearing balls was not the chief purpose of his strategy. He used bumpers scientifically to soften up their defences, to divide their attention between playing the ball and saving their skins. Once he got them ducking and hopping they were easier prey for a sudden, well-pitched, straight ball, especially if he could make them back away and leave their stumps exposed. In the five Tests in which bodyline was used almost half of Larwood's victims were bowled (16 of 33), two l.b.w., and 15 caught.

Before bodyline was outlawed its defenders and apologists emphasized Larwood's accuracy to give non-witnesses the impression of pace without peril. Those who could see for themselves knew better. After one ultra-short ball had whizzed over a batsman's head a Sydney barracker called: 'Eh, Harold! That would have been a yorker if you'd bowled it from the other end.' A Press pundit's advice to the batsman that what was needed to play Larwood was a straight bat and a stout heart was soon disproved; while those two things couldn't be done without, there was an even greater call for a cross bat and a tough hide.

With fast bowlers, accuracy is not a matter of pin-point precision; like Air Force bomb-aimers, the high-speed men do well if they land the ball in the target area. Larwood's rate of expense in Test cricket was 44½ runs per 100 balls. Half a dozen regular fast bowlers in Tests since the First World War were more economical. The point about Larwood was his control at pace: while bowling swifter than the others he was up among the best of them for command of the ball.

Even his haul of 33 wickets fell short of reflecting Larwood's power as a match-winner in 1932-3 with his new methods. He took them with 530 fewer balls than Tom Richardson had bowled to get 32 Australian wickets in 1894-5, and 330 fewer balls than F. R. Foster's loose-sleeved left arm had swung along to take 32 wickets in 1911-12. More than that, the reign of terror which Larwood set up with Voce's help undermined the Australian batting and made inroads by other English bowlers easier. Twelve summers later, when Notts men in Admiral Sir Bruce Fraser's fleet reached Australia they were surprised to find, instead of animosity towards Larwood, a feeling of regret that the great bowler should ever have been mixed up in such unpleasant business. Long before he was warmly applauded for his innings of 98 in the final Test, Larwood had needed no recorder of sound-waves to discover that the angry billows of noise from the crowd were directed not at him personally but at the methods used.

As a fast bowler in Test cricket he died with his boots on. The hard Australian ground took final toll of his thumping left foot in the last weeks of the tour. Though he bowled four overs per innings fewer in the 1928-9 Tests, his work under Jardine was more intense, his rests shorter; he was four years older and a heavier man (12 st. 5 lb.). For Chapman he had done less than one-fifth of England's bowling; for Jardine he sent down more than one-fourth of the overs bowled.

His breakdown came on the fourth day of the last Test. It was a heavy match for Larwood. In Australia's first innings, which lasted almost seven hours, he bowled 32 overs; then he batted for 2¼ hours in England's first innings. In eagerness to break a Woodfull-Bradman partnership in Australia's second innings Jardine kept throwing Larwood into the attack. The fast bowler had only two overs' rest before he was summoned to his third turn at the crease; his speed slackened, he began to walk gingerly on his left foot and he was taken off after one over. Less than a quarter-hour later he was called on again. With set jaw he bowled three more overs before Verity dismissed Bradman at the other end. Following Bradman from the field Larwood limped out of Test cricket.

Damage to the left big toe joint and fracture of two small bones beneath the toe kept him out of action for 14 months. After an operation he resumed county cricket in 1934, bruised his foot in Notts' first game, suffered a strain in the second, missed the third, blistered the toe in the fifth. I believe England's selectors were willing to gamble on his standing up to four-day Test play against the Australians, but as Fry put it, 'Larwouldn't'. In mid-season, when he was second in county cricket averages, he broke down again and bowled in only four innings in Notts' remaining fourteen matches. He was 33 and in his fourteenth year in first-class cricket when his form flickered out in 1938. On his retirement to his poultry run at the Notts village of Annesley Woodhouse I didn't hear anybody repeat the playful curse, 'May your chooks die'. Rather, Australians wished him hard shells and good hatchings.

Though most widely known as Larwood's partner in making batsmen's flesh creep, Bill Voce, five years younger, achieved much more success as a Test bowler in solo parts than by sawing away at a second fiddle of frightfulness. The powerful Notts left-hander, 6 ft. and 14 st. before he really filled out, was a hardy man of stamina. Despite a torn ligament in his left hand he bowled 32 overs in one innings against South Africa in 1931. After the Australians protested about his body-line tactics for Notts against them in 1934 he was withdrawn from the last day's play; the official reason was shin-soreness, but nobody ran for a doctor. When he took 6 for 41 at Brisbane in 1936 a London newspaper poster proclaimed: AUSTRALIANS HELD IN VOCE-LIKE GRIP. Voce holds two records for a Test fast bowler between the wars – most wickets (97, average cost 26) and most balls (5,678 in 24 Tests). On Army leave in 1946 he gained selection for the first post-war tour of Australia but at 37 more than his experience had widened and he could not reproduce his old sting.

Fastest of the left-handers, Northamptonshire's tall, fair Ted Clark varied his in-swinger with a paralysing ball that flashed across like a supercharged leg-break. His only Test tour abroad was to India, so Australian umpires were not called on for an opinion whether his pronounced wristflick amounted to a jerk within the meaning of Law 10.[1]

Learie Constantine, happy-go-lucky cricketer from Trinidad, bowled without removing his cap from his short-clipped, crinkly hair. He did not even bother to roll up his sleeves, but kept them buttoned at the wrist. Of middle height, he seemed in flannels to consist mainly of a pair of long legs surmounted by broad shoulders, with long arms dangling loosely from each corner. Constantine was the most brilliant fieldsman of his period, probably of all time, and ranked with Gregory as an eye-catching all-rounder.

On the West Indians' tour of Australia, 1930-1, Constantine bowled mainly fast-medium, with an occasional fast ball, but when he let himself go in one match his speed was close to Larwood's. He covered his 19-yard run-up with long, easy strides. Sometimes he began his delivery swing with his hand in front of his chest; sometimes it started higher than his forehead. Batsmen who looked to that difference for a clue to the ball's pace were fooled, because he bowled both quick and slower ones with either action. After he turned thirty Constantine

---

[1] I believe a doubt whether H. Ironmonger's action would satisfy English umpires kept the great Victorian left-hander out of more than one Australian tour of Britain. Ironmonger, who spun the ball more sharply than Rhodes, Parker, White and Verity, was passed by first-class umpires in Australia, as Clark was in England.

still had enough pace to give England an imitation of the
kind of attack which had caused the blue when Jardine's team
toured Australia. At Manchester, 1933, he and powerful E. A.
Martindale bowled fast to a leg field of up to six men. Though
they did not reach Larwood's heights of speed and menace
Hammond was hit three times; one ball from Martindale laid
his chin open. Hobbs commented: 'I am glad in one sense that
the West Indians introduced bodyline, because now English
people know exactly what it means.'

On the quicker West Indian wickets two summers later
England's batting crumpled before the fast bowling of Martindale, Constantine and L. G. Hylton, a massive Paul Robeson
of a man. The three Negroes shared 47 wickets in the four
Tests; England's captain, Wyatt, said they were the best combination of the kind in the world. Wyatt could speak feelingly
because Martindale had broken his jaw. England reached 250
only twice in eight innings, and *Wisden* reported: 'While the
West Indies never resorted to the packed leg side, and orthodox
placing of the field was usual throughout the tour, some of the
England players complained of occasional attempts at intimi-
dation in the matter of short-pitched deliveries and full-tosses
directed at the batsmen.' The tour ended in March, 1935, the
month in which the M.C.C. issued the first instruction to
umpires to stop 'direct attack' (since incorporated in Law 43,
empowering umpires to deal with unfair play).

Two years earlier the Australian Board of Control had
adopted a rule framed by three Test captains (M. A. Noble,
W. M. Woodfull, V. Y. Richardson) and R. J. Hartigan, who
scored 116 in his first Test in 1908:

> Any ball delivered which, in the opinion of the umpire at the
> bowler's end, is bowled at the batsman with intent to intimidate
> or injure him, shall be considered unfair, and 'no-ball' shall be
> called, and the bowler notified of the reason. If the offence be
> repeated by the same bowler in the same innings he shall be
> immediately instructed by the umpire to cease bowling, and the
> over shall be regarded as completed. Such bowler shall not be

permitted to bowl during the course of the innings then in
progress.

The first part of the rule was applied in an inter-state match
at Sydney in January, 1936, when short-pitched fliers from the
Queensland aboriginal, Eddie Gilbert, hit H. Mudge, R. H.
Robinson and A. Marks. Two of them retired hurt. After
warning Gilbert, Test umpire George Borwick no-balled him
once. The bowler sent down no more balls which Borwick
regarded as intimidatory.

Short in build but long-armed, Gilbert took only four or
five steps to the crease. There, he made a sudden bow as his
arm flashed over and down until his hand finished alongside
his left shin. Often his bowling was fast-medium but now and
again he turned on scorching speed. On an underdone pitch
at Brisbane, 1931, he began as if instead of an arm he had a
bazooka up his sleeve; the slips dropped back to nearer the
boundary than the wicket, and a bumper, sailing over the
distant wicket-keeper (L. Waterman), landed over the sight-
screen. Gilbert took 2 for 0 in his first over, one of them
Bradman, who fell down twice in avoiding fliers. In reply to
commiserations about his sudden dismissal Don said: 'Luckiest
duck I ever made.' Batsmen estimated that in his first few overs
that day Gilbert bowled faster than Larwood. He was then
twenty-three. A season later Gilbert and Larwood bowled in
the match between Queensland and England, but the abo, who
had been under diathermic treatment for inflammation of the
shoulder socket, hardly exceeded medium-pace.

Gilbert's ability to bowl fast after only a few steps brought
his arm action under suspicion. There was something flail-like
in the movement of his forearm, and at Melbourne in December, 1931, the leading Victorian umpire, A. Barlow, no-balled
him eleven times in three overs. Gilbert bowled his third over
from the opposite end but Barlow called him from the square-
leg position, and the abo was not put on again in the match.
Queenslanders were so sure that Gilbert did not throw that a
slow-motion film of his action was made. He was not sent to

play at Melbourne again but was passed by umpires elsewhere.

Perhaps there is something in the arm structure of the boomerang-throwing race[1] which makes their bowling action look dubious. Back in 1900-1 another aboriginal fast bowler, Jack Marsh (N.S.W.), was no-balled nineteen times by Test umpire R. Crockett in a match against Victoria at Sydney. After that Marsh bowled with his arm in splints in a trial to prove that he did not throw.

Tim Wall was the most gentlemanly of all fast bowlers. Don't imagine that when the Adelaide schoolmaster hit batsmen it hurt him more than it did them, but if he had that streak of savagery most fast bowlers possess it was faintly marked. Wall stood 6 ft. 0½ in. in his shoes, weighed 12 st. and had a good high action. He bowled probably the best outswinger of the lot, especially when a gentle breeze blew from mid-on. His debit rate was the lowest of all regular fast bowlers in Anglo-Australian Tests between the wars – a fraction less than 44 runs per 100 balls. He is the only man who has taken ten wickets in an innings in Sheffield Shield cricket.

Wall ran up with a dozen long strides, delivered as he came down on the thirteenth and – including five or six follow-through strides and his hikes back to starting-point – he covered about 50 yards for each ball. On an average he bowled 85 balls for each wicket in Tests, so he covered 2 miles 3 furlongs, half run, half walked, for each. In his eighteen Tests he travelled 133 miles for his 56 wickets (average cost, 35). His 294 balls in an innings at Lord's, 1934 (when he was 30), are a record for an Australian fast bowler in England.

In twenty-five innings against England, Wall dismissed only four opening batsmen in his first turn at the crease, but he was a great-hearted trier who never gave up. At Manchester, 1930, England had passed 100 without loss before he came on for a second time and in four overs took 3 for 6 (Hobbs, Sutcliffe, Hammond). In England's first innings at Melbourne,

[1] A Queensland tribesman, King Billy, made the longest throw recorded in Australia, 140 yards, at Clermont in the 1872-3 summer.

9a Larwood

9c McCabe

9d Leyland

9b Paynter

10a & b   O'Reilly

10c   Wellard, hitter of sixes

10d   Mushtaq Ali

1932, his 3 for 8 in four overs were taken after the tea interval. He skittled Hammond three times in Tests with balls that pitched on the leg and middle stumps and went away to hit the off stump. In all he got rid of Hammond for under 40 five times, thereby saving the Australians many calluses on the soles of their feet.

Harry Alexander, thickset Victorian fast bowler, was soon nicknamed 'Bull' because of a number of characteristics, most conspicuous of which were his charge to the wicket, his bellowed appeals for snicked catches, and the size of his chest, broad, deep and hirsute. The fine line of his Gable-style moustache betokened a steady hand in the morning but his bowling was more notable for speed than control. When Alexander entered first-class cricket in 1929 he made his mark in more ways than one. In his follow-through his boots scratched the pitch in the area where a roughened surface might aid a leg-spin bowler from the other end. One theory was that it was harder for him to slew away off the pitch because he ran pigeon-toed (a mischievous libel on the manoeuvrability of pigeon-toed men). Alexander was twenty-four, but well-meant attempts were made to remodel his follow-through strides by driving a stump in front of the crease on a practice wicket at Essendon, so that to avoid it he would have to make a quick detour after delivery.

After that there was seldom a complaint, but the thing remained a bugbear to Alexander and prevented him from letting himself go with his earlier vim. He took 74 wickets in twenty-five matches for Victoria. In his only Test, at Sydney, 1933, he broke two of Wyatt's bats (the second time, Fred Brown as twelfth man took out a child's bat as well as one of man's size). Jardine, twice, and Hammond were dropped in slips off his bowling. After Jardine complained to the umpire that Alexander's boots were cutting up the pitch the bowler tried around-the-wicket deliveries but was uncomfortable. Reverting to over-the-wicket he bumped one ball over Jardine's head and another struck the English captain a bruising blow

6

in the left side. For all that eventful bowling Alexander received the meagre reward of one wicket.

Fortune was kinder to fair-haired Laurie Nash, who in two Tests at Melbourne took 5 for 22 on a rain-damaged wicket against South Africa in 1932 and 5 for 104 against England in 1937. Nash raced up so quickly that he had to steady himself in delivery, but he made the ball bounce. A chunky athlete of 5 ft. 9 in. and 13 st. 9 lb. he was more famous as one of the most brilliant players of the long-kicking, high-leaping brand of football favoured in two-thirds of the Australian States.

Because he entered Test cricket when Larwood was in mid-career G. O. Allen was regarded as a stand-in for the Notts man, and it was some time before he was given wide recognition as a fast bowler of international class in his own right. The Middlesex amateur, about an inch taller, a couple of pounds lighter and two years older than Larwood, bowled wholeheartedly from the first step of his twelve-yard run. He produced an in-swing visible from the back row of seats and made the ball lift quickly. Allen's most startling Test figures were 5 for 14 in thirteen overs against New Zealand in 1931 on a drying Oval wicket. In all Tests, his striking-rate (a wicket for every 51.5 balls) is the quickest of all England's regular fast bowlers since 1919. His figures – 76 wickets in 21 Tests (average 28.6) – are little inferior to Larwood's; against Australia only, his wickets cost nine runs apiece more.

Complaints about running on the pitch were made about him, too. Perhaps Allen's endeavour to avoid cutting up the pitch had something to do with his entanglement at Manchester in 1934, when he bowled the longest over I have seen in a Test match. The trouble was that when he concentrated on placing his right foot to avoid being no-balled for dragging over the line he lost control of direction and pitched the ball too far off. When he concentrated on putting the ball within the batsman's reach, to save a wide, his feet played him false. In between he would bowl an unchallengable ball, then something would go haywire again. It began to look as if only an early sunset, or the removal of Allen on a stretcher in a state of collapse, would bring merciful relief, but after four no-balls and three wides had been called the distressed bowler completed the over with his thirteenth delivery. Heaven knows what would have happened if Test match rules had required an eight-bowl over.

Allen is the only English bowler who has handed 50 extras to the Australians – 32 no-balls and 18 wides, in thirteen Tests. I have heard that in some match in England in 1929 he had an avid batsman stumped off a wide. Perhaps that gave him an idea.

Queensland's tall H. M. Thurlow ran little risk of being no-balled for dragging over. He often finished his run-up so close in that his right foot kicked the stumps as he delivered the ball. 'Pud' Thurlow, who played in a Test against South Africa in 1932, enjoyed his cricket; his disposition was belied by the fact that in inter-state matches he gashed Kippax's forehead and put Woodfull out for a season with two broken bones in the back of one hand.

The thought of a fast bowler wearing spectacles in action seemed comical until Bill Bowes showed it could be done. I never saw or heard of the blond Yorkshireman's glasses falling off, but he did not bound like Gregory or tear up to the crease like Nash, Allen or Edrich (the only optical aid they could have kept in place would have been motor-cycling goggles). A man of Viking build – 6 ft. 4½ in. and more than 14 st. – Bowes lumbered up easily and delivered the ball at a speed not greatly above fast-medium.

In English conditions he made the ball change course more than any other fast bowler and was outstanding for cutting it back from the off or the leg. That enabled him to hit the stumps more often than the others – he bowled 38 of his 68 victims in Tests. Bowes did not get the same response in sun-dried Australian conditions. Thirteen of his fifteen Tests were in England, one in Australia and the other in New Zealand. Of all English fast bowlers since 1919 who have played in more than five Tests Bowes took his wickets at lowest cost (average

22) and his average of $4\frac{1}{2}$ wickets per match is the highest.[1] International batsmen found him the most difficult English fast bowler to score from; his expense rate for all Tests was $41\frac{3}{4}$ runs per 100 balls. Captured in North Africa, Bowes was a German prisoner for three years and was freed in 1945. He played in one more Test against India a month before he turned thirty-eight.

After Larwood, the English fast bowler who usually looked most likely to get wickets was Kenneth Farnes, the handsome Essex amateur. Why the selectors did not play him more than eight times against Australia was difficult to comprehend. Farnes weighed 15 st. 6 lb., was almost 6 ft. 5 in. tall, and his hand at peak of his action was estimated to have been more than 8 ft. up. With his lofty delivery he could make the ball jump from the pitch, and even on unhelpful wickets he was awkward to face. Once or twice he attained Larwood-like speed. Farnes ran eleven paces, not much more than half as far as Surrey's J. W. Hitch.[2] He could keep up his pace for eight overs on end. Batsmen felt he was at them all the time; in his last Test in Australia, at Melbourne, 1937, he took 6 for 96 while the Australians piled up 604. In fifteen Tests against Australia, South Africa and West Indies he took 60 wickets; against Australia only he got his wickets two runs cheaper apiece than Larwood and at a quicker rate (one in 57 balls). A schoolmaster and a man of personal charm, Farnes was fond of painting; on tour he never missed a worthwhile art gallery. He was thirty when he was killed in 1941, a fortnight after his return to England from qualifying in Canada as a R.A.F. pilot.

[1] Fast bowlers who had averages better than 22 in fewer than five Tests since 1919:

	Tests	Balls	Runs	Wkts	Av	Balls per wicket	Runs per 100 balls
G. Bisset (S. Af.)	4	989	469	25	18	40	47
W. Copson (Eng.)	2	420	185	12	15	35	44
L. J. Nash (Aust.)	2	311	126	10	12	31	41

[2] Hitch ran 22 yards, with a skip in the middle. When he came to the skip Australian barrackers used to call 'oo-oop'.

R. J. Crisp began his run of a dozen yards as if he intended nothing more menacing than a medium-fast ball, but he spurted in the last few strides and and made good use of his height to fire the ball down so that it would lift disturbingly. An outsize journalist of 6 ft. $3\frac{1}{2}$ in. and 14 st.7 lb., Bob Crisp took 20 wickets for South Africa in nine Tests against England and Australia. The most-wounded and the most-decorated cricketer in the war in the Western Desert, where he won the D.S.O. and M.C., he was thirty when he suffered the first of his wounds while attempting a rescue in a tank battle in December, 1941.

An inch taller, not so fast, but a trier whose determination won the admiration of Australian crowds was powerful A. J. Bell, who took 48 wickets in sixteen Tests for South Africa. He holds the record for any type of South African bowler in Australia with 23 wickets in five Tests in 1931-2. Passing his hand over his head, 'Sandy' Bell got a big in-swing but his action imposed a wearing strain on his arm and shoulder. Bell was twenty-nine when fluid on the elbow ended his Test career in 1935.

Jack Cowie's opportunities have been limited by New Zealand's short list of Test engagements yet he has consistently gained enviable figures. In the three Tests in England in 1937 he was easily the outstanding bowler, and his total of wickets on that tour (114) is the closest a pace bowler from any country has got to McDonald's 150 in 1921. Commenting on Cowie's accuracy, swing either way, lift and pace off the pitch and his stamina, *Wisden* said then: 'Had he been an Australian he might have been termed a wonder of the age.' The strapping Auck-lander was thirty-one when he first met Australians in a Test match in 1946 and captured six wickets for 40 with fast-medium bowling on a rain-affected Wellington wicket. Against England at Christchurch in 1947 he loosened up with an opening stretch of thirteen overs (broken by a spell for lunch) and pounded down thirty overs in the day in taking six of the seven wickets lost. Yardley and Compton played the ball on – evidence that Cowie's breakback was still awkward.

Until his feet began to come in on the wrong beat, Australia's fast-bowling jeweller, Ernie McCormick, approached the crease with an arrowy rush. The only criticism was that there was so much of it. When McCormick began marking out his run it looked as if he could do with a chain-measure, and perhaps a theodolite. His approach was the longest I can recall in Test cricket – thirty-one paces, which he covered with four preliminary skips and twenty running strides. When he missed count (maybe somewhere in double figures) in his first match in England in 1938 the 6 ft. Victorian was no-balled eight times in his opening over and 35 times in the twenty overs he bowled in the match. Batsmen scored off 16 of them. When a fast bowler's run-up came to bits like that there was a big risk that all the kingdom's sorcerers and psychiatrists couldn't put it together again. Without the confidence to gallop into the job full-tilt he might as well pack up and go home. McCormick's sense of humour saved him from a fate worse than death, as it were. In the middle of the no-balling at Worcester he wisecracked: 'I'll be all right after lunch – the umpire's hoarse.' He regretted having lacked the foresight to ask the sexton of nearby Worcester Cathedral to set the bells pealing a rhythmic air when he came on to bowl.

In the first three matches he sent down 54 no-balls in 48 overs, despite such expedients as bowling at three-quarter pace and lopping half a dozen yards off his run. He practised out in the middle with sweaters, caps and handkerchiefs marking the spots where his feet should pound. In his tenth match he reached his century of no-balls (49 scored from, 51 extras). In his other eleven matches his erring steps were fewer and pressmen lost count of the total but the scorers entered 17 more of his no-balls as extras. McCormick's fame preceded him to Glasgow, where onlookers nae-balled him, just for fun, when he bowled from legal range. Next ball he ran three feet past the line and the crowd roared again, only louder. But he had not bowled the ball and he held it aloft for the people to see.

In twelve Tests against England and South Africa he sent down 36 no-balls which were not scored from and three wides (an average of one extra for every 54 balls) but he gave away fewer extras than Albert Cotter, the Australian fast bowler who was killed in World War I. 'Tibby' Cotter's 93 no-balls and 18 wides worked out at one for every 49 balls.

In the four years before World War II McCormick's opening overs were the fastest on earth; nothing so swift has been launched by any post-war bowler. His arm action was high and fluent and his body swing energetic. He always looked where he was firing but did not always fire where he was looking. This caused mixed feelings among batsmen: it enabled them to score quicker off his bowling (51 runs per 100 balls) than off any other regular Australian fast bowler in Tests between the wars; it exposed them to the biggest risk of copping a gashed forehead since Larwood's hostilities ceased. Sometimes when McCormick hit batsmen in England barrackers shouted: 'Send him home!' or 'Bodyline!' but he never had more than two short-leg fieldsmen.

At full throttle he almost equalled Larwood's velocity. Larwood himself turned on few more destructive bursts in Tests than McCormick's 3 for 9 in nine overs and 3 for 10 in four overs against South Africa at Johannesburg in 1935-6, his 3 for 16 in four overs against England at Brisbane in 1936 and his 3 for 14 in four overs at Lord's, 1938. McCormick took a wicket with the first ball of an innings against England and South Africa (the first bowler to do it twice). Bowling in eleven innings against England he dismissed nine opening batsmen – eight of them in his first time on, the highest proportion of all.[1] He brought the ball back from the off but I never noticed him swing it away. In his twelve Tests against England and South Africa he took 36 wickets – one for every 59 balls, at a cost slightly below 30 runs each. That gave him a quicker

---

[1] Fast bowlers who dismissed most opening batsmen in Anglo-Australian Tests between 1919 and 1939 were Larwood 18 in 28 innings, Gregory 18 in 38 innings. Larwood got 12 of his first time on, Gregory 9.

striking-rate than Constantine, Larwood, Gregory and Mc-Donald and the best average of Australia's regular fast bowlers between the wars.

Though his spirit was willing, McCormick bowled fewer overs per match than the other great fast bowlers because of muscular strains and lumbago. He entered Test cricket older than the others, having been 29 years 7 months when he first appeared against South Africa in 1935. He was five months short of thirty-one when he played his first Test against England, opened brilliantly, but broke down after eight overs. He was on the casualty list when the third Test came on in 1937. The night before the match Keith Rigg, the competent Victoria batsman, was in the dressing-room nursing a tender ankle and hoping to be fit when somebody outside was heard limping up to the door.

Hearing knock, knock, someone inside called: 'Who's there?'

The outsider (voice recognizable as McCormick's): 'Rigg.'

Insider: 'Rigg who?'

McCormick: 'Rigor mortis.'

Mac made fun of his left-hand batting and told of an innings in which he lasted two balls. He played the first one and called 'Wait' resonantly to an impetuous partner. The next ball bowled him. As he walked away he heard the wicket-keeper say: 'McCormick, eh? Obviously the tenor.'

In an inter-state match the ball was returned from the boundary with stitches frayed, probably from having cannoned seam-first into one of the iron pickets around the Melbourne ground. The captain and an umpire studied the furry part, then beckoned to McCormick to get the fast bowler's opinion on whether the ball was fit for play. Mac took one look at it and said: 'Short at the back and sides and a little bit off the top.'

W. J. Edrich, the shortest fast bowler (5 ft. 6 in.) I have seen in first-class cricket, must have a heart disproportionately large. From a low-arm sling the Middlesex player converted his action into a more appropriate delivery in 1946, with extraordinary adaptability, in time to become an opening bowler for England in Australia. In his all-round play in those Tests we saw other facets of the courage and determination which won him the Distinguished Flying Cross as a bomber squadron-leader. One was at Brisbane, where he was hit ten times in 105 minutes' defiance on the sticky wicket. Another was at Melbourne, where a close-range blow near the left knee brought him down and his captain sent him hobbling off. Next morning, when the most likely news expected of him was an X-ray report, Bill tested his leg with a quick canter, delivered an imaginary bumper toward the ladies' stand, then faced right-way-about and took a wicket first ball. As Edrich races up with eleven strides he slews his left shoulder forward and gets up on his toes as if he has half a mind to take off. All his $11\frac{1}{2}$ stone goes into firing the ball along and he hurtles onward like one somehow caught up in his own slipstream.

Those who never saw Larwood can form some picture of his run to the wicket when they see Ray Lindwall go into action. Similarity in their colouring adds to the illusion, though the fair-haired Australian is a couple of inches taller and a few pounds lighter. As a boy of eleven Lindwall saw the Notts man bowl in Sydney; he never forgot the sight. He runs one stride fewer (thirteen) but his approach is like Larwood's in its sure-footed gathering of momentum and in the trailing of the right foot before the hand flings the ball on. Whereas the English-man planted his foot down squarely, parallel with the line, Lindwall points the toe ahead. To save the boot from being worn away by the slither along the ground he has an aluminium plate about two inches long around the outer sole below the toecap. In his first Test season he wore out two of these guards.

On his return from thirty-two months' service in an Army Signals unit in the jungles of South-west Pacific islands Lindwall had to be dosed with atebrin to ward off recurring malaria, but once he worked the fever out of his system it was the batsman's turn to get the shakes. Travelling fast when he delivers the ball, he gets his body to do its share in producing speed by towing his arm over. The direction and length of his bowling are so controlled that with the new ball he has impelled Brown, Hutton, Washbrook and other practised opening bats-men to chase out-swingers into the risk-filled air outside the off stump; when he brings the ball back and beats the bat he usually hits the stumps if no knee is in the way. In skittling Geffery Noblet (South Australia) at Sydney in 1947 Lindwall sent a bail 143 feet 7 inches. His stamina is attested by his capacity to bowl fast whenever he is summoned to the crease; after twenty-one wicketless overs on the dead Adelaide pitch in February, 1947, he was recalled from the outfield and dis-missed four Englishmen in two overs, the last three with four balls.

Possession of so many qualities has enabled this keen bowler to succeed without the high action that has been a hallmark of great fast bowlers. His arm swishes over about thirty degrees from the perpendicular – not recommended for making length balls lift from easy wickets – yet in numbers of matches he has made the ball fly quickly enough to hit batsmen. His bouncers are awkward for all except good hookers because usually they pitch in line with the off stump and bore in toward the batsman's throat. The highest frequency of bumpers I noticed in his four Test matches against England in 1946-7 was four in 24 balls on the last day of the fifth Test. Despite a post-war legacy of dermatitis in a place subject to chafing, the 25-year-old New South Welshman headed the bowling averages in that Test rubber – and in hitting up an exhilarating hundred at Melbourne he discovered more half-volleys in the English-men's bowling than were observed by most of Australia's leading batsmen.

Keith Miller must be the greatest unwilling bowler who ever stepped on a cricket field. From his all-round triumphs in the Australian Services' unofficial Tests in England and India in 1945 he returned with the reputation of world's fastest bowler – and a sore back. Seven weeks before the first Test of 1946–7

he announced that he would concentrate on batting and would
not bowl for fear of causing a recurrence of his back trouble.
But once Australia and England got to grips this handsome,
easy-going ex-pilot did not refuse duty when briefed to open
the bowling with Lindwall. A few days after he turned twenty-
seven, Miller's 7 for 60 in England's first innings at Brisbane
were the reward for twenty-two overs of intelligent bowling
on a sticky wicket; after a sighting shot which knocked Cyril
Washbrook's cap off he put accuracy before pace, kept the ball
up to make the batsmen play at it and rang in stabbing
breakbacks among his usual swingers.

This loose-limbed six-footer's approach is uncommonly
short. He runs little more than half as far as Lindwall, but not
because he is shorter in the wind – both are footballers and
non-smokers. There has been little between them in the speed
of their early overs, but when he was going flat out Miller's
bowling landed in a great number of spots on the pitch, the
frequency of his bumpers occasionally went to the limit allowed
by a fast bowler's licence and his over-the-top action made
them fly higher. As if in protest against the wicket's deadness
in the Adelaide Test, 1947, Miller launched an overhead full-
toss. Compton ducked involuntarily and Umpire Scott sig-
nalled a wide to indicate that he considered it out of the
batsman's reach. Keith is the only Test bowler I know who can
boast of that. The same match brought him another distinction
– the only bowler who has been stopped by a cat. To find the
cause of the crowd's sudden mirth in the middle of his
sixteenth over he looked to the outfield and stopped, shaking
with laughter, while an intrepid cat crept into the field,
scratched, and crept out again.

from BETWEEN WICKETS *1946*

W. J. O'Reilly

SIR DONALD BRADMAN

William J. O'Reilly first played against me on a concrete wicket, on what is now called the Bradman Oval at Bowral, in a Saturday afternoon fixture. I survived his first few overs more by good luck than good management and remained 234 not out at stumps.

We continued the match the following Saturday at Wingello, and in the first over he bowled me round my legs before I had added to my score.

I was amazed that a man could turn the ball from the leg at his pace with his grip.

That was in the year 1926.

Before many more years were past every leading batsman in the world was amazed at the same thing.

O'Reilly did not hold the ball in the fingers quite like the orthodox leg-spinner. It was held more towards the palm of the hand. He was advised by certain 'experts' to change his grip, but fortunately refused to be advised.

This grip did not enable him to spin the ball very much, but it did enable him to achieve phenomenal accuracy plus *sufficient* spin.

His stock ball was the leg-break, but now and then he would bowl a very well concealed googly or an overspin with a delightfully delicate change of pace and for good measure an occasional fast one.

This slower ball would often be played uppishly by batsmen because in addition to the deceptive flight O'Reilly's great height gave it much lift from the pitch.

The particular type of bowling he exploited enabled him to

adopt an attacking field embodying two short-leg fieldsmen and he would concentrate on the leg stump for hours at a time.

O'Reilly never gave the batsman any respite. He was always aggressive, had great stamina and courage.

To hit him for four would usually arouse a belligerent ferocity which made you sorry. It was almost like disturbing a hive of bees. He seemed to attack from all directions.

His record in Test cricket is amazing, for in the brief period from the 1932-3 to the 1938 series, he achieved the distinction of getting 102 wickets against England.

No other player can approach such a performance.

Some other figures of his should also prove illuminating. In Sydney First Grade District Cricket we find that over a period of 45 years from 1895 to 1939-40, only seven players have had a bowling average of less than 10, for 30 or more wickets.

Not one of those players did it more than once.

O'Reilly had a bowling average of less than 10 (with a minimum of 31 wickets) *seven times*.

Those figures I think are a true reflex of his greatness, especially as they were made during a period when the batsmen's averages all advanced considerably.

From what I have read and from conversations with old players, there can be no doubt S. F. Barnes was a magnificent bowler.

He must have been very similar to O'Reilly though I imagine slightly faster and without the wrong-un or googly.

It is impossible accurately to compare the two men of different generations, but my inquiries lead me to the conclusion that Barnes and O'Reilly were the two greatest bowlers who ever lived, and that each was undoubtedly the greatest of his time.

Their respective Anglo-Australian Test Match figures were:

| Barnes | 106 wkts | 2,288 runs | 21.58 average |
| O'Reilly | 102 ,, | 2,616 ,, | 25.64 ,, |

The late Sir Stanley Jackson once tried very hard to convince me that George Lohmann was a greater bowler than O'Reilly.

I listened intently. On every count (but one) I gave in to Sir Stanley that Lohmann might have been as good as O'Reilly.

However, I claimed as my winning point that O'Reilly bowled a googly as against Lohmann's orthodox off-break and on technical grounds must have been more difficult to handle.

With the tenacity which characterized his batting, Sir Stanley (not having played against O'Reilly) refused to concede the argument.

I am in no doubt on the point.

from FAREWELL TO CRICKET *1950*

Don Bradman

JACK FINGLETON

People will tell you that figures do not do justice to the super-
lative art that was Trumper's. Macartney was another whose
skill was not revealed by figures, and the same, in my time,
applied to McCabe. But as long as cricket lives, figures *will* tell
the revealing story of Bradman. They will not tell, perhaps, of
the murderous upsurge which happened whenever a ball was
pitched short and Bradman fell into his very individual pull
shot, but they will tell for all time how Bradman made runs
and how he went on and on making runs.

In his pen picture of Bradman Major Vincent, of *The Times*,
tells how many people found themselves with a desire to go
and have a beer after watching Bradman bat for some time.
That was true but it applied more to Bradman in the post-
bodyline period than before the days when Jardine and Larwood, the decision having been made that his batting technique
was above them, decided to probe him on the physical side.
Bodyline *did* leave its imprint on Bradman – as it did on all
other Australian class batsmen who struck its full fire. Seldom,
if ever, afterwards did Bradman's batting have the same jaunty
air, if one may so term it, which distinguished his batting in
1929, 1930 (in England) and 1930-1 and 1931-2 in Australia.
The bodyline scar was still there in 1934 in England when he
experienced the only known run of outs in his whole first-class
career.

Nothing I have experienced or read since has influenced me
to alter, in the slightest, the bodyline story which I told in
Cricket Crisis, and that historic happening in cricket was un-
impeachably because of Bradman's influence and dominance in

cricket. Bodyline was specially prepared, nurtured for and expended on him and, in consequence, his technique underwent a change quicker than might have been the case with the passage of time. Bodyline plucked something vibrant from his art.

It so happened, too, that soon after the bodyline period, Bradman became the Australian captain. This has to be considered in the general picture of Bradman's change of technique because it can be accepted that Bradman the batsman often became subservient to Bradman the captain. This was so, particularly, in the Australian season of 1936-7 when he had an up-hill captaincy fight after Australia had lost the first two matches of the rubber. I batted almost the whole of one Test day with him in Melbourne when he refused to take the slightest risk because of the state of the game, and he did that again, often, in the series of 1938 (in England), 1946-7 (Australia) and, finally, this last season of 1948 in England.

Yardley quietened him for over after over in the first Test at Nottingham with leg-theory. The 1930 Bradman would have thrived on such stuff; nor would the 1930 Bradman have adopted the 1948 technique of pushing his pads at the ball in negative answer to Bedser's threat of the fine-leg trap.

This, of a certainty, is not a criticism of Bradman. It is but another way of asserting that (a) nobody would have gone for a glass of beer while Bradman was batting in 1930 and (b) how successfully he changed his run-getting technique to suit requirements and the passage of years.

There were, I think, three periods of the Bradman era. One was pre-bodyline; the other was from then to the beginning of the World War, and the final was from 1945 to the end of 1948. In his first post-war game against England (for South Australia in Adelaide) Bradman found that his mind was moving quicker than his legs. He accommodated his technique to that, but in all periods of his era, though his technique changed considerably, Bradman retained to the last the most remarkable appetite for runs that the game of cricket has surely ever known.

As at Scarborough in his last innings, Bradman threw his wicket away on a number of occasions in England in 1948, but never until he had reached his objective, and Bradman, in all his career, never began an innings in any game without an objective. As I read his mind, he had two objectives before this 1948 tour started. One was to lead an unbeaten team through England (which had never happened before) and the other was to be cock of the batting walk until the very last. And he achieved both. No side beat this twentieth Australian Eleven, and Bradman, with 2,428 runs, was well ahead of the next batsman, Morris (1,922), though Morris and Barnes beat him in the Test averages.

I retain one vivid picture of Bradman's insatiable appetite for runs. It was late in the tour at Manchester and on the final day, when Bradman's decision to bat on denied the game any reasonable chance of a decision. All competitive interest had long since flown the game. Bradman had left his mark on it and Old Trafford by making a century, but in the 120's he scuttled as hard to run a three as a tyro would in running a three to make his first century in any tyro of a game. That was typical of Bradman. He never tired of making runs, even in his fortieth year. There was one previous occasion in this game when Bradman might have had a quick two, but the inimitable Sydney Barnes had his own ideas about the sharing of the strike. As Bradman turned for the two, Barnes had his broad back turned at the other end. It was a clear case of disagreement and, from the outside, it was apparent that Bradman rebuked Barnes down the length of the pitch.

Barnes, not easily rebuked, motioned to Bradman and made as if to walk out while the Lancashire men enjoyed the general situation. It transpired that Barnes said to Bradman: 'Here, you come and have it all. I'll have none.'

Bradman planned everything and, in his long career, I saw his complacency only twice rattled. Once was during the bodyline days and the other whenever a 'sticky' pitch happened along. Sir Pelham Warner writes of when Bradman scored a

masterly 71 on a bad Sydney pitch in 1932. To be true, that was
a lovely innings, but there was no fast English bowler playing
that day, and for each of the few times Bradman succeeded on
a bad pitch one could name half a dozen when he failed. It was
reputed of Dr Grace ('Strange to say, champion and all as
W.G. was, he was not in any way a wonder on a sticky pitch' –
Jack Worrell) that he had his limitations when the pitch was
not good, and Bradman, though possessed of all the funda-
mentals to succeed, certainly had his. Bradman's limitations on
a bad pitch were, I think, largely psychological. His whole
demeanour changed on a sticky pitch and the psychologist had
something to work on at Old Trafford on the final day of the
third Test when Bradman, after every ball, walked down the
pitch and energetically patted it, whereas, at the other end,
Morris barely worried about it. This pitch was not bad.
Something has happened to English pitches so that nowadays
one rarely gets a bad one, and the turf certainly did not lift at
Old Trafford this day. It was a sodden pitch, but Bradman's
exaggerated patting of it was as if to suggest that it was a nasty
business. Not a single ball flew.

That was one side to Bradman's batting nature and, to the
student and historian, an interesting one, but, on good pitches,
none will deny that this most amazing cricketer was the
greatest personality the game has ever known. Much has been
said and written of the 'jealousy' of those who played with and
against Bradman, but those best qualified to speak are those
who played with him, and I have never met a single first-class
cricketer of Bradman's age who was not ever ready, indeed
eager, to declare that the game of cricket had never known his
like before. He had his critics, and will always have, I suppose,
for his somewhat indifferent, cold and unfriendly attitude towards most of those with whom he played, but not one, I
repeat, has ever denied the greatness which rightly belongs to
Bradman. On good pitches, he stood in a class of his own as a
scoring machine; and, moreover, the game has never known
one to approach, yes, even approach, his miraculous con-

sistency. When you boiled Bradman down, when you analysed his eyesight, his footwork, his judgment, his range of strokes, there was still something left in which he was also superior to all others, and that was consistency.

What was the secret of Bradman's consistency? That is a subject which will be always fresh as long as cricket is played, but I am inclined to think that the answer is to be found not so much in anything physical as in the mind. With the exception of those two perturbing instances I have mentioned, Bradman's mind was always cool, calm and analytical and, in its sphere, was as great a taskmaster of the body as man could possess. His mind gave his body no rest. His mind called the tune and his body, gifted as it was in peerless footwork, eyesight, judgment and a perfect dynamo of ceaseless energy, danced to it. The only times the dance became agitated were against body-line and on sticky pitches.

One does well to try and analyse Bradman's mind because, in all cricket, I met no other like it. He was the only cricketer I knew who never tired of the game, who never became bored by it, who never became stale – or, if his body did, his mind would not allow it to be so.

from BRIGHTLY FADES THE DON *1949*

Bodyline

KEITH MILLER and R. S. WHITINGTON

Bodyline was given its name, as Ray Robinson tells in his book *Between Wickets*, because he and others felt that the term fast leg-theory misled people who did not see this type of attack for themselves. It was first bowled in the match between the M.C.C. and an Australian XI at Melbourne in November 1932.

Dr E. P. Barbour (a former Australian first-class cricketer) reviewed it as: 'The deliberate banging of the ball down less than half way so that it flies up around the batman's head is not cricket. If continued and extended to all grades of cricket, as they should be if they are fair, the result of such tactics will be the disappearance from first-class cricket of every champion after he has put up with three or four years of this assault and battery. Perhaps,' Barbour continued, 'a more serious aspect still is the imminent danger to the good fellowship and friendly rivalry that has always been associated with cricket.'

Australia's batsmen had proved valiant and able enough to withstand the fierce pace of Larwood and even his short bumpers in 1928-9 and 1930. Their defiance was muzzled in 1932-3, however, by the setting of seven and at times eight men on the leg side of the wicket in an inner and outer ring that prevented batsmen fighting back at the bowling without gambling with their wicket, and, some contend, with their lives.

Against the 1932-3 *bodyline* of Larwood, who was yards faster than Voce and Bowes, batsmen had several alternative courses of action to adopt. *The first* of these was to dodge or duck their heads and shoulders from the path of the bumpers and keep their bats out of the way. *The second* was to take the

bruising balls on their bodies. *The third* was to play defensively
at the shoulder and head-high fliers with their bats held per-
pendicularly in front of their faces and upper chest. *The fourth*
was to hook at the bumpers with a horizontally held bat sweep-
ing from the off to the leg in an attempt to bang the ball so
hard and so often against the legside boundary fence that the
bowler would be forced for economy's sake to try other
methods of attack. *The fifth*, the one Bradman tried, was to
step back some feet to the outside of the leg-stump and slash
crossbatted at the bumpers as they reared in front of the batsman, so as to force the ball to the unguarded offside field.

Because Larwood gained terrific pace on the Australian
pitches and because he was clever enough to vary his four or so
bumpers in a six-ball over with good length and *yorker* balls
aimed in line with the stumps, our batsmen had only split
seconds in which to make up their minds to their course of
action.

In fact, Larwood's *bodyline* was never mastered. Bradman
has written that it is 'questionable' whether it could have been.
It batsmen dodged, ducked or took the ball on their bodies

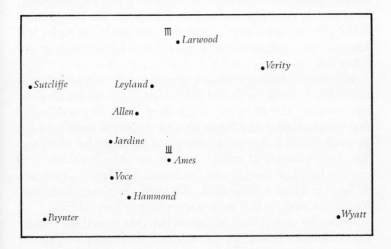

they would not score any runs. If they tried the defensively held bat, they took great risk of being caught by the four or five men in the inner leg-side ring which extended from leg-slip to close-mid-on. If they hooked, they ran grave risk of being caught in the outer ring near the boundary. If they stepped bask, as Bradman did, they took an undeniable chance of being bowled by the variant good-length balls and *yorkers*.

Despite the Press and public outcry at the introduction of *bodyline* at Melbourne, the Englishmen employed it in the first Test of that series at Sydney. Adopting method four – the hook – Stan McCabe, with the help of high courage and considerable good fortune, hammered Larwood and his colleagues to the tune of 187 runs and the jubilant cheering of the Sydney Hillites and members. On that December day of 1932 the young McCabe became a national hero. But after his glorious, defiant innings he himself said, 'I have got away with it once. But I couldn't get away with it again.' In his nine other Test innings against *bodyline* McCabe aggregated 198–11 more runs than he had made in the first innings at Sydney. Bradman, who was unavailable through ill-health for that first Test scored 396 runs in the remaining four at an average of 56.57 by adopting, for the most part, alternative five. Except for the Englishman Eddie Paynter, who only played five innings in the series and was twice not out, Bradman's was the best batting average for either side.

The climax of the uproar that greeted *bodyline* wherever it was bowled in Australia occurred at the beautiful Adelaide Oval on the Saturday and Monday of the third Test. England batted first on the Friday and Saturday and recovered from four for 30 to all out 341. Australia went in on the Saturday afternoon and, after a couple of orthodox overs to orthodox fields with the new ball, Larwood, under the direction of Jardine, switched to *bodyline* against Woodfull, Bradman, McCabe, Ponsford, Victor Richardson and even wicket-keeper Bert Oldfield.

It was the very timing of that switch that roused the usually very peaceful Adelaide people to anger, to mass outcry, almost to physical interference with the English players on the field. Larwood, bowling to his orthodox field, made a fast ball rise which hit the Australian captain Woodfull a painful blow in the region of the heart. For minutes Woodfull writhed in pain, first on the ground and then in a semi-erect position. When he decided he was able to resume batting, Larwood began his run to deliver the next ball. But Jardine called him to stop, then moved his fieldsmen into the *bodyline* leg-traps and ordered Larwood to bowl his bumpers. Even old men of conservative habits and normally most moderate tempers seated in the Members' Enclosure, rose to their feet, blood red in the face, as they first hooted and later joined in chorus to count Larwood and Jardine 'out'. And, for a time, it was touch and go whether the less conservative barrackers on the opposite side of the ground would jump the fence and mob the English players. Men out on the Adelaide mounds that day say that if one man had jumped the fence the whole huge crowd would have followed him.

from BUMPER *1953*

S. J. McCabe

RAY ROBINSON

In an era studded with batting triumphs, it was given to one man, Stan McCabe, to play the three greatest innings seen on Test fields in the decade before the War.

Any one of the three would have been a fitting crown to the finest batsman's career, but it was no accident that all of them were the handicraft of McCabe, not of other master run-makers of the Hobbs-to-Hutton period, such as Bradman, Hammond, Ponsford, Headley, Dempster, Nourse or Merchant.

In fact, none of McCabe's contemporaries attempted such batting – in Test matches, of all places – because nobody else thought it could be done. None had the blend of imagination and skill to feel capable of it; by all the standards of the times none would have dared to hope for enough luck to carry it through. The drama of these exploits by McCabe fascinated the crowds. Their delight at his graceful and venturesome stroke-making was sharpened by the piquant feeling that each moment might be the last, as if they were watching a bolting horse or a runaway train.

First of these breath-catching innings was his lone-hand 187 not out against England in 1932, the boldest innings ever played on the Sydney Cricket Ground, or any other ground. The situation when the twenty-two year-old McCabe walked in to bat was dispiriting. The Australians had entered the valley of the shadow of bodyline. Illness had robbed them of their out-standing batsman, Bradman, on the eve of their first encounter with the fast leg-side assault. Only 82 runs were on the board when McCabe, No. 5 in the batting order, came in to face

Larwood, who was in the middle of a bout in which he took three wickets for seven runs.

McCabe immediately showed his determination not to die a death of shame on a day of dark disgrace, though Jardine, Larwood and Voce were trying to set a noose about his neck. Without a flinch, he stood up to the fearsome bowling; he hooked the short balls as if there were no danger to his ribs or skull, and as if he were unaware of the battalion of catch-awaiting fieldsmen, covered by outer scouts ready for the lofted ball. When the direction of the bowling changed, flowing drives and crisp cuts kept him gliding along. Nobody thought it could last for long, yet when those daring hooks were lifted they continued to fall beyond the fieldsmen's reach. By the day's end he had scored 127 in a little more than three hours, with 17 boundary hits.

Fifty-five minutes on the second day brought the end of Australia's innings. In that time McCabe took command, manoeuvred to keep the strike, and scored 60 while four wickets fell for 10 at the other end. In going for the bowling bald-headed (or almost, for one so young) he was debited with a nominal chance at 170, when he cut Larwood behind point with such stinging power that it would have been captious to blame Voce for not making a catch. At an average rate of 47 an hour, McCabe scored his 187 while his seven partners made fewer than 90. It was like a blood transfusion for a sinking innings. Boundary hits brought him 100 of the runs. Nineteen of the fours were leg strokes, 13 of them hooks which rapped the fence between wide long-on and square-leg.

For audacity, skill, effortless power, and courage against the bowling that beset him, no other batsman on the active list could have equalled his performance.

In size, dominance and value to a team in difficulties, it ranks with three epic innings by Victor Trumper, Clem Hill and Ranjitsinhji in the period which men over sixty describe as the Golden Age of cricket. After England had led by 292 on the first innings at Sydney in 1903, Trumper made 185 not out for Australia while seven partners fell for 95. He hit 24 fours; his scoring rate was 49 an hour. At Melbourne in 1898, in an innings in which Australia's sixth wicket fell at 57, Hill scored 188 while seven team-mates were making 94. The left-hander made 21 boundary strokes and his hourly rate was 37. When England followed on 181 in arrears at Manchester in 1896, Ranjitsinhji made 154 not out (23 fours) at the rate of 48 an hour while nine partners were dismissed for 112.

No amount of debate will ever determine which of the four magnificent innings was the finest. McCabe's was played on a pitch of modern excellence, but he was up against a method of attack more unsettling than the other three had to face.

If McCabe's 187 was a blood transfusion for his side, his 232 in the Nottingham Test, 1938, was a heart-massage innings which revived the patient after hope had been given up. The Englishmen had led off by amassing the overwhelming total of 658 for eight wickets before Hammond declared the innings closed. After Fingleton had gone for 9, Bradman for 51 (after an unsuccessful appeal against the light) and Brown for 48 the Australians' position was desperate.

McCabe, who was vice-captain, had been out of touch for weeks (a few days before the Test he had raised the question whether it would not be better to choose another batsman instead). With about half an hour to go to complete the Saturday's play, he began in the gloaming, yet batted more firmly than his predecessors and scored 19 before stumps were drawn. On Sunday night he had a slight cold, but O'Reilly assured him: 'You'll sweat it out by 3 p.m. tomorrow.'

When two more wickets fell in the first quarter-hour on Monday, it seemed as if the innings would peter out before McCabe could work up a single bead of perspiration. Half the side was out, with Australia still more than 500 behind. Farnes was bowling at keen speed, and Wright was making leg-breaks snap from a boot-worn patch. McCabe's way of counter-ing the menace of that pitch was to skip forward smartly when-ever Wright tried to pitch the ball on it. He played watchfully for more than half an hour until the downfall of Badcock (9) left only the tail-end division of wicket-keeper and three bowlers to come.

That was the signal for McCabe to take the match in his own hands. For the next couple of hours his batting was enchanting. It held every one under its spell, bowlers as well as spectators. From the players' balcony, Bradman called to a few of his team who were inside the pavilion: 'Come and look at this! You've never seen anything like it.' In the Press box, Woodfull was moved to write: 'It is a pity that the whole cricket world could not see this double-century scored.'

The 30,000 who were lucky enough to be there watched wonderingly as the vice-captain added 170 while his last four partners scored 38. When he was 123 he gave a sharp chance to square-leg, but Edrich did well to get a hand to it and save a four.

The arrival of Fleetwood-Smith as last man was accepted as an infallible sign that the innings was drawing its last breath. Instead, his advent inspired McCabe to unfold the most dazzling half-hour's batting of the match. Hammond spread five fieldsmen around the boundary yet could not prevent fours – McCabe had so many strokes and guided them so surely. The Englishmen fared little better when, near the end of overs, they drew in to encircle him with a net of in-fielders, trying to block the singles he needed to get the strike at the other end instead of his vulnerable partner. While Fleetwood-Smith rose to the occasion by surviving 18 balls and collecting five runs, Stan scored 72 in the last enthralling 28 minutes – something unheard-of in Test cricket, even in the days when Bonnor and Jessop were denting pavilion roofs. McCabe's 232 in 235 minutes (34 fours, one six) is the fastest double-century in Test history. His 213 on the second day came up in 200 minutes, his last 127 after lunch in only 80 minutes.

For all the speed of his scoring – he skimmed through his last 100 at the dizzy rate of 109 runs an hour – each stroke was made with the artistry natural to him, each was properly chosen for the ball it had to meet. Despite the urgency of the chase for runs there was not one slogging hit, in fact no show of force, because of the precision of his timing. It was power without violence, dash without slap.

McCabe made his 232 while eight partners were scoring 58 – an achievement without parallel in international cricket. When at last Ames caught him off Sinfield, Australia's arrears had shrunk to 247 and the match had been plucked from England's grasp. He had taken the steam out of the English bowlers and given the Australians fresh heart to face the follow-on justifiably hopeful of keeping England from victory in the 8¾ hours before the time-limit expired.

When McCabe returned to the pavilion, Bradman greeted him with: 'If I could play an innings like that I would be a proud man, Stan.' Surely the highest tribute ever paid a batsman.

Two former English captains, A. E. R. Gilligan and R. E. S. Wyatt, agreed that it was the best Test innings they had seen, and their opinion was shared by a renowned cricketer of an earlier generation, S. F. Barnes, as this dialogue between Neville Cardus and the mighty bowler showed:

Barnes: 'The finest innings I have seen.'

Cardus: 'Think again; you saw Trumper.'

Barnes: 'I can only repeat it is the greatest I ever saw.'

Cardus: 'I'd have liked to see you out there bowling to McCabe.'

Barnes (after a moment's thought): 'I don't think I could have kept him quiet.'

The other striking instance of McCabe's indomitable spirit in adversity – for his deeds were as much a triumph of character as of skill – was his 189 not out at Johannesburg in December 1935, against the South Africans, who had won their first Test rubber in England earlier that year.

After a fine 231 by A. D. Nourse in South Africa's second innings of 491 the Australians were in a corner. To win, they needed 399 runs in the fourth innings, on a wicket worn by the traffic of three days' play. In Test history no team which had been set the task of getting more than 340 in the fourth innings had ever won, in England, Australia or South Africa. Precedent held out no hope for victory when the Australians began batting after the tea interval on the third afternoon, and, as another day remained for play, the South Africans had ample time to get them out. When the first wicket fell for 17, the Australians were in a tough spot.

The common policy at such times is to attempt a dogged, back-to-the-wall struggle in which the full weight of the task bears incessantly on the batsmen, taxing their nerves until every over is loaded with tension, every run becomes an effort. This psychological pressure and the wearing of the wicket are the two reasons why, dozens of times, 300 in the fourth innings has been beyond the power of Test teams. That was not McCabe's way of meeting the crisis. He never believed that the best defence was defence, anyway. He refused to give the bowlers the advantage of holding the initiative (as army communiqués put it) because he had the vision to perceive that it made the task more burdensome. That afternoon and next day he carried the fight to the enemy, not in a desperate, headlong sortie, but measuring each blow with cool judgment and delivering it with polished skill.

He sped to his first 100 in 91 minutes,[1] despite the class and variety of the attack by Langton (a great medium-pace bowler), Crisp (fast), Mitchell (googly), Robertson (ultra-slow off-spin) and Bock (medium-pace). Several times McCabe had to use his pads to fend off wide-turning balls. Before a sharp leg-break got past the patient Fingleton (40) McCabe made 148 of a second-wicket partnership of 177. He scored 100 before lunch on the last day. By then he had been joined by Len Darling, a kindred spirit in putting side before self and in inclination for free stroke-play.

Thunderclouds were banking up from the north-west.

[1] The only faster Test centuries have been by G. L. Jessop in 75 minutes at the Oval, 1902, and C. G. Macartney in 80 minutes before lunch at Leeds, 1926.

Whether the coming downpour would wash the match out or
would doom the Australians to finish their struggle on a sticky
wicket the batsmen did not know. They pressed on boldly in
failing light. Vivid lightning was flashing in the gloom as
McCabe, at 166 and 186, cut Crisp's fast bowling above ground
and was missed behind point by a fieldsman who had little
chance to sight the ball properly. Once Darling edged Langton
to the left side of second slip, who groped for the catch without
touching the ball. An appeal against the light came at 2.45 p.m.,
not from the batsmen but from South Africa's captain, H. F.
Wade, who said it was dangerous for the fieldsmen. Soon after
play had ceased the thunderstorm broke, so soaking the field
that the game was abandoned two hours later, with Australia
274 for two wickets, McCabe 189 not out and Darling 37 not
out.

McCabe's brilliance had so transformed the situation that,
instead of struggling to stall off defeat, the Australians were
playing like winners, with 125 more runs to get and eight
wickets in hand. He batted 3¼ hours for his 189 while 66 were
scored at the other end. He hit 29 fours, probably a record for
a Test innings under 200. As at Sydney and Nottingham, he
won his Johannesburg triumph by tackling a depressing situation in a way that the few other living batsmen possessing
enough skill for it would have regarded as too venturesome,
even foolhardy. There was something Churchillian in his
spirited resistance to his adversaries: he fought them in the
crease, and he fought them up the wicket.

McCabe's scores in those three innings were big – so big that
they were within the range of only the first flight of the world's
batsmen – but size was far from being the only element in their
greatness. Other batsmen have made more than a dozen Test
scores larger than his highest, but nobody made so many so
quickly to rally sides that had been beaten to their knees. As a
saver of lost causes he had no rival.

Many a time, bowling which looked troublesome before he
came in seemed to lose its terrors after a few overs of his

serene strokeplay. Often his dash lightened the burden for others by setting the ball rolling, as when Australia needed 478 to avoid having to follow-on at Manchester in 1934. McCabe scored his second 50 at run-a-minute speed and hit 22 fours in making 137 out of 208 for the second and third wickets.

He made a better fist of batting on rain-affected pitches than most Australians, and some of his match-rescuing feats were on difficult wickets. At Southend in 1938, turf which had not recovered from re-laying in winter had made such a vicious wicket that 40 Australian and Essex wickets fell in two days. The surface of the pitch looked as if, by some confusion in the toolshed, the groundsman had prepared it with a marcel-waving iron instead of a roller. When a bat was laid along it there was room to put the fingers under it in the valleys between the ridges. The Australians lost five wickets for 75 in the second innings and were in a precarious position until McCabe pulled the game around by knocking up 50 in less than an hour.

I think the reason why McCabe dared so much when others had lost heart is that he had no dread of failure. Despite the glare of publicity and the tension of international encounters, the sternest Test match never ceased to be a game of cricket to him. He went in and played in the way he felt the situation required. If he failed he accepted it as just one of those things. He came up smiling again next time. His character is reflected in this and in the sunny nature of his strokes. In McCabe the cricketer you saw McCabe the man – urbane, sociable, unpretentious, straightforward, incapable of anything mean-spirited. Of the players in the Test rubbers immediately before the War he was the best-liked by his own team and by the opponents. Even the bowlers on whom he operated so freely found his bedside manner so pleasant that they felt they had not been hurt much, no matter how he carved them about.

His nickname is 'Napper' – derived from Nap, because of his facial resemblance to Napoleon, even to a mid-forehead tuft denoting where the hairline used to be when he was nineteen.

As he neared thirty, the resemblance to the thickset Emperor spread elsewhere, but this chubbiness (weight about 12 st. 7 lb., height 5 ft. 8 in.) did not lessen the grace of his batting; it simply rounded it out.

Hundreds by McCabe were more infrequent than by other batsmen out of cricket's top drawer. He had not passed 90 in first-class cricket when, at nineteen, he was chosen for the 1930 Test tour of England, but – as with Denis Compton and Neil Harvey in their teens – anyone who saw McCabe make 20 knew he was watching a player of uncommon gifts. He scored 29 hundreds in first-class matches, an average of one in nine innings, compared with Bradman's one in three, one in five by Ponsford and Woodfull, one in six by Hammond and Kippax and one in seven by Sutcliffe and Hobbs.

McCabe's feet are small (Army doctors found that one was size 5, the other size 6) and he has been subject to trouble underneath the arches for years. Back in 1934 the Board of Control's doctors thought twice about passing him for fear that his feet would not carry him through five months' continuous cricket in England. They began to let him down just before the War, after he had played 24 Tests, the last when he was only twenty-eight.

Yet McCabe bowled more in international cricket than any other upper-bracket batsman of his day except England's champion, Hammond. In Test annals only two other players – Armstrong and Woolley – who scored as many runs as McCabe (2,748, average 48), did as much work at the bowling crease. McCabe bowled 3,746 balls (medium-pace, with an occasional nippy wrong-un) in taking 36 English, South African and West Indian wickets, and one-fifth of his overs were maidens. He was an opening bowler in several Tests, but the menace in his bowling was reflected less by that post of honour than by the average cost of his wickets, 43 runs. At second slip and other in-field positions he held 42 catches in Tests. Excepting that superb wicket-keeper, Oldfield, and that wizard slip-fielder, Gregory, McCabe took more catches (56) than any

11a Hutton batting in the Oval Test *v.* Pakistan, 1954

11b Washbrook   11c W. J. Edrich batting for Middlesex *v.* Surrey at the
                   Oval, 1956 (Macintyre keeping wicket, May at slip)

12a Compton batting against South Africa at the Oval, 1955

12b Evans attempts to catch Neil Harvey, Trent Bridge, 1956

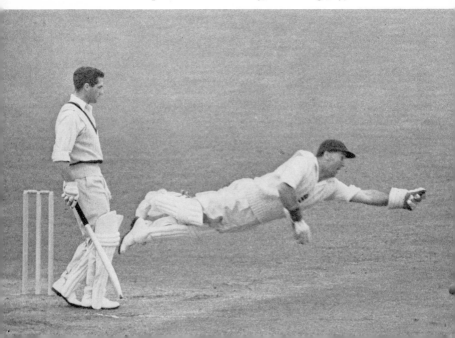

other Australian on tours of Britain since Tests were resumed after the 1914-18 War.

Apart from the calls bowling made on his energy, McCabe could have made more hundreds if he had gone after them, instead of so often undertaking the job of disrupting the opposition's attack. Time and again, in pressing the assault he got out unexpectedly when well on top of the bowling, in a manner fit to make Bradman and Ponsford rock with laughter. In Tests alone, 13 of his innings exceeded 50 without reaching 100, and he was dismissed eight times between 70 and 93. (When Bradman passed 50 in Tests, bowlers were able to prevent his scoring 100 only nine times, and not once after he got midway through the eighties.) In topping the Australian aggregates in England in 1934, McCabe scored eight hundreds, and needed only 12 runs for another when he sacrificed his innings because his side was hard-pressed for time to win the Nottingham Test.

He was the most adventurous Test batsman in the twenty years after Macartney retired in 1926. Bradman could be venturesome, too, but his disposition was different. When Don chose to cut loose there was usually something calculated in the daring of his whirlwind bursts. Sometimes, when nothing was hanging to the match, Don seemed to set himself to see just how hard and often he could hit without losing control, as if flexing a blade to see how far it would bend without snapping.

Outside Test cricket, Bradman often scored as fast as McCabe, even outpaced him – at Scarborough in 1934 Don made 132 in 90 minutes, four days after his 149 in 104 minutes at Folkestone – but in their century innings in Tests McCabe had the quicker rate, especially against England: 47 runs an hour and 14 boundary hits per 100 runs, compared with Bradman's 37 an hour and 10 boundaries.

McCabe was adventurous by instinct. The sight of the ball leaving the bowler's hand set him thinking of a stroke, not of keeping it out of his stumps. He could not play a cheap shot, even to save his wicket. He was beyond the ordinary measures of scoring, consistency and safety.

7

He passed 200 only three times, never carried on as far as 250. His big innings were masterpieces, not adapted to his side's pressing need. Many of his smaller innings were masterpieces too. When McCabe got out, the melody lingered on, and often it was some time before you noticed what kind of tune the next batsman played.

McCabe usually seemed to have a better bat than his companions. The ball went off it as if some craftsman bat-maker had chosen the choicest willow in the land and fashioned it into a blade of extra springiness. Some of his strokes were almost noiseless, particularly his glides to leg and his finest cuts. In between their chief shots, such great batsmen as Bradman, Ponsford and Hutton have not been above turning out pot-boilers – little pushes that were scarcely strokes but kept the scorers busy. Such commonplace nudges by McCabe would have been as out-of-place as if St Paul's Cathedral organist rang in a few bars of the *Beer Barrel Polka* at intervals in the *Magnificat*. I doubt whether a bat accustomed to being handled by McCabe would agree to have any part in them.

Possessing natural poise and aptitude for sport (he was several times both golf and billiards champion of the N.S.W. Cricketers' Club), McCabe used his gifts intelligently. One reason why he could apply power so effortlessly was that he used both sides of his body; his strokes were essentially two-handed. I have seen him practise swinging a bat through with the left hand only, so that the left wrist would do its full part in bringing the bat to the ball, not leave the job largely to the right hand pushing behind.

In cutting he could leave the downward slice of the bat so late that it would have been prudent for wicket-keepers to get their fingers insured, like Marlene Dietrich's legs. Cuts brought him one-quarter of his runs. More of them were placed square behind point than were steered finer. He seldom edged the ball – so rarely that Jardine once suggested that it might pay England to do without a first slip and place an extra fieldsman in the gully.

He did not grip the handle as high as Trumper, Macartney, Kippax, Bradman, Miller or Hassett, and several others of his day excelled him in driving straight and past mid-off. But he continued to play the forward cover-drive freely, long after other leading Australian batsmen decided that the stroke was not riskless enough to be worth while, except to give half-volleys their due punishment. More than half his strokes were to the off, but well over half his fours and sixes were hit to leg. The masterly range of his hooking enabling him to score more than two-thirds of his boundaries with this shot. For every ball he swung to the square-leg fence he hooked four farther forward, around an arc extending to wide long-on.

In boldly taking the ball on the rise, he sometimes lifted his hook, unlike Bradman, who always kept the ball down when he hooked from choice, and only put it in the air when he hooked by instinct, in self-defence. Field-placing to catch McCabe off his hook became a standing order in English captaincy, and nine of his 43 Test innings ended that way. For all its power, McCabe's hooking never looked so savage as Bradman's, almost as if one were using the bat as a wand and the other as a pikestaff – or a waddy. No matter how sudden the stroke, McCabe's pivot on his right foot was free from contorted effort, whereas Don sometimes threw his body and legs all ways in dealing the ball a terrific smack by hook or by crook.

When Voce first came into the line of Test candidates in 1930 the Australians were inexperienced against quick left-arm bowling to a leg-trap field. In a mid-season match against Notts, McCabe and Victor Richardson, another strong hooker, led the way in a bold plan to hit Voce out of Test selection. Of McCabe's 137 in the two innings 100 came in boundary hits, and 88 of Richardson's 119 were scored in fours and sixes. Voce took five wickets in the match, but his second-innings figures were one for 112 and his Test début was postponed for two years.

Beneath the smoothness of McCabe's forward and back play, his foot movements were decisive, and always to the line of the approaching ball. He could no more retreat from a ball, no matter how nasty, than he could show petulance at an umpire's decision. Of the Australians who remained regular Test players after undergoing the bodyline ordeal he was the only one who faced fast bowling with unblemished confidence as if he liked it.

At the peak of his career he was the world's most commanding player of high-speed bowling. There was no batsman whom fast bowlers – English, South African or Australian – were gladder to see get out.

Though the dashing game was natural to him, McCabe could throttle down if his side's welfare called for patient batting. In one such innings of 70-odd against England his scoring rate was only 25 an hour. But he was never hum-drum, never died a lingering death. His defensive technique was sound, and he was bowled only seven times in his 62 Test innings against England, South Africa and West Indies. But you could not picture him batting all day, as Sutcliffe, Bradman, Hutton and half a dozen others have done in Tests. McCabe was not built that way. He was too mettlesome, too prone to get out off a forcing stroke. Of his 43 innings against England, 31 ended in catches, 11 of them from cuts between point and second slip, nine from hooks and six from drives.

In all-time averages for Australian scorers of 10,000 only five (Bradman, Ponsford, Woodfull, Brown and Kippax) headed McCabe, who made 11,949 runs in 262 innings (20 not out). Judged on results alone he has been one of the world's most successful batsmen in a period when scoring has been higher than ever before, but he was more than that.

McCabe's batting possessed a lyrical impulse which made him different from all others of his generation – a spirit of daring uncommon in his day, compared with times when a batsman's innings did not have to reach 100 or 200 to be regarded as great. In outlook he was a throwback to the Trumper-Macartney-Woolley era. In spirit and charm of strokeplay he was fifth in the noble Sydney dynasty which has not been excelled in the world – a bearer of the torch kindled by Trumper, fanned by Macartney, and kept aglow by Kippax and, while his health lasted, by Jackson.

from BETWEEN WICKETS *1946*

George Headley

C. L. R. JAMES

What I want to draw special attention to here is George's play on wet or uncertain wickets. Here are his scores on such wickets in England.

		Other high scores in the innings
1933		
v. Northamptonshire	52 out of 129	32 and 15
v. Yorkshire	25 out of 115	25 and 16
v. Nottinghamshire	66 out of 314	54 and 51
v. Lancashire	66 out of 174	29 and 18
v. Leicestershire	60 out of 156	22 and 19
v. Leveson-Gower's XI	35 out of 251	70 and 44
1939		
v. Surrey	52 out of 224	58 and 52
v. Yorkshire	61 out of 234	72 and 28
v. England	51 out of 133	47 and 16
	5 out of 43 for 4	13 and 11
v. Somerset	0 out of 84	45 and 17
v. Gloucestershire	40 out of 220	50 and 28
	5 out of 162	43 and 26

In those 13 innings George passed 50 seven times. Three times only he scored less than double figures, and in his other three innings his scores were 25, 35 and 40. I believe those figures would be hard to beat. Look at a similar list made for Bradman by Ray Robinson in his fascinating book *Between Wickets*.

	Match	Total	Bradman	Top Scorer
1928	Brisbane Test	66	1	Woodfull 30 n.o.
1929	Sydney	128	15	Fairfax 40
1930	Notts Test	144	8	Kippax 64 n.o.
	Northants	93	22	Bradman 22
	Gloucester	157	42	Ponsford 51
		117	14	McCabe 34
1932	Perth	159	3	McCabe 43
	Melbourne	19 (2W)	13	
1933	Sydney	180	1	Rowe 70
		128	71	Bradman 71
1934	Lord's Test	118	13	Woodfull 43
1936	Brisbane Test	58	0	Chipperfield 36
	Sydney Test	80	0	O'Reilly 37 n.o.
1938	Middlesex	132	5	Chipperfield 36
	Yorkshire	132	42	Bradman 42

In fifteen innings Bradman passed 50 only once, 40 only twice and 15 only four times. His average is 16.66. George's average is 39.85. You need not build on these figures a monument, but you cannot ignore them.

Bradman's curious deficiency on wet wickets has been the subject of much searching comment. George's superior record has been noticed before, and one critic, I think it was Neville Cardus, has stated that Headley has good claims to be considered *on all wickets* the finest of the inter-war batsmen. I would not go so far. It is easy to give figures and make comparisons and draw rational conclusions. The fact that the odds were 10 to 1 that in any Test Bradman would make 150 or 200 runs, and the more the runs were needed the more certain he was to make them. Yet if Bradman never failed in a Test series, neither did George. I believe Bradman and Headley are the only two between the wars of whom that can be said. (Hammond failed terribly in 1930 in England and almost as badly in the West Indies in 1934–5.)

But there is another point I wish to bring out. Between 1930 and 1938 Bradman had with him in England Ponsford,

Woodfull, McCabe, Kippax, Brown, Hassett. All scored heavily. In 1933 and 1939 West Indian batsmen scored runs at various times, but George had nobody who could be depended on. In 1933 his average was 55.40. Among those who played regularly the next average was 23.83. In 1939 his average in the Tests was 66.80. The next batsman averaged 57.66, but of his total of 173 he made 137 in one innings. Next was 27.50. It can be argued that this stiffened his resistance. I don't think so. And George most certainly does not. 'I would be putting on my pads and sometimes before I was finished I would hear that the first wicket had gone.' This is what he carried on his shoulders for nearly ten years. None, not a single one of the great batsmen, has ever been so burdened for so long.

He had characteristics which can be attributed to less than half a dozen in the whole history of the game. He has said, and all who know his play can testify, that he did not care who bowled at him: right hand, left hand, new ball, old ball, slow, fast, all were the same. He loved the bad wickets. And his reason is indicative of the burden he carried. 'On a bad wicket it was you and the bowler. If he pitched up you had to drive. If he pitched short you had to turn and hook. No nonsense.' I sensed there a relief, a feeling that he was free to play the only game which could be successful under the circumstances, but this time his own natural game.

George was a quiet cricketer. So quiet that you could easily under-estimate him. One day in 1933 West Indies were playing Yorkshire at Harrogate, the wicket was wet and Verity placed men close in, silly mid-off and silly point I think. The West Indian players talked about bowlers who placed men close in for this batsman and the other batsman. George joined in the reminiscences. Someone said, 'George, if Verity put a man there for you—'

A yell as of sudden, intense, unbearable pain burst from George, so as to startle everyone for yards around.

'Me!' he said. 'Put a man there for me!'

They could talk about it for other players, Test players, but that anyone should even think that such fieldsmen could be placed for him – that was too much for George. The idea hurt him physically.

George was a great master of the game in many senses. He landed in Australia (1931-2) a boy of twenty-one who had never played or seen cricket out of the West Indies. As he has told me in great detail: 'I was an off-side batsman, drive, cut and back-stroke through the covers. Of course, I also could hook.' Australian critics were startled at his mastery of batting and of an innings of 131, played at Victoria in less than even time, one critic who had seen all the great players of the previous thirty years said that no finer innings had ever been seen on the Melbourne ground. An innings of 82 against New South Wales evoked the same admiration. Then, as he says, the word went round: keep away from his off-stump and outside it, you will never get him there. Henceforth in every match, on every ground, it was a leg-stump attack and an off-side field. George was baffled and I remember how anxious we were at a succession of failures. What he did, under fire, so to speak, was to reorganize his batting to meet the new attack.

This is what happened to George in Australia: 25, 82, 131, 34. Then he failed steadily: 27 run out and 16; 0 and 11 (Test, to Grimmett both times); 3; 14 and 2 (Test); 19 and 17. Nine successive failures. It is only by the Third Test that George is once more in control of the situation: 102 not out out of 193 (next highest score 21), and 28 out of 148 (again top score); 77 and 113; 75 and 39; 33 out of 99 (top score) and 11 out of 107 (Fourth Test); 70 run out and 2; 105 and 30 (Fifth Test).

He had so mastered the new problems that Grimmett considers Headley to be the greatest master of on-side play whom he ever bowled against, and he bowled against both Hobbs and Bradman. Yet of George's 169 not out in the Manchester Test of 1934, A. Ratcliffe, reviewing modern cricket (*The Cricketer* Annual, 1933-34), says, 'His cuts off the slow bowling were a strange sight to see and I had only seen such strokes once

7*

before when Woolley cut Roy Kilner's slow deliveries to the boundary time after time.'

George Headley, this West Indian, would be my candidate for a clinical study of a great batsman as a unique type of human being, mentally and physically. So far as I know no one has probed into this before.

Mentally. George is batting against an Australian slow bowler, probably Grimmett. To the length ball he gets back and forces Grimmett away between mid-wicket and mid-on or between mid-wicket and square-leg. He is so quick on his feet and so quick with his bat that Grimmett simply cannot stop ones and twos in between the fieldsmen. Every time Grimmett flights the ball, out of the crease and the full drive. Grimmett, that great master of length, can't even keep George quiet. He has a man at fine-leg. He shifts him round to square and moves square to block up the hole. Next ball is just outside the leg-stump. George, gleeful at the thought that fine-leg is no longer there, dances in front of the wicket 'to pick up a cheap four'. He glances neatly, only to see Oldfield, the wicketkeeper, way over on the leg-side taking the catch. The two seasoned Australians have trapped him. That sort of thing has happened often enough. Now note George's reaction.

'I cut that out.'

'What do you mean, you cut it out?'

'I just made up my mind never to be caught that way again.'

'So you do not glance?'

'Sure I glance, but I take care to find out first if any of these traps are being laid.'

'Always?'

'Always.'

And I can see that he means it.

Mark Twain was once a pilot on the Mississippi. The bed of that river is always changing and a man is sounding all the time and calling out the changes. Mark Twain says that a pilot, whether on duty or not, is always hearing these soundings. Even when playing poker his mind registers them automatically and days after uses the latest results when piloting. Great batsmen are the same, they are not like you or me. An experience is automatically registered and henceforth functions as a permanent part of the organism.

Similarly with placing. For George, to make a stroke was to hit the ball (he had a loud scorn for 'the pushers') and to hit it precisely in a certain place. He couldn't think of a stroke without thinking of exactly where it was going. Whenever he had scored a century and runs were not urgent, he practised different strokes at the same ball, so as to be sure to command the placing of the ball where there was no fieldsman. Those who know George only after the War don't really know him. In 1939 he was, in addition to on-side play, a master of the cut, both square and late, and though he was, like Bradman, mainly a back-foot player, half-volleys did not escape him. This placing to a shifting field must also be to a substantial degree automatic. Having taken a glance round, *and sized up what the bowler is trying to do*, the great batsman puts the ball away more by reflex than conscious action.

George had one quality that was paralleled by no one except Bradman. When he was run out in the Oval Test in 1939 he had scored 65 and, as one reporter wrote, if he hadn't been run out nothing was more certain than that he would make a century. He was not on the defensive but, according to *Wisden*, was cutting, forcing off his legs and driving.

Now physically. Headley has told me that the night before a Test he rarely slept more than an hour or two. (The night before the second century in the Test at Lord's in 1939 when he scored 106 out of 277 in the first innings and 107 out of 229 in the second he never slept at all.) But he isn't suffering from insomnia, not in the least. This fantastic man is busy playing his innings the next day. The fast bowler will swing from leg. He plays a stroke. Then the bowler will come in from the off. He plays the stroke to correspond. The bowler will shorten. George hooks or cuts. Verity will keep a length on or just outside the off-stump. George will force him away by getting back to cut and must be on guard not to go too greedily at a loose ball – that is how in Tests he most fears he will lose his innings (a revealing commentary on his attitude to bowlers). Langridge will flight the ball. Down the pitch to drive. So he goes through every conceivable ball and makes a stroke to correspond. This cricket strategist obviously works on Napoleon's maxim that if a general is taken by surprise at anything that occurs on a battlefield then he is a bad general.

Morning sees him in the grip of processes he does not control. He rises early and immediately has a bowel motion. At ten o'clock he has another. And then he is ready. He is very specific that these automatic physiological releases take place only on big-match days. He is chain-smoking in the dressing-room. But once he starts to walk down the pavilion steps he would not be able to recognize his father if he met him halfway. Everything is out of his mind except batting. Bumpers? Bodyline? He is not concerned. He gets out to good balls (or bad), but such is his nervous control that no bowler as such has ever bothered him. Near the end of an English tour he is physically drained except for batting. He has a few days' leave, he sits and smokes. His companions plan expeditions, make dates to go out with girls. George sits and smokes. From where he sits he doesn't want to budge an inch. But when they return to the tour, as soon as he has a bat in his hands, he is as fit as ever; fit, however, for nothing else except batting. When the season is over the fatigue remains and it takes him weeks to recover his habitual self. I watched the West Indians in the nets at Lord's in 1933 before the tour began. George never to my knowledge practised seriously. He fooled around playing the ball here and there. It was his first visit to England, but he was as sure of himself as if he were in Jamaica. In 1933 he ended the season with scores of 79, 31 (run out), 167, 95, 14 and 35. He was third in the averages for the season, Hammond and Mead averaging 67 to his 66. If he had thought about it in 1933 he would have made the runs needed. With him batting was first, not second, nature. In 1939 he was 72 with Hammond next at 63. He was a fine fieldsman and of the great batsmen of his day only Bradman was faster between the wickets.

His only unhappiness on the cricket field was that he was allowed to bowl only on the rarest occasions. George used to watch batsmen and detect their weak points. But from there he went on to think that he could get them out with his leg-break. Which does not at all follow. In 1933 he took 21 wickets. Alas! in 1939 he was allowed to bowl only 10 overs for the whole season. He spoke of it with feeling. In 1948, in a series of intercolonial matches in Jamaica, George made, out of 356, 203 not out; out of 151 for five, 57 not out; out of 456, 79 retired hurt. But he also took four for 40 and three for 53. Whereby I deduce that George captained the Jamaica side.

What does he remember most? Or rather what do I remember most about his talk on cricket? George rarely raises his voice. He never raised it louder than when he spoke of the West Indian failure in Australia (1951–2) to deal with the bumpers of Lindwall and Miller. 'West Indians couldn't hook,' he says, his eyes blazing. '*West Indians!*' To this day he remains adamant in his view that as far as he is concerned bowlers can drop the ball where they like and put fieldsmen where they like. 'If they catch it when I hit it they are welcome.' There is not the slightest trace of braggadocio; I have not known a more genuinely modest cricketer. For all I know, George may be quite wrong in his views of short fast balls, though he had plenty of them in his time and dealt faithfully by them. He speaks as he does because it is part of his outlook: never to have his equanimity disturbed by anything that a bowler may do.

That is why he speaks so soberly of the two balls which he did not see out of the bowler's hand. He had a kind of night-mare vision of having to bat without seeing the ball out of the hand. And one more catastrophe, a real one. A celebration match in one of the leagues. Mayors and corporations, dignitaries and their ladies. George, the star attraction, opens the innings, taking the first ball. An unknown medium-paced bowler sends one right up on middle-and-leg. Right up. George plays comfortably forward, a thing he rarely does, only to see the ball move away in the last inches and hit his off-stump. George is horrified. He has disappointed everybody. But there is more to it. He goes behind and observes the bowler carefully. Yes, it was not an accident, he is swinging the ball very late. George makes inquiries. Yes, he is a good league bowler, always moves the new ball well. It is years since it has happened. But George cannot get over it. He has been caught napping. He should never have assumed that any bowler with a new ball in whatever kind of cricket was not able to move it so late. Ordinary humans don't play cricket that way. Few people in this world do anything that way.

Such strange human beings as George Headley fascinate me not only for what they do but in themselves. There was a time when I read every biography of Napoleon I came across, and I still read some. He looks over a map of gun emplacements on the coast of France and points out that the investigators have left out two. I have known a few men who could do similarly. He could sleep instantaneously at any time for any length of time available. I have never met a man who could do that. And I have met very few men who can concentrate on anything as George concentrated on batting. I am sure he never had to learn it. I wonder if he had gone to America to study medicine (and had got interested in it) if he would have become a great surgeon, seeing everything, remembering everything, hands deft and sure, without nerves before the most distressing case. These qualities were not remote from those which made George the batsman he was.

I once talked for two hours with C. B. Fry. Technicalities all the time. But I added to my store of curiosa. While we talked there was cricket on television, a rather small screen.

He looked at me and gesticulated a great deal, watching the cricket, if at all, only out of the corner of his eye. But he seemed to see and judge every stroke and he always showed why a batsman got out. He was at the time over eighty and was not wearing glasses. It was Mississippi piloting in London, N.W.2. (When I was leaving he told me, 'Come in again'.) To many thousands of people a great batsman is a man who makes a lot of runs. Not to me. A really great batsman (*there are not many*) is to me as strange a human being as a man seven feet tall or a man I once heard of who could not read but spoke six languages. It is, however, only when you are aware of this that you begin to see. In scientific investigation you see as a rule only what you are looking for.

I read many books on cricket about and by great batsmen. Even the very few good ones tell more about the writer than the player. If life were not so urgent I would be willing to spend a year talking to a great batsman, asking him questions and probing into all sorts of aspects of his life on and off the cricket field. If he and I hit it off the result would be a book such as had never yet been written, which physiologists, anthropologists and psychologists would read more eagerly than cricketers. Such an investigation of Worrell, Walcott and Weekes would tell us as much about the past and future of the people of the West Indies as about cricket. But it will not be done. Late and soon, the world is too much with us.

No, I have not forgotten the third reason why I wanted to write about George Headley. And note it well, you adventurous categorizers. I know Constantine and Headley pretty well, as cricketers and as human beings. Contrary to all belief, popular and learned, Constantine the magician is the product of tradition and training. It is George the maestro who is an absolutely natural cricketer. We West Indians are a people on our way who have not yet reached a point of rest and consolidation. Critics of a sociological turn of mind had proved that we were a nation which naturally produced fast bowlers, when in 1950 Ram and Val, both under twenty-one, produced the greatest slow-bowling sensation since the South African team of 1907. We are moving too fast for any label to stick.

from BEYOND A BOUNDARY *1963*

A. W. Wellard – Hitter of Sixes

GERALD BRODRIBB

The world of first-class cricket has never seen a more consistent hitter of sixes than A. W. Wellard of Somerset. In the course of a county career lasting from 1929 to 1949 he scored over 11,000 runs, of which over a quarter came from his 500 sixes. This is a greater quantity of over-the-boundary hits than ever achieved by any other players, with the possible exception of Jessop, whose number of such hits can never be known. Wellard's aggregate of sixes is even more impressive when particular seasons are considered. In each of four seasons he reached a total of over 50 sixes:

> 72 in 1935
> 57 in 1936
> 57 in 1938
> 51 in 1933

No other batsman has ever reached as many as 50 sixes in a season, and only a dozen or so batsmen have recorded as many as 30.

These figures are so overwhelming that it is not easy to know where to start in any survey of Wellard's hitting feats. But since we have broached the subject of 'records', we might first deal with the two occasions when Wellard hit 5 consecutive balls for six. Several batsmen have hit 4 consecutive sixes, but Wellard is the only one to go one better by hitting 5[1], and he did this twice. The first occasion was in the match Somerset v. Derbyshire at Wells in 1936. Wanting 274 runs to win the match on an uneasy wicket, Somerset seemed beaten when their fifth wicket fell at 143. At this point Wellard came in, and was

[1] Written 1960. Sobers has since gone one better still!

promptly dropped in the deep off Armstrong, a slow left-hander. But in that same over he drove 2 consecutive balls over the screen and out of the ground for six. Armstrong was then taken off, but soon came back again, much to Wellard's delight. The first ball he played quietly to leg; the second and third he sent over the heads of the spectators into the car park, the fourth went straight out of the ground and was lost, and the fifth and sixth were also driven high and straight right out of the ground. When Townsend caught him off Copson, Wellard had scored 86 out of 102 in sixty-two minutes, the game had been pulled round, and Somerset eventually won a great match by one wicket. Wellard's score was composed thus: 1 4 6 6 1 1 1 4 1 4 4 1 2 6 6 6 6 6 3 4 1 4 4 4 . All 7 sixes came off two consecutive overs bowled by Armstrong – 0 4 6 6 1 0 0 6 6 6 6 6 – but, as has been explained, the first of these overs ended one spell of bowling, and the other began another spell. Despite that gap, the fact remains that 10 consecutive balls which Armstrong bowled to Wellard cost him 47 runs, one of the most devastating onslaughts a bowler has ever suffered.

The ground at Wells is a small one, and two years later, against Kent, Wellard again made the most of it, this time at the expense of F. E. Woolley, then playing in his last season. Wellard had already hit 2 sixes out of the ground off Lewis when Woolley was brought on to see what he could do. Wellard swept his first 5 balls for six – 4 of them right out of the ground – and 3 were lost in the gardens. This led to a shortage of balls, and no sooner had the Secretary produced a replacement than another one was needed. The last ball of the over Wellard attempted to despatch like the rest (he himself thinks Woolley sent him an easy one on purpose), but he failed quite to get hold of it and it fell in the neighbourhood of the screen, where the fielder got a hand to it, but dropped it, and a single was taken. Wellard says that if the fielder had not touched it at all it would have carried over the line for another six. So Woolley's over ended up with 31 runs – 6 6 6 6 6 1 – to surpass by one run Wellard's previous best of 30 runs in an over. When out, Wellard had scored 57 runs, including 7 sixes, and in the second innings he scored 37, with 4 more sixes, making 11 sixes in the match, an extraordinary proportion for a match aggregate of 94.

On two later occasions Wellard hit 3 sixes off consecutive balls: off D. V. P. Wright, when he scored 21 against Kent at Maidstone in 1939, and off E. Hollies, when he scored 34 *v.* Warwickshire at Birmingham in 1949. No other batsman has appeared as frequently as four times on the list of those who have hit 3 (or more) consecutive sixes. It is at the best of times a difficult feat against an experienced bowler, but Wellard hit the ball with that controlled power which made such feats possible. He stood 6 feet 2 inches, possessed very strong hands (he sometimes used a bat weighing 2 lb. 11 oz) and increased experience enabled him, unlike many other natural hitters, to develop from a crude slogger into a scientific driver of extreme consistency. Anything pitched up he drove, with the knowledge that if he really got hold of the ball it would safely carry the boundary. All round the country there are recollections of his hitting. . . .

Though Wellard was such a frequent six-hitter, he cannot be said to have been such a consistently *long* hitter as Thornton or Bonnor or F. T. Mann. From time to time, however, he produced a hit of extreme length, and it would seem that the longest hit he ever made was one at Brabourne Stadium, Bombay, during Lord Tennyson's tour of India in 1937–8. In the fifth unofficial Test he scored 33, and his hit was made off the bowling of Amar Singh. He had just sent a six off Mankad into the Club House, and then, batting at the opposite end, he drove Amar Singh towards the North Stand and out of the ground. W. J. Edrich in his book *Cricket Heritage* describes the hit:

'Wellard straight drove Amar Singh sky high over the sight screens, over the top of the stand behind it, and out of sight. I was sitting with Lord Tennyson at the other end of the ground, and I said, "Good heavens, that one's gone right over the top!" Lord Tennyson said, "Don't be a damn fool; no one could do it." This was interesting because Tennyson himself was a tremendous hitter. I confirmed my statement, and Tennyson said, "I'll lay you a pound you're wrong." I took his bet and his money. It was 97 yards when we measured the distance from the wicket to the edge of the turf where the sight screen stood; then there was a cinder track, then a series of terraces, then the stand, over 60 foot high. The ball had skied over the whole lot into the blue Indian distance.'

Wellard himself considers that hit the biggest he ever made, and both N. W. D. Yardley and Alf Gover rank it as the biggest hit they ever saw. Gover recalls it as a low, skimming hit which made the umpire duck, and then went on and on and on, until it finally rose to clear the stand and vanish for ever. It was obviously one of the greatest hits in the history of the game.

from HIT FOR SIX *1960*

Mushtaq Ali

RAY ROBINSON

Now that they have mechanical brains working, scientists could probably build machines to bat. Well oiled and wound up, their robot run-getters might win batting averages but they could not produce one to bat like Mushtaq Ali.

Even Nature has done that only once, and has endowed him with a kind of perpetual motion at the wicket. The only time this tall, slender Muslim is still in his momentary pause is to take guard from the umpire. Why he goes through this formality is one of the mysteries of the Orient, because after making his mark he takes no notice of it.

He is like a tiger on hot bricks. One moment, making up his mind in advance, he will spring along the wicket before the bowler delivers. A ball or two later will find him over near the slips, swinging the bat like a tulwar, impatient for a cleaving stroke to the leg boundary or a glance past his bails. All this is to put the bowlers off, like Denis Compton's up-pitch forays, except that Syed Mushtaq Ali in full flow makes the Englishman comparatively a stay-at-home.

The mobile Mussulman's name is pronounced Mooshtahk Ahlee (except by Australian Servicemen, who called him Muchjack Alley because of his liking for the strike). It means 'fond of Ali' – the fourth Muslim caliph who succeeded Mohammed nearly 1300 years ago after marrying the Prophet's daughter, Fatima. At the wicket Mushtaq Ali personifies lines from Islam's poet-philosopher, Iqbal:

> And behold yonder the mountain stream leaping . . .
> Rushing forth in spite of many a curve and twist.

The way Mushtaq Ali (and Compton sometimes) rush forth defies all odds of probability on their being stumped, regularly and ruinously. More often than stumping, the Indian's excursions to unsuitable balls have cost him his wicket in mishits. In one Test at the Oval he survived one fate to meet the other in the same over.

Mushtaq, son of a police inspector in Indore, Central India, is by the principle of action and reaction the least law abiding Test cricketer, always delighting to break the rules of batting. With eyebrows aslant and a smile flickering on his dark, handsome face, the idol of Indore has enjoyed disconcerting both bowlers and Anglo-Saxon watchers accustomed to more orthodox behaviour by first-class batsmen. After a six as high as a muezzin's tower, he would be just as likely to pat back a couple of half-volleys. Then he would pick the straightest length ball of the day for a cross-hit aimed at his batting partner wondering why a man with so many brilliant shots in front of the wicket should swing across the flight of the ball so much. Yet his best stroke has been made by keeping the bat truer and using his wonderful wrists to deflect medium-pace balls off the stumps past mid-wicket or squarer. It and his glance are full of risk but have brought him hundreds of runs when they would have been disastrous to less agile men – as they have often been to him when attempted against fast bowling.

Fellow-players estimate that in nine-tenths of his innings he got himself out, saving the bowlers that trouble. But for that, he would have made runs by the lakh. Sometimes the fatal stroke looked almost careless, as if his attention had been caught by something in a sari passing the sightscreen. He loved to swing a four near the tree adorning the square-leg boundary at Delhi and to cause a flutter among the women who watched Test cricket there in such numbers that Shree N. S. Phadke said of them: 'Hundreds of yards of ninon, silk and georgette and tons of greasepaint, powder and lipstick have graced the occasion.'

His old opening partner at Lahore, Muni Lal (later director of Indian Information Services at Sydney and Washington) said Mushtaq was no stickler for the grammar of batsmanship – he coined his own strokes and used them with stirring effect.

The flamboyant façade has been supported by essential struts. Speed of movements and sight have given him time to bring off feats of black magic, and a high grip of the bat has helped give him commanding height in stroke-play.

Neville Cardus no sooner saw him than he said: 'Here is the real Indian batsman,' as if he regarded the others as Asians conforming to British ways.

The example of his old counsellor, Colonel C. K. Nayudu, who was never bound by the conventional, probably encouraged Mushtaq Ali to follow the path of daring originality. When a friend asked Nayudu whether he felt he ought to advise Mushtaq that his cross-hitting indulgences were suicidal, the veteran shook his greying head and answered: 'I believe in letting him play his own game.'

Mushtaq was born on the twenty-ninth day of Muharram, 1333 A.H. by the Islamic calendar (December 17, 1914). At fifteen he entered first-class cricket with a hat-trick and 65 runs in a Hyderabad tournament. The Maharajkumar of Vizianagram, one of Old India's princely patrons of cricket, took the boy into his team at Benares and sent him to Bengal Dola High School. At sixteen Mushtaq played with Hobbs and Sutcliffe for Vizianagram's team touring India and Ceylon. As a left-arm spin bowler and smart infielder from Aligarh University, he was still in his teens when he appeared for his country. It was in the dawn of India's day as a Test nation, the second Test played on Indian soil. At that time the outside world knew little of Indians as cricketers except for the deeds for England of the princes Ranjitsinhji, Duleepsinhji and Pataudi.

A fine band of young cricketers stood ready to carry the banner – ripening batsmen Armarnath and Merchant, bowlers Amar Singh and Mohammed Nissar (All-India's fastest),

teenagers Mushtaq Ali and C. S. Nayudu. In the opening Test
Amarnath, 22, danced his way to India's first Test century and
left the ground heaped with honour, money, jewellery, gold
and silver cups. Today India needs another rich crop, especially
to refresh the national outlook on batting. A fore-runner may
be Vijay Manjrekar, youngest of India's 1952 side in England
and first of his race to score a Test hundred under the age of 21.
He bats with much the same ease of foot and stroke.

At 19 years 19 days Mushtaq Ali became the youngest
cricketer ever to play for India in a Test. He was one of those
introduced to international cricket against an English team led
by D. R. Jardine. . . .

At 21 he was playing for All-India in England [in 1936].
No batsman can achieve consistency while he is subject to
sudden promptings to cart well-pitched balls to leg. Though
Mushtaq Ali scored four centuries, his 1,048 runs were made
at the unflattering average of 25. The standards of consistent
mediocrity are a hopelessly inadequate measure for the inspiration of genius and many a man who would never be guilty of
throwing his wicket away is equally incapable of challenging
fortune successfully on a great occasion.

One of these came at Manchester when the Indians began the
second Test one down. Mushtaq Ali and Vijay Merchant
opened the innings, a pair as dissimilar as curry and rice, and
just as effective in combination. No couple less alike in mind
and method ever batted together. Mushtaq Ali, a Muslim over
6 ft. tall, clean-shaven, airy in manner as in style; Merchant
padding beside him, a short, quiet-spoken Hindu who, six
years before, had entered big cricket from Sydenham College,
Bombay, at the age of eighteen.

Vijay Madhowji Merchant's first name means victory in
three languages, Hindustani, Gujarati and Marati. He wears a
moustache much more restrained than the Ranji style with
gravitating ends and he looks rather like a younger edition of
General Franco, only slighter and taller (5 ft. 7 in.). Always well
balanced, he had complete mastery of modern batting science,

from solid back play right through to the forward dead bat in defence. Impetuosity and lack of concentration were given as basic reasons for a number of Indian failures but there were no such faults in this trustworthy batsman.

Mushtaq Ali did not care a rupee for any bowler's reputation. As they walked in he would sometimes say in a tone of resolve: 'I will knock the stuffing out of that bowler, you just wait and see, Vijay.'

The pair had four attributes in common: strength in onshots, artistry in cutting, sharp eyes and nimble feet in getting along the pitch to drive. Mushtaq got farther and drove harder.

In the first innings at Old Trafford they had made only 18 when a straight drive by Merchant cannoned off his partner's pads to mid-on, who threw the backer-up out. Back in the pavilion some sympathizers suggested that Merchant was to blame for the run-out. Mushtaq smiling asked: 'What could Vijay do if I got in the way of his drive?' It was typical of him that he would never blame anybody for any bad luck that came his way. He was always genial, whether he made a century or failed. He never expected to make a blob but was never upset if it did happen.

When they walked in for the second innings, England's declaration with a lead of 368 had left India a struggle for a draw, with no chance of winning. To his partner, three years older, Mushtaq Ali said, not for the first time: 'Vijay, please stop me whenever I am taking any undue risks.'

In the first over he charged a couple of yards forward to meet a fast ball from England's captain, Allen. Taking him at his word, Merchant made a cautionary remark between overs, but Mushtaq replied, 'Well, Vijay, it puts the bowler off and that is exactly what I want.' This theory often let him down, but it worked this day at Old Trafford. He carved 15 off one of Allen's overs. Strokes unorthodox and unpredictable upset England's field-placing. Whenever his onslaught seemed to be tempting fate too much, Merchant would give him a gentle reminder that India's chief purpose was to draw the match and so keep the Test rubber alive. Every time Mushtaq Ali would say, 'Yes, Vijay, I will be careful now,' but after a couple of overs he would forget. All the time England's bowlers expected to get him, yet his quickness of foot and luck helped him get away with the risks. C. B. Fry hailed his spectacular batting with: 'Here's another juggler from the country of Ranji and Duleep.' With Merchant playing classic cricket at the other end, 190 appeared on the board at the rate of 80 an hour.

Merchant realized that India's standing in international cricket would be given a much-needed lift if they could add 134 next day and thereby annex the proud record of the world's highest Test opening partnership. Going to Mushtaq Ali's room that night, he mentioned that there was just a possibility of their beating the Hobbs-Rhodes 323 not out[1] against Australia if they got set. Mushtaq promised that he would take no risks in the morning until he settled in again.

In the third over of the morning he pranced along the pitch and drove Robins hard and straight. Merchant half turned to watch the ball hit the boundary but Robins flung a hand out and brought off a memorable catch. As Mushtaq Ali departed he smiled wryly at his partner, as if to say, 'Sorry for letting you down.' As it was, he had contributed 112, with 17 fours, to a partnership of 203 in 150 minutes, still a Test record for any team visiting Britain and 23 higher than Australia's best opening against England.

from THE GLAD SEASON *1955*

---

[1] Since exceeded by Hutton and Washbrook's 359 for England against South Africa at Johannesburg, 1948.

Sir Leonard Hutton

A. A. THOMSON

It must always have been hard for the severest of his critics to
find fault with his batting technique. In the very first place it
was frankly based on defence, not from excess of wariness, but
because of the simple precept that you cannot score runs, however aggressive your intentions, if you get out first. One of the
two Australian bowlers who fought duel after duel with
Hutton in post-war Test cricket was heard to say ruefully: 'Len
worried me most when he wasn't seeing the ball properly,
because then he would dig in and, when he did that,
dynamite couldn't shift him.' This was true enough,
no doubt, on certain occasions, but nobody ever made
2,428 runs against Australia by merely declining to be
shifted.

In a young player he first looked for soundness before brilliance, but this did not mean that he was an enemy of brilliance.
The brilliance of May and Cowdrey in their early England
careers owed much to his personal encouragement and there
are countless examples in both county and Test cricket of his
own glorious artistry.

It would be absurd to believe that his batting was confined
to the business of keeping the ball out of his wicket. He was the
master of every stroke, and, like a true master, appeared to have
all the time in the world in which to play them. His batting was
a thing of beauty, not with ornament or flourish, but with
grace, directness and the art that conceals art in apparent
effortless ease.

'He is indeed a beautiful player,' that fastidious critic J. M.
Kilburn has said. 'His every movement at the wicket has a

tidiness, an economy, a "rightness" that stamp him among the truly great.'

His strokes were not 'contrived' towards beauty; they were executed in the best possible way; they were, in both a technical and an aesthetic sense, just what the ideal coach would try to teach you, if he was a sufficiently skilful instructor. Every stroke carried an air of perfection, and nothing more beautiful has ever been seen on a cricket field than his cover-drive. But manipulation of the bat is only part of the stroke. What made it possible was his superb footwork, an art which marks the master in all ball-games. His movements were the movements of the cricket text-book, but he gave to each text-book action a sheen and a polish rarely seen before except among the truly great and hardly ever seen since.

In the art of batsmanship he never seemed to need a lesson, but in the grand strategy of the game he was willing to learn all the time. If one outstanding quality had to be singled out from his many gifts, it was his concentration; not only the concentration which formed the steel framework of his 364 runs at the Oval in 1938, but the concentration which gave strength to his every visit to the wicket. From Pudsey to Adelaide and back again, he never played a slap-happy innings. Carelessness was wholly outside his nature.

Many excellent craftsmen belittle their own skills, by aspiring to an artistry beyond their powers. Hutton's genius could be looked at from the opposite direction. An artist of the highest possible standing, he would have thought it a sin not to be a good craftsman.

I am a good deal older than Sir Leonard Hutton and it is difficult for a man who as a boy saw Trumper, Ranji, and Jessop to enjoy some of the cricket he sees at the present time. I find it hard to listen politely to those who say, not without complacency, that none of the old masters would get a run today and that Ranji would be caught at leg-slip first ball.

The first answer to this is that it is nonsense. Are we to suppose that Hirst, Rhodes, Barnes, Lockwood, Richardson, Braund,

Trumble, Saunders and Faulkner did not really know how to bowl? The fuller answer is that, while the mediocre would fall by the wayside, the truly great would adapt their talents to the new conditions or the new conditions to their talents. The best are the best – in any age, and Leonard Hutton played the supreme part in the development of modern batsmanship, studying, facing and mastering all the considerable contemporary arts of bowling and field placing, and eventually coming out on top.

The two most illustrious names in England's post-war cricket were Hutton and Compton. Not only were they the greatest batsmen of their period, they were diametrically contrasted in their styles and characters. They were natural examples of their own separate breeding and background, north and south. They were examples, too, of the broad divide in human character, or at least English character: the traditional north and south; the Roundhead and the Cavalier; the steadfast and the dashing; the sternly virtuous and the irresistibly charming; the completely reliable and the gloriously unpredictable. Both kinds are completely indispensable in cricket, as in more momentous walks of English life; they are complementary and together they are almost invincible. Moreover, men of each of these kinds can overlap in their talents: Hutton, the purist, has sometimes batted in the utmost freedom, as in his glorious 122 (retired ill) at Sydney in 1947 and his fantastic 37 on the same ground in the same series. Compton, the exuberant, the magical, has in at least two of his Test hundreds defended with a barn-door stubbornness, entirely foreign to his nature.

'They were as different in type as in temperament,' E. W. Swanton has commented, 'the one often puritanically correct, yet in his more expansive moments putting a rich bloom on the orthodox, and occasionally releasing all his inhibitions in a glorious cascade of strokes. If Len Hutton was the pride of the north, Compton epitomized the Cockney gaiety and wit of the

London crowd; defiance, daring, improvization, charm . . .'

But however great the pleasure that Compton gave – and no post-war cricketer could have given more – the balance in sheer value to county and country lay with Hutton, on the score of soundness, reliability and devoted leadership. In the last resort the Roundhead virtues last a little longer.

from HUTTON AND WASHBROOK *1964*

Cyril Washbrook

A. A. THOMSON

Washbrook is forthright on the subject of fielding.

'Everybody can't be a Len Hutton for batting or a Brian Statham for bowling, but everybody can be on his toes in the field. If he can't, he has no business to be in a team at all.'

Much as he scorned what he deemed to be lazy fielding, it is only fair to say that there might be room for a slightly different view. Though I agree with Washbrook on the necessity for the highest standards in fielding, I could quote one of his close colleagues and ardent admirers, who said something like this: 'Of course every man should try his best in the field and of course even the worst fielders can do better if they practise, but Cyril's standards are terrifying.

'He is not just an ordinary good fielder, he is out of this world. He judges everybody by his own near-impossible standards, but although you can learn a lot, there are things that can't be taught: especially that sense of anticipation, that sixth sense that you'll find in tennis champions, international goalkeepers, and all great ball-game players. It is not a thing to be picked up: it is an instinct, a purely reflex action. Hobbs had it, Bradman had it, and Washbrook had it to a remarkable degree. That's why he was a bit hard on us ordinary chaps.'

If he was hard on his fieldsmen because of his own immaculately high standard, he was also hard on his bowlers, judging them by the equally high standards set by Brian Statham. Hard, I should say, because cricket is a hard game played with a hard ball, but he did not consider himself unjust in this, and neither do I. He was, in his strictness, which was courteous and not ill-tempered, more like the older amateur captain than the senior professional. Indeed, his was something of an aristocratic outlook, in the sense that he demanded a good deal, though never more than he would give himself. Despite this somewhat stern demand, he would never interfere with, or upbraid, anyone who was genuinely trying. You could think of him as someone akin to the good public schoolmaster whose most hateful bugbear is the thing called 'slacking'. He never courted popularity, but was popular all the same, and he exerted more influence on his county's cricketing affairs than any player of recent years.

When as a cricket-watcher you think of him in retrospect, you see him marching briskly to his post at the end of the over with a step that is nearer to a light-infantry regiment than that of the R.A.F. in which he served, his cap inevitably set at the gay angle which had brought him a solemn rebuke after making 152 in his second county match, but which he never deigned to alter. Or perhaps you remember his stance at the wicket, lightly poised and eager, unsmiling but at ease. When he was making his name, the Old Trafford crowd called him 'Smiler', which was an expression of their own unsubtle irony. After all, who could live in Manchester at all without a sense of irony? But if they thought that here was an over-solemn person they were wrong. He was not solemn, only serious in the sense that every professional man, every entertainer (including every genuinely gifted comedian) must take a serious view of his work. He has always seen the cricketer, especially the batsman, as an entertainer.

'You begin,' he told me, 'by playing for the love of the game and, if you lose that love, you will neither be a good player nor a happy man.'

But his view has always been that this idealistic sentiment must expand. He wanted to make strokes and to make them with an individual attractiveness; in fact to give pleasure as an entertainer, just as an actor gives pleasure. As he progressed, he came to believe, and still believes, that a cricketer's duty is to be an entertainer, first, last, and as nearly all the time as makes

13a *above* Lindwall
13b *above right* Miller
13c *right* A. V. Bedser

14a   *above* Walter Hadlee

14b   Reid of New Zealand

14c   *left* Bartlett (Griffith keeping wicket)

no matter. He must play to win matches, fairly, of course, but, winning or losing he must play as entertainingly as the state of the particular game permits. And if he is captain, he should encourage everybody to do the same.

He has some revolutionary views on cricket's future, though he thinks that almost everything depends on the player's attitude and willingness to be an entertainer. He is not greatly in favour of altering the Laws, but agrees with Sir Donald Bradman and many other famous cricketers in believing it would be a help to revert to the old leg-before-wicket law. On the question of covering wickets, he is against covering the actual pitch, but in favour of covering the square, especially the bowler's run-up. There are, he argues, two good reasons for this: the first is that the square takes hours to dry. The Old Trafford groundsman says: 'If it stops raining, I'll dry the pitch!' The second reason is that if the pitch has been covered, the batsman will play every ball carefully while the wicket is well behaved. If not, he may fail to punish a bad ball and be out to an unplayable one the next. This proves that it would have amply repaid him to hit the bad ball while the hitting was good. . . .

Washbrook's reputation as a good business-man is well deserved and wholly creditable. History has moved a long way since the days when Lord Hawke used to take elaborate precautions to prevent the old-type hard-hitting professional from dissipating the whole of his benefit in the four-ale bar. In the old days they were not all of the tremendous integrity of George Herbert Hirst. The modern professional, though not a finer character than, say, Wilfred Rhodes or Johnnie Tyldesley, is as different as possible from the cruder type of old pro who played in his grandfather's time.

He is better paid, better turned out, considerably better educated, and normally an excellent example of the well-mannered, sophisticated young citizen of his period. Almost every one of them has an opportunity of obtaining a good post

8

in industry at the end of his career; those at the very top of the tree, admittedly only a few, derive a pleasing additional income from advertising or journalism of the ghosted or do-it-yourself variety, and enjoy a grateful and gratifying benefit, the proceeds of which can be sensibly and legitimately invested in a sound business which should safeguard the retired player's future, with that of his family, for the rest of their lives. Such success has been achieved by both Sir Leonard Hutton and Mr Cyril Washbrook and it would be worse than churlish not to say good luck to them.

Yet when all is said and done, Washbrook's reputation with the wider public rests upon the respect and affection which his cricketing skill and personal integrity have won him. As a cricketer, he made his way on merit and ability. He received no special favours, but from the very first he impressed the most intelligent judges that here was Test-match material of the highest quality. From early days he could, perhaps paradoxically, concentrate with all the necessary caution and yet enjoy every minute of the play.

If, under Makepeace's instruction, he curbed his natural exuberance in the interests of the side, he would still take every chance of making forceful and charming strokes. These strokes, which he made particularly his own, gained him praise from the beginning to the end of his career and there has never been any doubt about either their power or their beauty. 'Sometimes,' Neville Cardus has said, 'I think he was unlucky to come into cricket when he did. In the epoch of MacLaren and J. T. Tyldesley his swordlike stroke-play would have stood comparison even with MacLaren and Tyldesley.'

From a Lancastrian about a Lancastrian, this is the most reverential praise.

from HUTTON AND WASHBROOK *1964*

Walter Hadlee

JOHN ARLOTT

On a Test Match Monday morning in 1937 at Manchester, New Zealand went out to bat against England on a wicket made spiteful by week-end rain and in face of an English total 358. The English bowlers were 'Big Jim' Smith, Arthur Wellard, Hammond, F. R. Brown and Tom Goddard – a powerful and varied attack supported by some brilliant fieldsmen. Half the New Zealand side was out for 119. Number six was a tall, lean, quiet young man of twenty-two – Walter Hadlee – who, in the words of *Wisden* 'had accomplished little up to that stage of the tour'. Not always certain in playing Wellard early on, he went coolly about his rescue innings and gradually played himself in. Then he used his height and reach in fierce driving of any ball pitched up to him. He stayed to see the score more than doubled before, in turning a ball from Wellard 'round the corner', he slipped and kicked his wicket down. His 93 – more than a third of the runs scored from the bat in the New Zealand first innings – gave his side a fighting chance.

That coolness in trouble and courage to attack were characteristic of Hadlee's batting, and implicit in the New Zealand team he led in England in 1949. He captained that side by right, fitted as few touring captains have been for his post. He was worth his place in the side as a batsman, irrespective of whether he was captain or not – and was an experienced cricketer who had been playing Plunkett Shield cricket for seventeen years. Only twenty when he first played for New Zealand – against G. O. Allen's side in the M.C.C. team in 1936 – he came of age while on the tour of England in 1937. He was made captain of New Zealand against the Australians in

1945-6, and against Hammond's English team a year later. This experience, coupled with a thoughtful manner, made for real appreciation of the strategy of the game and an understanding of his men as men and players. He bridged the gap which had existed in some touring teams, between manager and players, so that his party was, in fact, a party. Here he was fortunate in having – in Jack Phillips – a manager with a sense of humour who, like Hadlee, identified himself with the party rather than governed it from above.

If Hadlee needed to do more to establish himself among the members of his own team, he did so in the third game of the tour, against Surrey. New Zealand began their second innings on a crumbling wicket which might have been made for the Surrey bowlers. The pace of young Cox, the spin of Laker's and Eric Bedser's off-breaks and McMahon's 'Chinaman' were made doubly difficult, but most dangerous was the bowling of Alec Bedser. Bedser always has something in reserve for the wicket which really helps him, his pace seems to increase on a lively pitch, and every variation on the theme of fast-medium bowling is at his finger-tips under immaculate control. On that Monday at the Oval, his leg-cutter, pitched to a blind length on the middle or middle-and-leg stumps, was darting away outside the off-stump – perfect slip-bait. Or his late inswinger would strike back at the wicket like a whip-lash. The ball was lifting – often waist-high from a good length – compelling a stroke, but investing the stroke with danger. Bedser conceded less than a run an over for thirty overs. Defence alone was a full-time job on such a pitch. Yet, his left side a mass of bruises from the rising ball, Hadlee made 119 not out – no other New Zealand batsman scored more than 20. To hear the New Zealanders speak of that innings was to realize that here was that unusual cricket captain whose appointment had the unqualified approval of all his team.

from THE ECHOING GREEN *1952*

W. J. Edrich

TREVOR BAILEY

The County Championship is normally won by a team with a powerful attack, but when Middlesex carried off the title in 1947 it was largely due to the exceptional quality and strength of their batting. They had a formidable opening pair in the elegant Jack Robertson, who made over 2,700 runs, and the efficient Sid Brown who also topped 2,000. Then came those incomparable cricketing twins, Bill Edrich and Denis Compton. In that golden summer this pair amassed between them 7,355 runs, a feat which will surely stand for ever. In the circumstances it is easy to appreciate the batting opportunities of the rest of the side were somewhat limited.

In those days bowling against Middlesex was more of a problem than bowling against many Test teams. Not only did they score heavily, but they aimed, and often succeeded, in having four hundred runs on the board soon after tea on the first day. I often felt that the best chance of removing either Bill or Denis was for one to run the other out. It was a case of runs and roses all the way for that wonderful duo. How did these two compare as players? I would rate Denis as a genius and Bill as a great player, who (in his prime) would have been an automatic selection for a world eleven.

Bill was a complete batsman with a magnificent defence (few in my experience have watched the ball so closely) and a wide range of attacking strokes. All the outstanding small players have hooked and pulled well, because they are in position for these strokes a shade quicker than bigger men, and Bill was no exception. He was a superb, and absolutely fearless hooker of the fastest bowling. I have always maintained that seeing this chunky little man hook Ray Lindwall was one of the most exhilarating sights I have ever witnessed on a cricket ground.

Again in company with most small, nimble batsmen Bill was very quick on his feet against the spinners and his cutting was of the very highest order. He also perfected a lofted stroke wide of mid-on, which was a cross between the on-drive and the 'cow-shot' which brought him a vast number of sixes on even the largest of grounds.

As the years went by Bill lost some of his freedom and though, because of his sound defensive technique, he was never easy to dismiss, it was possible to keep him relatively quiet by bowling a full length on and just outside his off stump, something which could never have occurred during those memorable days in 1947.

When Bill eventually retired from the first-class scene he returned to his native Norfolk, found a new lease of life, and has rendered them great service both as a captain and as a player. He is of course the most famous member of the greatest cricketing family of this generation.

Bill was a born fighter and this characteristic was, in my opinion, the most outstanding feature of his batting, and indeed of his life. The bowling could be fast with the ball lifting off a length, but you could guarantee that Bill would be right behind every delivery. He accepted the hardest knocks without flinching and they only served to increase his determination. His pugnacious chin would simply be thrust out a little further and he would battle on. I would like him on my side at any time, but especially when the going was rough. He was just the type of player England needs now to combat Wes Hall and Charlie Griffith.

In these circumstances it is hardly surprising to find that Bill had a distinguished career in the War. Not for him the quiet little sinecure far removed from the main scene of the conflict. He learned to fly and became a bomber pilot in a squadron that specialized in daylight raids. Real courage is needed for this particular job and this priceless virtue shone through his cricket.

Perhaps, because I am a romantic at heart and lived through those turbulent days, I have an intense and passionate admiration for those who flew with the R.A.F. during the War. To me they will always represent the best that this country has produced.

Bill first played for Middlesex as a professional in 1937 and was quickly recognized as one of the most promising young players in the country at a time when there was no shortage. Playing at Lord's undoubtedly helped, but there was no disguising the class, and he went on two overseas tours before the War. When at last the hostilities ended, Bill, with a D.F.C., a decoration never lightly awarded, returned to Middlesex and after one season decided to become an amateur. It was the early days of the social revolution when it was still considered essential to have an amateur captaining England. At that time it seemed quite probable that Bill, who was an automatic choice as player, might lead England when Wally Hammond retired. Wally had, of course, taken the same step (of turning amateur) before the War. For a variety of reasons, including a disregard for the hierarchy, a certain wildness and impetuosity, and an unconventional outlook, he never achieved this particular honour. However, his decision to join the amateur ranks undoubtedly cost him at least a ten thousand tax-free benefit.

Bill lived hard and played hard. He believed that life was for living and was prepared to let tomorrow take care of itself, a view which his experiences as a combat pilot had helped to develop. I always felt that he needed a thirty-six hour day and inevitably there were clashes with authority from time to time, because he was a colourful, controversial, and sometimes headstrong individual. I remember how he upset one rather sedate Selector who simply could not understand the ethical gulf that divided the two of them, and never would. This Selector was utterly and completely dedicated to cricket, to Bill it always remained a wonderful game, but he never allowed it to interfere unduly with his private life. As a result England went to Australia in 1950-1 without him, and this piece of selectorial folly could well have cost us the Ashes.

Bill loved parties and he brought to them the same zest and enthusiasm which epitomized his cricket. He was also firmly of the opinion that a good one should never end before dawn, and, if there were indications of this unhappy event occurring, he was prepared to provide his own cabaret act which always delayed the break up. His party piece took the form of either a vocal, or a conjuring act. He had acquired his repertoire of songs during long forgotten nights in the mess and I think it is fair to say that his memory of the lyrics was considerably more impressive than his voice which was, fortunately, unique in my experience. It was an off beat, husky whisper, but sufficiently penetrating to reach everyone in the room. He also had another favourite party piece involving an egg which was always far more entertaining when it failed than when successful, a view not shared by one distinguished cricket correspondent whose white tuxedo never looked quite so immaculate again.

It is sometimes forgotten that in his younger days Bill was a more than useful fast bowler. There was nothing beautiful about his bowling, a quick scurry up to the wicket, followed by a slinging action (rather reminiscent of a catapult), but he did propel the ball through the air at a considerable speed and with enormous zeal. His own lack of height combined with his action ensured that he did not achieve much lift, in fact he tended to skid off the wicket. He was essentially a shock bowler, to be used in short bursts, when he was always liable to surprise the batsman by his speed. For a few overs he was genuinely quick.

Originally a cover and a good mover, as one would expect from a professional soccer player, Bill gradually developed into a very effective and unspectacular first slip. His captaincy was in a similar mould to his slip fielding, sound rather than showy. He did not miss many tricks, but he was always willing to take a gamble if there was the slightest hope of victory.

from PLAYFAIR CRICKET MONTHLY *October 1966*

Denis Compton

TREVOR BAILEY

Of all the great English batsmen I have bowled against Denis
Compton was the most unorthodox and the most brilliant.
When he was in his prime, and in the mood, he was not only
very difficult to dismiss, but his wide and often unconventional
range of strokes, combined with his ability to extemporize,
made him hard to contain. An outstanding example of his
capacity to *ad lib* when at the crease occurred when he was
playing for Middlesex against the Rest. Denis, as was so often
his wont, had advanced down the wicket to that fine off spinner,
Tom Goddard. He slipped and fell. Quite unperturbed by this
mishap, he was not merely content to make contact, but proceeded to hit the ball to the boundary from his prone position
much to the indignation of the understandably incensed bowler.

Against the faster bowling the initial movement of Denis
was the same as that of the majority of overseas players, back
and across. No doubt that this was to some extent due to the
fact that he was brought up on the fast, true pitches which prevailed at Lord's before the War. He also had the good fortune
that in his formulating years the net wickets at Headquarters
were outstandingly good, and almost lived up to the ideal of
being better than the middle. When he became established,
nets had little appeal for him, except as looseners, after all he
did spend a not inconsiderable portion of his life at the crease,
but they helped originally.

His initial movement back and across, combined with his
wonderful eye, quick reactions, backlift towards third man,
and physical courage meant that he was an exceptionally good
hooker and a fine player of really fast bowling. It is interesting

to note that today when there is not all that amount of genuine pace about most batsmen wear one and often two thigh pads, but Denis never bothered with one even when facing Lindwall and Miller at their peak.

Like all great players Denis used his feet and he was never happier than when gaily trotting down the track to some unfortunate spinner. Conversely when he played back he gave himself the maximum time by going right back to the stumps, and indeed this did on occasions lead to him treading on his own wicket.

Denis used rather more right hand in his batting than a classical stylist, but this did not prevent him from being able to cover drive with ferocity as I know to my cost. Young and naïve, I allowed myself to be stationed at silly mid-off with Denis batting and the eight stitches I had to have inserted in the webbing between my fingers are a permanent reminder of the power of his drive.

Although he had all the shots, both defensive and offensive, the stroke that will for ever be associated with his name is the sweep. This can be a dangerous shot if a fieldsman is stationed at deepish backward short leg for the top edge and the South Africans did, rather optimistically, plan to trap him in this way. However, Denis overcame the problem as a result of his own interpretation of the sweep. He played the shot later and hit the ball down with the blade of his bat slanting and not parallel to the ground. In addition he had an almost uncanny ability to place this very difficult stroke. On one occasion at Lord's I watched him sweep three successive boundaries off Peter Smith. I was stationed at deep square leg and the first one went to fine. I was moved there, only for the next to go to the exact spot I had vacated. This was the signal for another fieldsman to join me, but it made no difference as he smote the final delivery to very fine leg.

Denis had a long career which would have been even longer, but for the famous 'knee' which was to restrict his mobility in his later years. Despite a handicap that would have caused a less determined individual to retire, he did still make runs, because he could afford to forget about quick singles and rely on boundaries, but it could make batting with him for ordinary, limited players like myself rather difficult. However, there is no doubt that the golden year for the golden boy was 1947 when he scored more runs and made more centuries than anyone in the history of the game, records likely to stand for eternity. At the close of that summer when it was 'roses, roses all the way' I found myself batting with Denis against the South Africans in the Hastings Festival. Thousands turned up mainly in the hope of seeing him break the record. My one fear was that I should run him out which seemed to be the only thing likely to prevent him achieving this feat. I was also aware that an event of this nature was by no means improbable as the 'golden boy's' calling was unpredictable in the extreme, and it had been re-marked, with every justification, that his first call merely meant that he was prepared to open negotiations. Fortunately we managed to avoid this calamity largely through some un-expected co-operation from the South African fieldsmen. It was a less satisfactory story some years later in a Test match at Old Trafford, when Denis had me half-way down the wicket after his first affirmative, halted me there with a frantic 'wait', and had me slightly puzzled as he passed me at full speed saying 'no'. On my way back to the pavilion I realized that I had merely become yet another victim of the Compton three-call trick!

Denis was infinitely more than just a great batsman. He was an entertainer and one of the biggest box office draws ever to have played the game. Some of the more dour of the North-erners may have regarded with suspicion the light-hearted way he tackled the serious business of amassing runs, but in general he was a source of delight to crowds all over the world. The feature of his play I most admired was its essential gaiety. He not only made batting look easy, he also made it look fun. It contained a mixture of genius, mirth, and more than a sug-gestion of schoolboy impishness.

Like all entertainers he thrived on situation and a large audience. These brought the very best out of him, so that he tended to sparkle more brightly in a tense Test match at Melbourne than in a comparatively unimportant, badly attended county match in the Midlands.

Although it is sometimes forgotten, Denis was a useful 'chinaman' and googly bowler. He spun the ball considerably, but lacked the discipline and singleness of purpose necessary to reach the heights of this department. He might produce the unplayable delivery, but his length and direction tended to be wayward. Until increasing age and the handicap of the 'knee' took their inevitable toll, Denis was also a brilliant and decidedly unpredictable fieldsman. Away from the bat and when the game was proving somewhat dull he had a tendency to wander both mentally and physically which somewhat increased the problems of captaincy. Close to the wicket he liked to stand nearer to the batsman than most fieldsmen. His theory was that it was better to run the risk of putting down a possible chance through being too close than not to have the opportunity because the chance did not carry.

Quite apart from his ability as a cricketer Denis would always be one of my first selections for an overseas tour, because so much of the charm of his batting is reflected in an essentially sunny disposition. In consequence he is a pleasant and easy companion. It is easy to disagree with him on occasions, but I find it difficult to believe that anyone, who knows him well, could dislike him as an individual. Few people have possessed so much charm, a charm moreover that appealed to young and old, male and female, friend and foe.

Of course Denis has never been famed for his punctuality, reliability, and sense of responsibility and these have from time to time led to minor disagreements with the authorities, but even these august bodies have always been content with the mildest of rebukes. As one perplexed official once remarked to me, 'You can't be cross with Denis for long.'

There is a certain amount of truth in the idea that it is com-

paratively easy to be a good tourist if you yourself are enjoying a successful trip, but I was with Denis in Australia during
one of his very rare periods of cricketing failure. It is almost
unbelievable, but in 1950-1 he had a Test batting average of
7.5, yet despite the disappointments he still retained both his
sense of fun and his perspective.

My own affection for Denis was increased by the fact that
we are both kindred spirits in the virtue of being thoroughly
untidy. Changing next to either of us is a well-known cricketing
hazard, but I did not appreciate the full extent of his aptitude in
this direction until I shared a room with him in the West
Indies. It was a quite unforgettable experience for both of us.

Not only did Denis possess the golden touch on the cricket
and football fields, but it tended to remain with him on other
occasions. He just happens to be one of those people who
automatically pick up good cards, who receive tips that really
come home, and whose putts wobble on the lip and then drop
in. I shall always remember the day I went racing with him at
Sydney and provided a classic example of his luck. For once the
magic failed to work and in an effort to recoup his losses Denis
decided to have a 'tenner' on the final race. The bookmaker
first advised him against his bet, suggested horse number 7,
scrawled out a quite indecipherable ticket, and handed it to
him. A few pre-race inquiries elicited the information that
mysterious number 7 was merely a country hack without a
hope. Needless to say it romped home at ten to one.

After the race Denis approached the bookmaker a trifle
circumspectly as he really was not certain whether he was on
the winner or not. He need not have worried as the friendly
bookie paid out £100 with a smile and a 'didn't I tell you so'.
We were on our way back to the car when suddenly there was a
shout of 'Denis'. We turned and saw in the distance a short, fat
man sprinting towards us. On reaching us he apologized pro-
fusely for having omitted to pay the stake money and handed
Denis a further 'tenner'.

When a professional bookmaker does not take your money

for your original choice, gives you the winner, accepts the bet, pays out contentedly, and then chases half a mile to give you more, you rightly deserve the tag of golden, eighteen carat!

from PLAYFAIR CRICKET MONTHLY *February 1967*

H. T. Bartlett – The Hero as Cricketer

ALAN ROSS

Carlyle, in his famous series of lectures, allowed for six categories of hero – the hero as divinity, as prophet, as priest, as man of letters, as King. It is an exclusive list, making no mention of statesmen, explorers, scientists, soldiers – or, for that matter, sportsmen... The hero, for him, had to be a great man....

Yet the idea of a hero today, a hundred years after Carlyle lectured, has become something much more intimate. A cricket hero in this case could legitimately, of course, still be one of the legendary names of cricket: Grace, Hobbs, Hammond, Larwood, S. F. Barnes, Fry – an Olympian figure, almost without mortal failings. Any such would be a reasonable choice. Myself, I have never had the affection – admiration, respect, yes – but never that warm glowing regard, for the lordly great, which my conception of hero worship regards as necessary. I prefer local heroes to national ones, on the whole: once they progress from the county to the country arena, I feel they can do without my secret dispensations of passionate advocacy.

I believe that heroes are necessary to children and that as we grow up it becomes more difficult to establish them in the increasingly responsive soil of our individual mythology. Occasionally, the adult imagination is caught and sometimes it is held: but the image rarely takes root. I do not know that we become more fastidious, more cautious; I think it is simply that we become less whole-hearted.

If I accept then that a cricket hero must belong to adolescence, I find myself choosing from among those that haunted my mind during the 1930s. It would be unthinkable that he should not have been a Sussex cricketer, though I confess I was much enamoured once of C. F. Walters (as who, having seen him bat, could not have been?). I might well have settled for Tate, the true idol of my youth, or Duleepsinhji, or J. H. Parks, especially during the year [1937] of his 3,000 runs and 100 wickets, or Alan Melville or James Langridge. My hero-worshipping really was in the plural: my heroes were, without reservation, the Sussex cricket team. I could have chosen George Cox, who has given me greater qualitative pleasure than any living batsman, not least for his habit of driving successive pairs of Yorkshire fast bowlers through every inch of cover boundary in the country and of cutting fast or slow ones through every compass bearing between wicket-keeper and gully. I could watch him field all summer, as with the Sussex bowling of his day, he nearly did!

Then, again, there is John Langridge, of the ritualistic gestures, more hieratical in preparatory movement than any African witch-doctor, whom I have probably observed, with bird-watcher's patience, over a greater period of time than any other player. John Langridge was not quite in the heroic mould, but, because of his value to Sussex, I forgive him anything, while in the summer of 1949 he had more than a fair share of my adulation.

Any of these could have done as symbol for the pre-war Sussex of my youth. That I have, in fact, chosen as my figure-head H. T. Bartlett represents in some ways a perverse and contrary decision, for generally we seek heroes in our own image: idealized, but also to be emulated. Bartlett was a left-hander, I a right-hander; he was batsman *tout simple*, and for all my sudden batting cravings and hallucinatory phases of success, I was indeed a bowler. I imitated Tate as a boy, I spent two formative summers coached by A. F. Wensley. By the time Bartlett, in 1938, descended like a comet on the fairly sleepy fields of Sussex cricket, I was already absorbed at Haileybury in devising plans to bowl out Cheltenham at Lord's. What could Bartlett have especially for me? There was nothing possibly I could hope to emulate in his play. Yet, if I am to be honest, I have to admit that for two whole summers I could think of practically nothing but of H. T. Bartlett. Subsequently, he provided a number of disappointments: but at the peak period, both of his career and of my fevered imagination, he was a sight to behold.

I have never cared for my heroes to be either solemn or strait-laced. I know very little about Hugh Bartlett, and then I knew absolutely nothing at all. But he always gave the impression of having a healthy detachment from the game, of having an existence outside cricket that made his excursions into it both more perilous and romantic. Perilous his first few overs at the wicket certainly were; romantic he became, because not only was he pleasing in appearance, but the very nature of his genius was transitory. He made of this ephemeral, dashing, apparent recklessness a lasting quality: to those who tend to be attracted by the elusive, he was all they could ever require. I cannot remember, even in 1938, that he at any time exuded an air of comfort.

As a cricketer, domesticity was just not in his line. He began his innings usually as one who, suffering from violent astigmatism, has not only mislaid his glasses, but has in addition a fearful headache. He made a pass or two after the ball had gone past him: he lunged fitfully and missed: he stabbed down just in time at the straight ones: he sliced the rising offside ball over second slip: he snicked hazily past his leg stump. So, for about a quarter of an hour, it went on: or, to such an agonized onlooker as I, it seemed to go on. Then, suddenly, he would catch a half-volley or a long hop such a crack that the bowler, fearful of his own safety, lost all aggressive intention, and, with it, any idea of length.

Phase two then began. One no longer felt that the bowler was remotely interested in the stumps, but, having scattered his fielders round the boundary, relied now, in the form of bait, on a species of poisoned chocolate. Bartlett paid scant heed to these exiled boundary creatures: at alarming rates he drove between, over, and if needs be, through them. He was a firm-footed hitter, possessed of a long reach, and the trajectory of his drives was low and of a fearful power.

Something of his particular magnetism came perhaps from this violent transformation of calm into hurricane, not only in his own person, but in Sussex cricket generally. Sussex had on paper a handsome batting side in those days, but the two Parks, J. H. and H. W., were effective rather than ebullient, and in any case rather past their best; John Langridge took his time, as did his brother James, and there was only George Cox to stave off periods of total becalming.

Bartlett began that summer of 1938 quietly enough; it was at Leeds on 21 May that he played his crucial innings. Going in at No. 7, with Sussex five for 106, he set about Bowes, Verity, Smailes, Robinson and Turner to such effect that he scored 94 out of 125 in 75 minutes. He was magnificently caught by Leyland off a hit that would otherwise have gone for six. Before that he had twice hit Verity for three sixes in an over!

Of course, Bartlett's hitting powers were not exactly unknown. He hit fantastically hard at Dulwich as a schoolboy, playing for Surrey before he went to Cambridge, and he had his moments over the next three years at Fenners. But in fact – he failed in each of his three University matches – there was not the same exhilarating, annihilating quality about his batting, and it had begun to look to many as if the best was behind, not before. In the winter of 1937–8, however, Bartlett spent many painstaking afternoons at an indoor cricket school, and the effect was immediate.

Curiously, after Leeds, Bartlett did not play again for Sussex for a whole month. It was a period of unbearable anticipation. Then at Worthing against Worcestershire he returned to make 76 and 64, and one knew that envious men of the West Riding had not spirited him away for good. He followed this with 91 not out against Essex, and Sussex began a wonderful winning run. Bartlett's next appearance was at Lord's when he scored his now legendary 175 not out for the Gentlemen. Nicholls was hit for two vast sixes, then five fours in an over, Smith (P.) for two fours and two sixes in the next.

It was evident now that there was no fluke about it, though since they had not been made for Sussex, I could not but feel at the time that these runs had been squandered unwisely. Who could have possibly predicted they would continue? When Bartlett came down to Hove to play against Lancashire the following week-end he was a celebrity. His scores in that match were 72 and 63. Next came the Bank Holiday game against Middlesex, the first county match of the season I was myself able to see. Bartlett scored only 27 and 16, Gray bowled him in the second innings, and I have loathed Gray ever since.

But then followed one of those magic weeks whose events even now, twenty years later, I can remember in detail. Daily I took the train from my home in Ardingly to Hastings, daily the fortunes of Sussex exceeded the wildest prayers of the night before. There was in fact a certain Mephistophelian contract undertaken in those prayers. In them I vowed willingness to surrender any potential 50 or 5 wickets if Bartlett could be empowered to make a hundred and Sussex to win. I was playing two weeks of cricket that month, one of them for a club called the Vandals. I made no score of over 10, nor took more than two wickets in that first week. Sussex in the relevant week at Hastings beat Northamptonshire by nine wickets and Kent by an innings and 15 runs. Bartlett scored 114 in each of his two innings. I made no spiritual compact the week after, when I scored the first hundred of my life against Tonbridge on the Angel ground, and then followed this with 75 and 77 against the Bluemantles. Bartlett during those innings managed 8, 9, 0 and 0. I did not dare to bat again that summer. Without question – such heights can adolescent fanaticism reach – Bartlett's centuries gave me more pleasure than my own.

There was even greater joy in store! On 27 August the Australians came to Hove and Bartlett, batting only two hours on the second day, hit 157. He went to his hundred in under an hour – the fastest hundred of the season – and then took 21 in an over off Ward. Altogether he hit six sixes and eighteen fours. That season Bartlett finished fifth in the first-class averages; above him were Hammond, Hardstaff, Hutton and Paynter. His own average was 57.33. It could not, of course, ever be like it again. Not that it was all over, by any means. That winter Bartlett went to South Africa with M.C.C., and though he did not play in a Test, he averaged 51 in first-class matches. 1939, too, had its rewards. Indeed, it started rather better than the previous year for Bartlett. He opened up with scores of 49, 49, 48, 24, 33, 60, 31, 74; he made 114 (a heraldic figure for Bartlett) against Nottinghamshire, 81 against Northants, and then rather fell away. As in 1938 he played almost entirely in home matches.

He had disappointing weeks at Hove and Hastings, and then I saw him at Eastbourne later in August against Worcestershire. Sussex, facing a score of 372, were about five for 180 when Bartlett went in with Jim Parks as his partner, Bartlett raced to 89 in 44 minutes. He was caught then by C. H. Palmer off Martin at deep extra cover, and, as at Leeds the year before, had not Palmer held the catch it would have been a six. I do not ever remember such unconstrained driving. It was not only the ball up to him that Bartlett hit: he hit as often as not on the rise, without prior reference to the length of the ball, and with little care for the correct placing of the feet. It was largely a question of perfect timing.

By now, this joyous performance apart, Bartlett was a more responsible – if that is the right word – kind of batsman. He hit less in the air; he built up an innings more in the approved style. He was a remarkably accomplished player, swift to hook, with a steely square cut, a solid, thoughtful air to his back play. There remained the usual left-hander's failings outside the off-stump. By the time cricket got properly going after the War, Bartlett was in his middle thirties. He captained Sussex, but with no great success, personal or otherwise. He was a memory, not a hero.

Heroes in fact die with one's own youth. They are pinned

like butterflies to the setting board of early memories – the time when skies were always blue, the sun shone, and the air was filled with the sounds and scents of grass being cut. I find myself still as desperate to read the Sussex score in the stop-press as ever I was; but I no longer worship heroes, beings for whom the ordinary scales of human values are inadequate. One learns that, as one grows up, so do the gods grow down. It is in many ways a pity: for one had thought that heroes had no problems of their own. Now one knows different!

Hugh Bartlett was not the greatest of Sussex cricketers, and it might have been better if he had not played after the War. His parting from the county was not of the happiest. Yet, for two seasons, he made of every Sussex ground on which he played a place of enchantment. You do not often hear these days the buzz of anticipation that habitually preceded his emergence from the pavilion. Sometimes when Godfrey Evans goes out to bat in a Test match, or when Frank Tyson comes on to bowl, but not often otherwise. We hear a murmur at Hove on behalf of David Sheppard, and sometimes for Jim Parks, or Don Smith. But it is nothing to what we felt when Bartlett, tall, brown, bareheaded, a little Byronic around mouth and chin, but fairer, more casual, walked with toes turned a shade inwards towards the wicket.

Perhaps simply it is that one is older, less roused to excitement. I do not know. But I remember the sea glinting, the flags fluttering, the crowd settling itself, and those terrible first overs when Pope or Copson or Smailes or whoever it was, fizzed the ball over Bartlett's waving bat – the agony of it, the unbelievable survival, and finally that great ecstasy.

from CRICKET HEROES *1959*

T. G. Evans

JOHN ARLOTT

He is the most unquenchable man in all cricket. He will greet the batsman at the crease with a wink, pull his leg, stump him with an appeal paralysing in its speed and sharpness, commiserate with him, replace the bails, and be waiting impatiently for the next man in – all within bare seconds. Never, surely, was a cricketer so boiling over with vitality or so prodigal of energy. Compact of muscle – not muscle for muscle's sake, but the muscle of purposeful activity – he seems almost to bounce as he moves. If he throws himself ten yards to take a catch, you may be sure he will be on his feet, throwing up the ball before the echoes of his appeal have died in the pavilion rafters. If he whips off the bails in an attempted stumping which finds the batsman's foot still grounded, then the bails will be back in position before the umpire can shake his head.

Until the Kent cricket committee, anxious for the safety of his eyes, demanded that he choose between cricket and boxing, Godfrey Evans had an unbeaten record as a professional boxer. I suspect he chose cricket because it promised longer and more frequent periods of activity and, as a cricketer, took to wicketkeeping because the wicket-keeper never gets any rest.

No one has ever seen him tired. Sometimes on the South African tour of 1948–9, the English team came off the field virtually sun-stunned after an entire day battling for a win on an iron-hard pitch in the pitiless glare of the Rand or the steam-heat of Durban. Very humanly, they wanted a cool bath and an ocean of rest – except Godfrey Evans, to whom a day keeping wicket was no more than a prelude to a swim, a party, a drive, a walk on his hands, a few cartwheels and, to crown the evening, his own rendering of 'The German Band' – with actions – the most physically exhausting song in the world.

He has the fastest and cleanest hands for the ball that the mind of a cricketer can imagine, and he tries for everything. He takes his innings as if he were certain of hitting any bowling out of sight: he does not always succeed, but when he does, the spectator sees the champagne of batting. Yet, when the game demands it, he can bat the other way. England had almost lost the Adelaide Test of 1947 when Denis Compton was joined by the number ten batsman – Evans – who batted for an hour and a half before he scored. That innings was historic: it saved England – and it is almost the only time Godfrey Evans has admitted, even tacitly, that a bowler *might* be worthy of respectful batting.

 . . . Godfrey Evans would bowl, simultaneously if he could, *and* field in the deep. For this very reason wicket-keeping alone can seem to him – as we may fancy – almost an unsatisfying day's work. He makes chances and he misses them, but, faults included, he is the finest wicket-keeper in the world by a clear margin.

from THE ECHOING GREEN *1952*

A. V. Bedser

NEVILLE CARDUS

Alec Bedser is a big man, squarely shouldered, with the gentlest face, frank and kind eyes, and the smile of a friend – that is when he is talking to you off the field of play. I have seen him waiting in the 'middle' for a new batsman to come in, and then his brow has seemed shadowed with thunder, and his mouth grimly closed.

When a game is about to begin, he measures his run as deliberately as once on a time boys measured paces in the street when playing a game called 'Piggy'. He strides the last two lengths, then rolls up the sleeve of the right arm, and with the other signals his wishes to his captain as the field is placed.

He moves into action as though going slightly uphill; it is not a flowing rhythmical action like Lindwall's. Bedser runs to bowl in small galloping strides until the ball is released by energy at the shoulders, which swing round from a classical left side pointing to the batsman's position. The right hand follows through full, or nearly full, circle. The hint of stiffness before the ball goes its stinging, swinging way is the proof of compressed, concentrated power.

He is a natural bowler. He learned his cricket less from instruction than from the example of others while playing entirely for fun. As a boy his first love was 'soccer', as it was mine. He then played at Woking, and after they had looked at him (and at his brother) at Kennington Oval, he was encouraged by advice and pats on the shoulder from Alan Peach the Surrey all-rounder, who not many years ago would arrive at the wicket at five o'clock on a warm afternoon and thump runs all over the field, pavilion or Vauxhall end, gasholder, Tenison's Grammar School, or Westminster and the Houses of Parliament. For years Bedser remained a bowler by instinct and steady application of muscle. But nothing distinguished can be done in this world without some amount of hard thinking thrown in.

Bedser was a splendid bowler when first he visited Australia with Hammond's team in 1946–7; but though he put all his skill and determination into his every arduous over during that tour, he was coping with Bradman, with Barnes, with Morris at his best, with Hassett also at his best. Since those gruelling days he has often found success coming to him after efforts less strenuous or challenging than those given so wholeheartedly to the ill-starred cause of Hammond. A cricketer's career, like that of any public performer, may easily change direction by hazard; a single wind turns fortune's weather-cock.

Bedser came into his own once and for all during the Australian rubber of 1950–1, under the captaincy of F. R. Brown. In the summer of 1950, against the West Indies in England, he was not outstandingly a great bowler. Critics in fact, were saying: 'Look at his arm. Getting low.' In Australia in 1950–1 he began indifferently. Illness handicapped him. On the eve of the first Test match at Brisbane, his bowling was hit about right and left by Miller and Morris in the match M.C.C. against New South Wales at Sydney. If Bedser had failed in this first Test match of F. R. Brown's campaign is it certain we should today agree that he is the greatest 'new ball' bowler since Maurice Tate – and perhaps the equal of Maurice Tate?

But we must be careful if we use the phrase 'new ball bowler' with reference to Bedser; for it suggests mechanical dependence on the seam. Bedser resents constant allusions to himself as essentially an inswinger. He exploits the inswinger cleverly enough, goodness and Sir Donald Bradman knows; it does not follow, however, that whenever Bedser sets his short-leg field he does so merely with inswingers in mind.

A few years ago he began some private experiments with the ball's seam held horizontally; after much diligent practice he

was able to pitch between leg and middle and cause the ball to
turn to the off and remain dangerously near the stumps. The
effect was that of a genuinely spun leg-break; it was not a case
of cutting under the ball. Bedser at his best brought this superb
ball – the best of any bowler's tricks – under almost sure command. At Melbourne in 1950 I saw him pitch it between
Harvey's off and middle and just miss the leg – Harvey, of
course, is a left-hander.

With this ball, known of old as the 'Barnes ball', Bedser has
taken his place among the truly great of his craft. No bowler
can live on inswingers alone. Every batsman will agree that
the really dangerous spin is that which 'leaves the bat'.

Bedser believes in the direct attack on the wickets; he does
not use his slips and short-legs as so many hopeful accessories;
he likes to see catches sent to them from strokes played mainly
in defence of the stumps. Naturally, being human, he likes to
take a wicket as soon a match begins. And being frank and
open of disposition he shares the Englishman's love of a
'grouse' and also his love of a hint of encouragement.

from CLOSE OF PLAY *1956*

Keith Miller

IAN JOHNSON

It is not difficult to know or to understand Keith Miller. It is, however, a difficult thing to put that knowledge and under-standing on to paper.

There are times when I like Keith immensely. There are also times when I dislike him intensely. He can be quite delightful because he can be so charming. He can be quite impossible, because he can be so selfish. And he is quite unpredictable because he has a touch of genius. He can be incredibly disin-terested because he has a goodly portion of temperament. You can never be certain, on the field, whether he will put his heart into the job or act like a mechanical automaton. He is a bad example to young players. Yet he can be such a help to them. All of which adds up to a rather complex character who is essentially an individualist rather than a team man.

I suppose I know Keith as well as anyone in cricket. I have seen him graduate from an undersized lad in short pants to a cricket giant, both in stature and deed.

We met for the first time at a cricket ground in a Melbourne suburb. I was thirteen and had been picked for the Victorian schoolboys' under-fifteen team. At the final practice, we 'senior' members were standing back with a very superior attitude, typical of lads of that age, looking at one or two of those who had failed to make the team and who were still at practice.

A small twelve-year-old captured our attention. This boy looked like an Alan Kippax in miniature. There was a charm and artistry about his play that impressed us slightly older cynics. He was obviously a polished cricketer of talent and style rarely associated with one so young. He was, of course, Keith

Ross Miller, so named because when he was born, in November 1919, the brothers Sir Keith and Sir Ross Smith were creating world history with the first flight from England to Australia.

The choice of names could not have been more appropriate, because flying has often gone hand in hand with his cricket. It was while serving in the Royal Australian Air Force that he first became known to the cricket public of England.

Our lives have taken an almost parallel course. We went to the same club in Melbourne – Keith went to live in New South Wales *after* the War – and were selected for Victoria almost at the same time, subsequently rooming together on trips whilst Keith was in Victoria.

When the War began we both became R.A.A.F. pilots, Keith on Mosquitoes and myself on Beaufighters, and, after the War, we were in the first Australian team to tour New Zealand. So started our international careers.

In the early pre-war days Miller was small and somewhat delicate and, when he played his first game for South Melbourne as a boy of fifteen, he still wore short pants and looked at least two years younger than his age. Even so, he was already a fine cricketer and, in his first match, greatly impressed the former Australian captain, Bill Woodfull, who, as well as an opponent on that day, was also his schoolmaster that year.

At that time Keith lived near the Caulfield Racecourse and, being so small, hoped to become a jockey. Between about sixteen and seventeen, he grew almost a foot and his dreams of jockeyhood ended, but he has retained his love of racing and mixed it freely, possibly too freely, with his cricket.

Few players in the game's history have cut such a striking figure in the middle. He appears to exude confidence. Yet in reality, he is exceptionally nervous.

A player who professes the couldn't-t-care-less outlook, and sometimes acts it, he is just as keen as, or possibly even keener than, most others to do well personally. On the surface he may appear devil-may-care, thrilling the crowds with his cavalier hitting, devastating bowling and deceptively casual catching, but underneath it all Miller has an almost ruthless determination to come out on top.

This transformation possibly dates back to the time when he was not originally picked for the Australian team that toured South Africa in 1949–50. Keith's pride was shaken and, ever since then, he has applied himself to the game with an increased intensity and will to produce figures.

Of course, there have been all sorts of stories circulating about Miller's carefree attitude. He is the type who naturally lends himself to such stories, but often they are without more than a grain of truth.

For instance, take that match against Essex in 1948 when a record score of 721 was made in a single day. Keith is said to have made no attempt to score, but just lifted his bat and allowed himself to be bowled first ball, indicating that he thought there were more than enough runs on the board without his having to make an effort. That is nonsense, and is unfair both to Miller and the team. What happened was that Keith had been sitting in the dressing-room through a long partnership and, when he was suddenly summoned to the middle, the first ball he received from Trevor Bailey was a fast yorker. Just as with many other batsmen, the yorker got through before he could get his bat down.

Before the War, Keith was solely a batsman, and possibly his finest performance of that time was a century he made in one of his early Sheffield Shield games for Victoria against South Australia, at a period when Clarrie Grimmett was still bowling with all his great artistry and guile for the South Australians.

Keith never bowled for the State in those days, but, at the nets, he would often grab the ball and run up and bowl spinners like a budding O'Reilly, or hurl down some genuine express deliveries. It was apparent even in those days, when he regarded his bowling merely as an opportunity to give his colleagues batting practice, that he had more than ordinary ability. He could bowl off any run up and yet still hit a length; in other words, he was a natural.

How he began serious bowling with the Services side is now history. His bowling developed to such a degree of brilliance that, allied to his batting, he has become recognized as one of the finest all-rounders the game has known.

I cannot vouch for his being the greatest of all, but I do know that he is by far the best all-rounder I have seen. It was inevitable that, when a man had such ability in both batting and bowling, conflicts of opinion would arise whether he should be used primarily as a batsman or as a bowler.

I have always felt that his bowling has greater match-winning potentialities than his batting. Under pressure, Keith is a devastating bowler. As a batsman, he is unreliable and often fails under the same pressure.

Probably the reason for this lies in his temperament. He is exceptionally highly strung and, to a great extent, he lives upon his nerves. When the pressure is on his batting, this condition causes him to be tense and strained, and so interferes with his natural approach to the job on hand. Bowling, on the other hand, offers an outlet for his pent-up nervous energy; this provides a driving force which lifts him well above the ordinary.

Don Bradman was criticized in 1948 for using Miller so much as a bowler. It was felt that this affected his batting. The fact is that on that tour Miller bowled so well that he became more valuable as a bowler than as a batsman in a team containing batsman of the calibre of Bradman, Hassett, Morris, Barnes, Brown, and Harvey. In fact, I feel that his bowling has always been of greater value to Australia than his batting.

The alleged dispute between Bradman and Miller about Keith being over-bowled is supposed to have flared up in the Lord's Test of 1948. It was reported that when Bradman threw the ball to Miller, at the end of Lindwall's opening over, Keith just threw it back, refused to bowl and walked straight on.

. . . The real story of the Lord's incident is that Miller had hurt his back (the same injury that has troubled him since) during the First Test at Nottingham and had rested it until the

Lord's Test. Incidentally, Miller had also been troubled by his back in pre-war days.

During Lindwall's first over, Keith stooped quickly in the slips to stop a snick, then turned to me, fielding beside him, and said, 'Hell, I think my back's gone again.' I asked if he would be able to bowl, but he was not sure. At the end of the over we walked down the pitch together and when Bradman, as a matter of course, threw him the ball, Miller mentioned his back. Bradman replied, 'If you have any doubt at all I'll give the ball to Bill. Don't take a chance.' Miller agreed, and Bill Johnston took the ball.

This was the innocent start of many stories inferring dissension between Bradman and Miller. The two, in truth, are such diverse types that a close friendship between them was hardly likely. Yet each did respect certain qualities in the other.

In the latter stages of the 1948 English tour and in the Test matches of that year, Miller's batting had been very moderate; in fact he could almost be described as a failure with the bat. Some suggested it was because he had been over-bowled. I will deal with that point later.

When Miller returned to Australia, he apparently shared the view that his bowling affected his batting and he made a statement at the opening of that Australian season that he had no desire to bowl but wished to be considered only as a batsman from then on.

At the end of that season the side was selected to tour South Africa. The important thing in considering the selection is to remember those words of Miller: 'I wish to be considered only as a *batsman*.' Following his lack of success in the latter stages of the English tour with the bat, Keith averaged only thirty-three during the Australian season, making four hundred runs for twelve completed innings.

It has been suggested that Sam Loxton was preferred to Keith for the South African tour. But Loxton was an all-rounder, so that the only players to whom Miller, by his own statement, could have been preferred were batsmen. They were Harvey,

Hassett, Morris, Moroney and Ken Archer. Of these Hassett, Morris and Harvey virtually picked themselves, leaving only Moroney and Archer.

Both were openers and Moroney, that Australian season, had made 897 runs in eleven innings at an average of eighty-one, while Archer, a young and promising player, as well as being an opener, had made 552 runs in thirteen innings at over forty.

Had Miller played as an all-rounder that year, no doubt he would have been selected. But facts suggest that his omission, when he had asked to be regarded solely as a batsman, was not open to the criticism it received.

When Miller eventually went to South Africa as a replacement after Bill Johnston was injured, he played the part of an all-rounder with the success that one would expect from a player of his all-round ability. Yet, once again, his batting was not dominating. I give all that as a factual account based on actual performance.

Now, what about the truth behind the suggestion that Miller's bowling has affected his batting? My own version is that Miller undoubtedly would have made more runs had he not been called upon to bowl, but I do not think he would have gone down in history as so talented a player had he been only a batsman, as he will now do because of his all-round genius.

His name is indelibly carved in the hall of cricket fame as an all-rounder. As a batsman, it would merely have been one of hundreds in that hall of fame.

I feel that the Australian tour of the West Indies in 1955 disposed of the suggestion that excessive bowling did considerable harm to Miller's batting potential. On that tour, in hot tropical conditions, on grounds that were brutally hard and wickets that were most unhelpful, Miller bowled possibly more than ever he has done, and, to my mind, better than ever.

He took twenty wickets in the Test matches. In addition he made three centuries. In the prevailing conditions his was an almost unbelievably magnificent performance. I think Miller emerged from that tour a better cricketer.

15a   Worrell
15b   'Collie' Smith

15c & d   Sobers

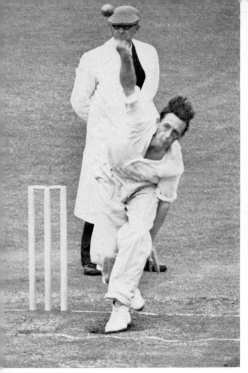

16a *above left* Statham
16b *above right* Trueman
16c *left* Hall

Certainly, he showed more responsibility and a sterner resolution in his outlook on the game whilst there. He did, in fact, play up to the unparalleled potential which he possesses. This was probably because he had so much work to do, for Miller is a type who must be in the game all the time, else his interest flags.

He has a keen sense of humour. I recall an incident one day when he was playing golf with Alan Walker, now a Nottinghamshire player, in South Africa, at a time when talk about the deadly South African snake, the black mamba, was fairly common. Alan hit into the bushes and went to retrieve his ball.

Miller waited for Walker ahead of a ladies' four-ball but suddenly there was a scream from the undergrowth and Walker emerged holding the leg of his trousers, yelling 'Keith, Keith, a snake's up my leg and he's bitten me. I've got hold of it. What'll I do now?'

Keith, startled, looked back at the ladies, who were now quite close, and suggested that all Alan could do was take off his trousers and shake the snake out while he himself waited with a golf club. Keith helped the trembling Walker undo his pants, then stood back ready to deal the death-blow.

Walker took off his trousers, shook them . . . and out fell a lizard, six inches long. Miller solemnly presented both lizard and trousers to the lady golfers!

Miller has a passion for music and likes nothing better than to sit through an orchestral concert. He is not musically gifted himself, but his knowledge of music rivals even that of the famous critic of cricket and music, Neville Cardus.

One of my biggest sources of amusement and enjoyment is to see Keith and Neville in a corner trying to find out the other by whistling a musical extract and hoping the other will not recognize it. It is a tribute to their musical knowledge that one can always recognize any tune that the other may be whistling.

Keith is undoubtedly a personality; but he is a *born* showman, rather than one by intent. Earlier his mannerisms stemmed

9

more from his highly-strung nature than from any deliberate attempt to hold the scene on the field, although in recent years he himself has realized his tremendous attraction to spectators and played up to it because he realizes its value to himself.

He is a keen student of cricket but does not talk easily about the game. He has many theories, several of which change with his moods. He admits that the pleasure he derives from cricket is moderate rather than extreme, and he prefers to relax on the golf links.

Miller is a natural athlete. He excelled at Australian Rules football and represented Victoria, and, later, New South Wales. He is possessed of immense natural strength and a constitution that has rarely been equalled in sport. He does not appear to do any special training to fit himself to his various activities, yet he is never out of condition.

Because of a knee injury, he had been completely inactive for about a month in Melbourne just before the Third Test with England in 1954–5. On the eve of the match he asked me if I would mind if he did not bowl as his knee was still not a hundred per cent. I fully understood the position and was quite agreeable. Next morning, just before the match started, he came to me and said he had tried his knee out in the bedroom and that it seemed all right. If I liked, he would bowl a couple of overs to see how it stood up to the strain, and if all was well he would go on for a normal spell. He bowled the full pre-lunch session – beautifully, too, taking three wickets for five runs in nine overs.

One reason for his amazing reserves of energy lies in the fact that he is such a sound and good sleeper. Despite his highly-strung nature, he can lie down and sleep almost at will. On tour he often sleeps as much as ten hours a night and he must always be awakened in the mornings.

From a captain's viewpoint, he can be very good and very bad. On occasions he is a wonderful help. On others he can be most exasperating. I have always found it best to 'give him his head'. I know him well enough not to be too exasperated, because he has usually been with me when the chips are really down.

That is the Keith Miller I know and have known for twenty-five years. He can be more serious-minded than most people imagine and, if he is unpredictable, that is, no doubt, part of his greatness as a cricketer.

from CRICKET AT THE CROSSROADS *1957*

Ray Lindwall

J. M. KILBURN

Keith Miller will forget his own cricket long before it is forgotten by those who watched it. He is a man of many talents and interests and he will always be tossing his head and tumbling into some further iconoclasm.

Ray Lindwall, companion and contrast, was primarily a cricketer's cricketer. His major bowling virtues were not discernible by untutored observation and he had not the appearance or playing character to create a popular sporting figure. The cartoonists could make little of him; neither could most batsmen, though he was one of the least alarming of fast bowlers – from the ringside seats.

His surname suggests Scandinavian stock but he was born in Sydney, a second-generation Australian, and nature granted him the physique and quick co-ordination of mind and muscle that are primary advantages in a games-player. The young Lindwall was Rugby footballer as well as cricketer and his cricket lasted all the longer because of a native toughness carefully preserved. He rarely began a spell of bowling without preliminary flexing of the muscles of back and legs; he rarely attempted any action beyond the limit of his poise and control. He was fortunate in his captains, but on tour he was his own best nurse during an uncommonly extensive career.

At first sight on the field he was not obviously the fast bowler of the side as, say, J. M. Gregory was the fast bowler or Kenneth Farnes. Even in action his magnificence remained partly disguised. His run-up looked leisurely and had no terrifying flamboyance of final leap to the crease. His arm was low, in defiance of classical principles. He could have been mistaken, from a distance, for a commonplace bowler.

Batsmen twenty yards away knew better and spectators in careful analysis revised opinions. Lindwall's bowling was, in fact, superbly designed. Not a step in the run-up was wasted, not a shred of energy was unnecessarily expended. Acceleration was progressive, culminating in a long delivery stride with a marked drag of the right foot. The right arm may not have been vertical but it made a wide sweep, fully stretched from beginning to end of the swing. The head remained steady and the back was arched, though never with any sense of strain. From first movement to last the whole action was under control.

It was in his control that Lindwall's bowling greatness originated. His variation of pace could be properly appreciated only from the batting crease or by the wicket-keeper, but his variation of length, direction and swing were on view for the delight of any watchful connoisseur. Lindwall, as much as any fast bowler who ever lived, knew where he was bowling. If he wanted to bowl a yorker, nine times out of ten he did bowl a yorker. If he wanted to remind a batsman that cricket is played with a hard ball his point was usually made clear. His bumper rose less steeply than Miller's but it was no less disturbing to complacency or dignity. Lindwall was perhaps the only bowler whom Jardine would have found acceptable as substitute for the Larwood of 1932-3.

In his first-class career there were few occasions when Lindwall looked less than a good bowler. When neither pitch nor the state of the game offered him any incentives he strolled through the formalities with accomplished ease and deliberate conservation of energy. At a time of crisis he was menace unmistakable, thunderous and thrilling as the ocean surf on Sydney beaches. With Lindwall 'on the kill', cricket became an enthralling, breath-taking spectacle, magnetic to players and watchers alike; drama charged the atmosphere.

Lindwall seen in a match without meaning could be forgotten;

Lindwall concentrated upon a purpose stays in the mind for ever. When England were 455 for 6 wickets in the scorching heat of Adelaide in 1947, Lindwall suddenly caught and bowled Compton and then took a new ball to end the innings in one swift over. In 1948 at the Oval England were all out for 52 and Lindwall's figures were 6 for 20. In 1953, after an Australian batting collapse at Trent Bridge, Lindwall's retort was the dismissal of Kenyon, Simpson and Compton in the space of eight balls while the England total stood transfixed at 17.

How much Lindwall enjoyed his chosen game or was conscious of his own splendour lay hidden from the general gaze. Only in the fierce appeal when breakback or inswinger thudded against obstructive pads did the inner passion show, though once, at Old Trafford in 1948, he was driven out of temper, to judge by the snatch of sweater from the umpire and the haste of his captain to speak soothing words. Without some hardness, some roughness of character, Lindwall could never have been the bowler he was. Great fast bowlers are not of apologetic inclination and by the very nature of their attack they must live in some isolation of spirit. They need to feel a little haste when a batsman faces them.

On the field Lindwall carried an air of detachment between assaults. He held, or assumed, a philosophy of contemplation, born, no doubt, of slip catches gone astray or the inability of batsmen to touch his outswinger or the imperfect sympathy to be found in umpires. His gestures of disappointment or satisfaction were few and became fewer with the ripeness of years. The more he played in England the more he accepted the English disinclination to demonstrate, yet he could not have been mistaken for anything but an Australian. The stamp of independence, of equality between Jack and master, was firmly upon him. He looked as though he knew how to look after himself.

It is Lindwall the bowler who will always be remembered in cricket, but Lindwall was also a batsman above despising. At

Melbourne, England once found that he had scored a century before the field-placing could be adjusted to cope with his hitting, and at Lord's in 1953 he was a batsman of distinction as well as a bowler. His fielding was invariably competent in an unobtrusive manner.

Ray Lindwall would have been a useful cricketer without bowling at all; as the world's worst batsman and fielder he would still have won cricketing immortality for his bowling.

from CRICKET DECADE *1959*

Sir Frank Worrell

JOHN ARLOTT

Frank Mortimer Maglinne Worrell was born at Bridgetown on August 1, 1924. As nearly a natural cricketer as may be – for he was never coached and rarely practised – he was a leading figure in the remarkable upsurge of Barbadian cricket in the 1940s. He was an outstanding player from boyhood; at Combermere School he was primarily an orthodox slow left-arm bowler and as such – and a number eleven batsman – was first chosen for Barbados – when he was seventeen. A year later while still at school, sent in as 'night watchman' he went on next morning to make 64 and to establish himself as a batsman. In the same West Indian season he scored 188, the first of his 40 centuries against Trinidad. In 1943-4 at nineteen, he made 308 not out in an unfinished partnership of 502 with John Goddard, a record for the fourth wicket which he and Walcott broke two years later with an unbroken 574, also against Trinidad. When world cricket recommenced after the Second World War, he and his fellow Barbadian batsmen, Walcott and Weekes, were the legendary 'three Ws'.

Worrell was the most orthodox of the three: his self-taught technique was so correct that he seemed incapable of a crooked stroke. Lithely built and superbly balanced, he was a stylist with an elegantly unhurried air, although his wide range of strokes, off front or back foot, was based on rapid movement into correct position. His cutting was delicate, his driving, for all its easy execution, powerful: he was strong on both sides of the wicket: and he combined ability to relax when not actually playing with the unremitting concentration of those who build long innings.

The demands of League cricket changed his bowling method from slow to fast-medium left arm; he exploited English conditions in sharp movement off the seam and his pace from the pitch was so hostile as at times to be little short of genuinely fast. Latterly his speed declined but to the end of his Test career his experience and control enabled him to seal up an end. He was a safe fieldsman and a clean catcher anywhere and latterly his fielding at silly mid-on was a considerable tactical asset for his bowlers.

As a young man he was markedly sensitive to criticism and some schoolday bitternesses rankled so deeply that, in 1947, he made his home in Jamaica. So it was as a Jamaican player that he established his Test place in the series of 1947-8 against England.

His performances brought him the offer which few West Indian cricketers have found it financially possible to resist and in 1948 he joined the Central Lancashire League Club, Radcliffe. There, and subsequently with Norton and Church, he spent some dozen happy and successful years as a league professional. Meanwhile, he read first Optics and then Economics at Manchester University. He contrived, however, to take part in all the West Indies' Tests of that period except those of 1958-1959 in India which coincided with the final terms before he took a B.A. (Admin.) degree. He made three tours of India with Commonwealth sides.

For the team of 1950, which was the first from the West Indies to win a Test, and a rubber, in England, he was top of the batting averages with 539 runs at 89.83 and made an important contribution to team-balance by his fast-medium bowling. At Trent Bridge after taking three important English wickets he scored 261, then the highest innings by a West Indian in a Test in England.

In the West Indian side which was beaten in Australia in 1951-2 he emerged as a genuine all rounder of Test standard. Apart from his technical ability, the quality of his temperament was strikingly apparent in Goddard's defeated and dispirited

9*

team of 1957 in England, when he made good the lack of an opening batsman and opened the bowling. He took seven English wickets in the innings at Headingley and finished second in the batting and first in the bowling averages for Tests.

It was now apparent that only internal politics could prevent him from captaining the West Indies. He himself wisely took little part in the occasionally acrimonious controversy which ended when he was asked to take the 1960-1 team to Australia: the first time a coloured West Indian had been appointed to the captaincy of a touring side.

On that tour, which included the famous tied Test at Brisbane, cricket in Australia was raised to such heights of public esteem as it had not reached since the days of Bradman. Australian opinion was reflected in the institution of the 'Worrell Trophy' for all future series between the two countries.

When he captained the touring side of 1963 to England, he was almost thirty-nine, a veteran by West Indian standards; indeed, all his famous contemporaries of the 1940s had retired from Test cricket. He himself was no longer the player he had been but, as batsman, bowler and fielder, he was still useful and he was one of the few men whose captaincy was so outstanding as to make a major contribution to a side's strength. He declared his purpose as not merely to win the Test series, but also to make such an impression as to bring West Indies to England again appreciably before the 1971 season of the Conference schedule. He achieved both his aims. The West Indies won the rubber three-one.

Worrell's captaincy was outstanding. Sharp in tactical perception, astute in attack and defence, quietly spoken, yet firm to the brink of ruthlessness, he outwitted his opponents and sustained his colleagues. As lately as 1957 a West Indian team had crumpled psychologically in face of defeat. Now, at one crisis after another, Worrell, with what sometimes seemed exaggerated calm, held them steady. His achievement may best be described as instilling in his players a professional attitude and stability which has endured. As in Australia, his side's cricket roused such immense public interest as achieved his second design. In the following winter the tour programme was revised, bringing another West Indian team to England in 1966.

By the time that decision was taken, Worrell had returned home to a magnificent public reception, the Post of Warden in the University of the West Indies at Kingston and a seat in the Jamaican Senate: a knighthood followed in the New Year Honours of 1964. In 1966 he was appointed Dean of Students for the branch of the University of the West Indies in Trinidad.

He was a non-smoker who kept enviably fit with a minimum of training. Convivial and conversational, he would talk gaily far into the night in his pleasant, slightly husky voice: he was quick and flexible in debate, fond of England and his many English friends, courteous in manner and he only rarely revealed the depth of his feeling on racial matters.

In 51 Test Matches he scored 3,860 runs at an average of 49.48 and took 69 wickets at 38.37.

Obituary notice from THE TIMES *14–3–1967*

J. R. Reid

BERT SUTCLIFFE

Any discussion on New Zealand cricket today cannot but be based on the character and achievements of John Reid. It is not just coincidence that in three successes in representative matches in recent years – the fourth Test against the West Indies and the third and fifth unofficial Tests against South Africa in 1961-2 – the New Zealand team was captained by Reid.

England has seen much less than the best of Reid, so far. But he is now [1963] only thirty-three and there appears to be every prospect that he will lead the side due to tour England in 1965. He has twice been a visitor. In 1949, he was the baby of the team, if one can apply such a description to a young man of twenty whose wide shoulders and great power were even then remarkable. On that occasion, he scored nearly 1,500 runs in first-class matches, averaged 41, and throughout the most golden of summers offered clear evidence of his ability to demolish good bowling – an aptitude now developed to an extraordinary degree. Reid secured a place in the third Test, scored half a century in his first innings and 75 for the match. Prior to the fourth and final Test, Frank Mooney, our wicket-keeper, was injured and Reid took his place. Conceding only six byes in a total of 482, he took a couple of catches and in New Zealand's second innings his 93 helped to ensure a very reasonable draw. In this brief period Reid emerged as his country's great all-rounder and if I assert that he is now in the class of players of the calibre of Keith Miller I am not just being wildly patriotic.

Reid's second visit to England was less happy. In 1958 he

was the captain of a side that was short of experienced batsmen and this in a summer that was, I regret to say, typically English. He again scored well, 1,400 runs giving him an average just below 40, but in common with the rest of us, he failed abjectly in the Tests. With New Zealand wickets meeting sudden death from stem to stern, Reid came to the fatal conclusion that Tony Lock had to be collared. But the Surrey spinner, bowling on pitches that were tailor-made for his skill, could not be hammered into obscurity and Reid's bold pretensions were quickly settled.

During this phase of his career Reid was by no means as popular at home as he is today. His Test displays did not, of course, do him any good, but at Wellington he had needled his fellow-players because of his devotion to the game. He was a dedicated player, giving all that he could of his exceptional skill and enthusiasm and he could be very terse and imperious with those who had less regard for the demands of the game than himself. Today Reid is still the perfectionist, but he has matured psychologically, and if he drives his side as fiercely as ever, he does so with much more understanding than he was able to bring to bear in the early, impatient days. Nobody now stands in higher esteem from cricketers and public alike than does New Zealand's captain.

With due respect to those who have a claim to consideration, I do not know of any player to whom the term all-rounder more properly belongs than to Reid. He again acted as reserve wicket-keeper in South Africa in 1953-4, and despite his muscular build, again displayed the speed and agility the position demands. He is, in fact, a magnificent fielder in any position. Early in his career Reid spent much of his time in the covers and, being a very young man, was not above demonstrating, quite often unnecessarily, the strength and speed of his returns. Lacking finesse, he did not realize that his pointed prowess served only to discourage the batsmen, chancing a quick single. In 1949 his wicket-keeping stints were limited, but he played a notable part as a cover fielder, especially when

Tom Burtt was bowling slow left-arm spinners. I, too, had the privilege, on occasions, of fielding in the covers and I make so bold as to say that our offside fielding was as good as I have seen anywhere. I can remember watching with pride the way in which Martin Donnelly, Mervyn Wallace and John Reid cut off shot after shot from such fine drivers as Hutton, Compton, Simpson and Edrich. It was thrilling to watch – the graceful curve of the left-armer's accurate placing, the flowing drive that followed, the swift interception, and the arrow-like return.

Reid was none the less great in the slips and with Geoff Rabone made the best pair I have seen. As for bowling, Reid was as versatile as ever. In his early days he used about a nine-yard run and his deliveries came through at a brisk pace. He bowled very little in 1949, then being as fast as anyone in English county cricket, but although he has, for some time now, cut down his run-up he still produces the most formidable bouncer to be met with anywhere in New Zealand. One is familiar with the fast bowler using plenty of space before turning and racing in to deliver a short one, but Reid, exhibiting at that time a mixture of off-cutters and out-swingers, always suggested that he had something in reserve. It worked out that way, for without any noticeable change of action, the batsman would suddenly find one flying at him.

These days, Reid is handicapped by a serious injury he received to his left knee – in fact, he announced at the commencement of the 1962-3 season that he would not be bowling at all – and has been forced to moderate his pace still further. This injury caused him much trouble throughout the tour of South Africa in 1961-2, and by his own exceptional standards he did nothing very much with his bowling, except in the Tests, where he headed the New Zealand averages. How typical of him it was. When New Zealand won the third Test, Reid's two cheap wickets represented vital successes. He bowled well, too, in the fourth Test, won handsomely by South Africa. It was in the fifth that he achieved one of the great feats of his career by taking two for 26 in the first innings. In the second, his persistence and courage allied to extraordinary accuracy (he was in constant pain from his injury) brought him the remarkable figures of 45 overs, 27 maidens, 44 runs and four wickets. Reid, and New Zealand, won the day.

Today Reid's first-class batting aggregate stands second in the list of all New Zealand players, and in bowling averages he is fourth. An all-rounder, without question, but it is as a batsman that he has done most for New Zealand cricket. After his 1949 successes in England, he had a lean period in Tests, with something like a dozen consecutive failures. But the faith New Zealand had in him was to be amply justified. He laid the hoodoo with a century at Newlands in 1953, one of the finest innings I have had the privilege of watching. He scored 116 of his 135 runs between lunch and tea, with a simply superb display of power batting. There is no denying, however, that for a good many years Reid did not quite appreciate his great potential. He loved to flay bowlers, but used his many fine forcing strokes without proper regard for a situation, and without reasonable discretion. Now he mixes aggression and discretion in the proper quantities, and I honestly think he is twice the cricketer he was. And he has always been good.

On his first South African tour, Reid became the first tourist ever to score 1,000 runs and take 50 wickets in the season. It was a notable performance. But on the recent tour of the Republic, he astonished the South African crowds not only with his batting successes, but by the manner in which they were achieved. He frequently scored at a tremendous rate, and he broke many records. His first-class aggregate for the tour exceeded 1,900, and it left behind the best efforts of players of the calibre of Hobbs, Hutton, Compton, and Harvey. It simply became a matter of Reid coming in, tapping away ominously at the block-hole, and setting about the best bowling South Africa had to offer. In the provincial matches, he had many good scores until half-way through the tour, when he really struck it rich. The sequence started with a double century against Western Province and a little later he ran up a succession of innings of 101, 118 not out, 165, 0, 60, 142, 112 and 117. And always, he thrilled the crowds with his bristling aggression and the tremendous power of his stroke-making.

John Reid is quite the strongest and most rugged cricketer of my time, a magnificent example of how to play the game between 11 a.m. and 6 p.m. I can think of only one other player who displayed such tenacity and power and he is South Africa's remorseless little Jackie McGlew, who, off the field, is friendly and very likeable. Reid has always had boundless energy, because of his high peak of physical fitness. Yet it is remarkable that he was able to play any games at all. As a schoolboy at the Hutt Valley High School, he was a champion sprinter, boxer, magnificent first five-eighths in the first Rugby fifteen and, of course, a cricketer of outstanding ability. But twice in his youth he contracted rheumatic fever, an illness that has put paid to the pretensions of many young athletes.

I played nearly all my Test cricket in company with Reid, but strangely, and quite unaccountably, we shared very few partnerships of consequence together. For two players to have been associated for so long, and yet never really to have clicked, defies explanation and I must leave it at that. Of our rare successes in partnership the most notable was at New Delhi in 1956 when our third-wicket stand produced 222 before the innings was declared closed. Following the retirement of so many of our top players after the English tour of 1949, both John and I were well aware of the new responsibility that rested on us. For a while it was left to one or the other to steer the side along and it is an undeniable fact that the cricketing public looked mostly to us to stabilize the New Zealand batting. Consequently, far too much importance was attached to our successes and failures, not that this affected our relationship which was always happily free of jealousy or acrimony.

I have always entertained the warmest regard for John Reid – the cricketer and the man. No touring team ever boasted a more devoted player or one who observed a stricter code. He did not care for alcohol, but was never the ghost at the feast. At team gatherings and parties John Reid was ever a popular figure, lively, amusing and good company. He appeared at the Glamorgan match wearing a cloth cap, muffler and a villainous expression, and his weapon was a water-pistol of which he made great play.

A cinema fan, Reid loved Westerns, particularly the sanguinary kind. He never really asked you to go to the cinema with him, but would casually ask, 'Who's for a film?' and not expect a reply. A moment later, though, he would seize somebody in a crippling grip and simply say, 'You', and to have refused would have appeared to be like mutiny. A fellow tourist remarking on Reid's immense strength, told him, not without reason, that he was 'all hair and teeth'. He is certainly remarkably hirsute and on one occasion when he walked off a county ground in England, a woman in the stands turned to her companion and asked why it was that Reid was wearing a dark singlet!

In the last year or two Reid has become a much more relaxed person. There were times when I felt that he had become a fire that burned too intensely. He tried so hard to be the complete cricketer and expected to find the bright flame in others, without realizing that we are not, heaven be praised, all made alike. Now he has discovered that he can enjoy a glass of beer with his fellow-players at the end of the day. He is that much the better for it and has come closer to his ideal than before.

What a debt New Zealand cricket owes to him. He still has a few years at the top left to him, but it is disturbing to realize that there is nobody in sight to take his place. I defy anyone to name a player today, save perhaps Rohan Kanhai, who can set a ground alight as Reid does when he comes out to bat. He is not a tall man, and his width of shoulder tends to reduce his height. He has a slightly rolling sort of walk, but he is a player wholly without affectation. Only one idiosyncrasy marks him out from his fellows: his habit of whipping off his right glove after starting out for a single, or what looks to be a three. He likes to be free of it when he is the non-striker, apparently because he fears perspiration could affect his grip. He is a dominant, as well as a demanding figure in New Zealand cricket. The world knows now how he can wreck good bowling with a steady stream of clean, perfectly-timed hammer blows; even last season Neil Adcock suffered the indignity of having the first ball of the day hit over the fence. But he has been just as much of a one-man hurricane as a bowler, in the lesser world of the Plunket Shield.

from BETWEEN OVERS *1963*

Trevor Bailey

JIM LAKER

You have to tour with Trevor to understand him. First impressions are that he is a somewhat affected individual, prone to 'act' and even play his cricket selfishly. And, to be fair, there are times when Trevor, in his batting, tends to play for himself.

Yet he has a load of guts, a flair for the big occasion, and is very popular with his England and M.C.C. touring team-mates. Far from being a snob, he mixes well, and counts some of the professionals among his best friends.

It is said that he dislikes Australians. I think he probably *thought* he disliked them in his earlier days, and I believe he even said so at a party in Australia on the 1950–1 tour. He irritated the manager of that side, Brigadier M. A. Green, by his mannerisms, and later Green wrote that at one juncture early on Bailey was told that he would be ordered home if he did not make greater efforts on behalf of the team.

I was not in Australia at the time, so I would not know the strength of this report, but I do know that Trevor is less headstrong now than in his early days, and has mellowed with the years. With his great knack of rising to the occasion, he has served England well. In my opinion he has been hard done by in not receiving more responsibility in recent years.

Trevor went to the West Indies in 1953–4 as vice-captain, and did an excellent job as skipper when Hutton was resting. But since that time he has been side-tracked. He got into trouble at Lord's for some comments in a newspaper article about that tour. They appeared before the M.C.C.'s twelve months' embargo on writing had expired. But this was due to a misunderstanding in the newspaper office, not to any deliberate flaunting by Trevor of his contract.

Sometimes, I feel, the M.C.C. are too reluctant to forgive. This has been a mistake, certainly in the case of Bailey. I know he has not been 'blackballed' as a touring cricketer. He has continued to receive full recognition in that direction. It is merely that his ability as a captain or vice-captain has been discarded. A pity, because he is a keen student of the game, with a ready knack for summing up a situation and the weaknesses of opponents.

Of course, Trevor has been favoured in Test cricket through a lack of opposition from genuine all-rounders in post-war England. The tendency is more and more to specialize, but Trevor, though now well into his thirties, has maintained his bowling speed and seems still to enjoy bowling as much as batting.

One man who might have challenged Trevor for his place if he had played regularly was the Merseyside dentist, Ken Cranston, captain of Lancashire. Cranston was a very useful number six, and an accurate and aggressive medium-paced bowler with a lot of nip off the pitch. I feel that if he had joined a county ground staff and taken cricket seriously as a livelihood, he would have developed into another Keith Miller. He was as strong as a bull, with great vitality, but after playing for England around 1947-8 he dropped out of the first-class game to concentrate on dentistry.

Cranston was vice-captain under G. O. Allen in the M.C.C. tour of the West Indies in 1947-8, my first tour abroad. I remember that in the heat of Trinidad, Cranston could bowl forty overs or so and then go out and play a useful innings. But he knew his days in first-class cricket were numbered, and he made the most of them. He was a gay, party-going type, and never really took the game seriously. Who can blame him? He did not *have* to take it seriously.

Trevor Bailey, on the other hand, plays cricket very seriously, with the studied approach of a professional. . . . This trait was already evident when he was at school at Dulwich. As a fourteen-year-old he skippered one side in a house match, which he allowed to end tamely in a draw. He was called before his master, Mr S. C. Griffith, to explain why he had not gone for victory.

'I thought the risk of defeat was too great, sir,' young Bailey stated.

'Never mind that,' replied Griffith, 'you must play to win.' Griffith was then an experienced county cricketer, who had toured Australasia with a M.C.C. side. But Bailey was undeterred. 'That's not the way I play cricket,' he retorted.

You can see how this attitude was bound to be as a red rag to a bull as far as the volatile Miller was concerned. . . . Trevor has traded on Keith's impatience.

In one Test match in which I was batting at the other end, Keith bowled a bouncer to Trevor. It hit him on the finger. Trevor immediately put on an absolute 'Hamlet'. He shook his glove, walked round the wicket half a dozen times, removed his glove, replaced it, prepared to take strike, then took off his glove for a second examination. The longer the delay, the greater Miller's anger.

The next ball was a 'beamer', straight for Trevor's skull. Bailey swayed out of harm's way and grinned impudently down the wicket. Keith said two emphatically uncomplimentary words, and hurried back to his bowling mark. He came in towards the wickets like a bat out of hell. He was about three paces away from releasing one of the fastest balls of all time, when Trevor stepped away from the stumps and began to look at his 'damaged' finger again. That was too much for Miller, and afterwards, his usually spot-on bowling was all awry.

In the Brisbane Test of 1954–5, Keith reached 49 by beautiful batting. Trevor, who was bowling, suddenly switched all but two of his fielders to the on side. Then he bowled leg theory in exactly the same way as he had done to save the Test at Leeds the previous year. Keith, who could not get near them, was hopping mad. The next ball was wide of the off stump, perfect for cutting. Keith slashed at it with all his might, got it on the side edge of his bat and dragged it on to his stumps . . . bowled Bailey 49!

Matters did not always go Trevor's way, however. At Lord's in 1953, the forward defensive prod stalled Australia in the second innings, but not in the first. Keith bowled a slower one, Trevor pushed forward too soon and popped up a simple return catch. Keith made sure of holding it and then, as Trevor tore off his gloves in annoyance, drop-kicked the ball, Rugby-fashion, into the covers as a gesture of triumph.

But Miller missed the pleasure of seeing Trevor's one big Test match 'failure'. After being originally dropped for the Fifth Test against the South Africans in 1955, Bailey was reinstated at the eleventh hour through an injury to Tyson. There was quite a hue and cry in the Press about Trevor's original omission and, when he went in to bat, he received a terrific ovation. Incredibly, Bailey seemed to allow the wine of the moment to go to his head. He had a dip at Tayfield before he had scored, and was caught off a skier. Miller would not have believed his eyes, especially when Trevor was l.b.w. to Tayfield in the second innings with only one run to his name.

'I would have given fifty quid to have been there,' was Keith's comment when next I saw him.

Actually, the 'feud' is not carried beyond the cricket field. Trevor really admires Keith's gay abandon as much as Keith admires Trevor's tenacity. All the Aussies love a fighter; that is why Bailey is not so unpopular in Australia as we are sometimes led to believe.

Both Miller and Bailey are good fields. You could not wish to see a better catch anywhere than the one Bailey took 'round the corner' off Trueman to get rid of Neil Harvey in the second innings of the Lord's Test in 1956. Indeed, Trevor is often as much a source of irritation to Harvey – so often does he have a hand in his dismissal – as he is to Miller.

Keith, of course, has also picked up some blinding catches in his time. He still catches well in the slips in spite of his disarming manner of standing bolt upright, often with arms folded, as the bowler delivers the ball. Here again is an instance where Miller should not be copied!

He is a fine mover, and thrower away from the wicket, too, and all round he is better in the field than Bailey.

Yes, no matter which way you look at it, the vote for that all-rounder berth in our All-Star team must go to Miller.

Yet there can be no finer tribute to Bailey than that he can seriously be considered in the same light as a cricketer of Miller's almost unrivalled skill.

from SPINNING AROUND THE WORLD *1957*

Jack Iverson

A. G. MOYES

Jack Iverson of Victoria was Australia's Bosanquet. The father of deceit learned to bowl the 'bosey' by using a tennis-ball. Iverson mastered his form of mystery with the aid of a ping-pong ball, bowling it at a tent-pole defended by a colleague with a foot-rule. All this happened in a Y.M.C.A. tent in Port Moresby, and so out of the War came a species of bowling which was to tie in knots some of the finest contemporary batsmen and to have a marked influence on one series of Test matches.

This six-foot-two-inches, fifteen-stone giant began life as Bosanquet did, bowling fastish stuff which exuded enthusiasm, but lacked any touch of guile. At Geelong College, Victoria, he took Hassett's wicket one day, the edge of the bat deflecting the ball into the stumps. It is one of the schoolboy memories of a future Test bowler. On leaving school he gave up cricket for thirteen years.

Suddenly his name began to appear in the news. Then he hit the headlines, and the story of his grip and his methods were so graphic as to cause laughter among those who had not seen him and did not know. My first real knowledge of him came during a conversation with Vernie Ransford and Bill Ponsford in the office of the Melbourne Cricket Club. 'This chap should be in South Africa with Hassett's team,' they told me. I pointed out that Iverson had not yet been chosen for Victoria, and that the Australian selectors could scarcely select him for an Australian side until they had seen him in action in first-class cricket. But I came away convinced that Iverson could bowl. Neither Ransford nor Ponsford was likely to make a mistake, for they were superb batsmen, and Ponsford has not been excelled by any Australian as a player of spin-bowling.

The story of Iverson is as fascinating as that of Bosanquet. Both evolved their species of witchcraft when idling away the time, and in both cases the first ball bowled by each of them caused ribald mirth and some anger. Iverson's experiment landed outside the batsman's legs and disappeared like a snake in the long grass, while the captain tersely told him to stick to his fast-mediums. But Iverson kept on experimenting and prospered.

Of course, his curious grip was such that it could not fail to bring weird results until it was mastered. He bent back the middle finger of his right hand, gripped the ball between it and his thumb, discarded the other fingers, and used the bent finger as a spring to discharge the missile. He found after a time that if the thumb pointed to the left the ball would turn from the leg. If the thumb pointed straight, then it was a top-spinner. Again, if the thumb pointed to the leg-side the ball would turn from the off-side, a peculiar 'wrong-'un' bowled with the wrist over the ball instead of underneath it, as is the rule among the more orthodox three-card-trick artists. It was a confusing business, and the only one who enjoyed it was Iverson.

But he let it go at that. He returned from the War without any thought of playing cricket until one afternoon he saw some blind men in action. He and his wife watched them, and Iverson reckoned if they could make such a fist of it with their handicap, then he could polish up his tricks, and convert them to worth-while use. His wife urged him on, and so he turned out one day at practice with a Sub-District side, hit the stumps a few times, was chosen in the third eleven, took twenty-seven wickets at less than six runs apiece in his first three matches.

Iverson stuck to the job. He practised assiduously – and no bowler can succeed without hard work. He began to develop, took seventy-nine wickets for the first team at an average of 10, and attracted attention in higher circles. Melbourne Cricket

Club, of which Vernon Ransford, former Test player, is secretary, invited Iverson to play with them. They took him seriously. He bowled his off-spin and his top-spinner. 'Give me a silly-point, a silly-mid-on, and a wicketkeeper. I don't care where the other fieldsmen are,' he told them. They did, and he took sixty-four wickets at 12 runs apiece. This was the season in which Ransford and Ponsford told me of his outstanding ability – 1948–9.

Iverson was sent to New Zealand with a side led by W. A. Brown. Over there he added the leg-break to his armoury, took seventy-five wickets at about 7 runs apiece. He also had forty wickets for Victoria in first-class cricket. Iverson had arrived – perhaps too late, some thought, for he was in the middle thirties, was something of a liability in the field, and his batting was mostly optimism. But his bowling performances were so good that in 1950–1 he was an obvious choice for Australia.

At Melbourne for Victoria against the M.C.C. he took three wickets for 71, not startling figures, but he confused Compton several times, and should have had his wicket. Then he went into the Australian side for the first Test at Brisbane, did not bowl in the first innings, but had four for 43 in the second innings. At Melbourne he took four for 37 and two for 36, bowling thirty-eight overs, conceding slightly less than two runs an over. Then came the Sydney Test. The Englishmen in their second innings batted on a wicket which took spin. The opening partnership hit 32 off the fast bowlers, but when Iverson appeared it was the end. In nineteen overs and four balls he took six wickets for 27 runs, and hit the stumps four times. Batsmen of the quality of Washbrook were so thoroughly confused that it caused wonder – and admiration for the bowler. No one made any effort to hit Iverson off his length, and none of them could master him by playing from the crease. In fact, rarely have I seen Test players so hopelessly inadequate for the task in hand.

The fourth Test was played at Adelaide, and Iverson had

three for 68 off twenty-six overs in the first innings, during which he trod on the ball when using his big boot to stop it. His ankle was twisted, he did not appear in the second innings, and was then unavailable for the return match, Victoria against the M.C.C. However, he played in the fifth Test under some handicap, took two wickets, and so finished his first international season with twenty-one wickets at 15.23 runs apiece, having the most wickets and the best average for Australia.

Unfortunately Iverson could not play in the 1951–2 season against the West Indians. He had announced that business responsibilities would force his retirement from big cricket, but the urge to have a try against Worrell, Weekes, Walcott, and others caused him to turn out for his club. The ankle, with his bulk weighing down on it, would not stand the strain of bowling, and so Iverson was not seen in big cricket during the season. In 1952–3 he was back in the game, keen to try his skill against the South Africans, and desperately eager to tour England in 1953.

It isn't easy to judge a man on one season's performances, especially as he bowled at a batting side which lacked substance. Only Hutton maintained his reputation, and none of the new men impressed, except, on occasions, Simpson. Compton fell far below his former standard, and Washbrook, with all his experience, was a sitting shot for Iverson, who made him stretch, and then either beat the bat or caused him to pop up an easy catch. Hutton played Iverson better than anyone else, and in the fifth Test Simpson mastered him, but that is likely to happen to any bowler once in a while, and it may not have been a permanent mastery.

To an extent Iverson was negative, in that he concentrated a good deal on the leg-stump and spun his off-break into the pads. He had four or five fieldsmen on the leg-side, and this made it extraordinarily difficult for the batsman to get him away. It was often an open invitation to commit suicide, and modern batsmen don't do that. Furthermore, Iverson could spin the off-break appreciably – more than the leg-break, which was his surprise ball in contra-distinction to the habits of the 'bosey' bowler proper, whose leg-break is the stock delivery.

from AUSTRALIAN BOWLERS *1953*

Tom Graveney

TREVOR BAILEY

The recall of Tom Graveney to the England team against the West Indies in 1966, after years in the wilderness when he was written off as not up to the required standard and indeed over the hill, proved to be an unqualified success. It was not only a romantic move, but a logical one, because nearly everyone in the game, other than the selectors apparently, knew Tom to be the most dependable batsman in the country, and that he ought to have been picked several seasons earlier. What our selectors had failed to appreciate, until it was almost too late, was that, once Graveney had settled down at Worcester, he became a far more consistent player than he had ever been in the past. He has always been a very fine batsman, but with maturity he became a great one.

Tom reached his peak in 1964, when Worcester won the title for the first time. Although Middlesex in 1947 were an exception, the Championship is decided mainly by bowlers; however, it is doubtful whether one single batsman has ever exerted as much influence on the Championship as did Graveney for Worcester that year; he elegantly bestrode the scene that summer and without him his county could never have triumphed. He carried Worcester's batting, scoring well over 2,000 runs, hitting numerous centuries, and making fourteen other scores of over 50. However, it was not only the runs he scored, but the number of occasions he steered his side to a reasonable total when the pressure was on and the pitch was poor. Against Essex on a lively wicket Tom made 106 out of 229, and because of that fine innings, which was beyond the capabilities of practically any other English player, Worcester won the match.

This was a typical example of the mastery he exerted, but our selectors omitted him while we lost the Ashes to one of the poorest Australian teams to visit this country. It did not make sense at the time, and in retrospect appears even more nonsensical. The final irony of Tom's belated recall to international cricket was that, afterwards, he was chosen on merit to play for the World XI in Barbados. Yet he had not been considered good enough to be even a member of three M.C.C. parties who toured Australia and South Africa, when he was in fact batting better than he had ever done!

I first met Tom Graveney when Essex went to play on the lovely school ground at Cheltenham which has a beautiful batting wicket. This match became stamped in my memory because the luncheon interval was lengthened and enlivened by a remarkable speech. The orator, a local dignitary, commenced by telling everyone, and apologizing for the fact, that mediocrity was the outstanding feature of both teams. He went on to say that Gloucester had done nothing of note since the prewar days of Walter Hammond. The Gloucester skipper, Basil Allen, was, not surprisingly, very, very incensed, as only two years previously his team had failed to carry off the Championship by the narrowest of margins. The speaker continued by welcoming us, 'the men from Exeter', and then was generous enough to suggest that there was an element of hope for both sides. Gloucester, for example, possessed two promising young cricketers, 'The Brothers Gravity'. From that day I always thought of Tom as 'Gravity'.

On the field I was immediately impressed by Tom's style and also noticed that high flowing backlift which suggested that he might be susceptible to the bouncer. In those days he was comparatively naïve, accepted my challenge, and swished at a head-high delivery which later he would have contemptuously ignored. The result was a catch at the wicket. I need hardly add that Tom was to take his revenge on numerous occasions in the years ahead; I have lost count of the number of centuries he has made against Essex for both Gloucester and Worcester, not to mention the fifties.

My first of many tours with Tom Graveney was to the West Indies in 1953-4, and it was then that I really began to know him as a person and not merely as a talented batsman from another county. We both liked hot weather and beautiful beaches, rum and Coke and impromptu parties. We were both fascinated by the calypsos, though Tom sang them rather better. We both were keen, though far from expert bridge players and on the way back from the Caribbean once played from 9 a.m. until 2 a.m. with breaks only for refreshments. We were both prepared to go on to the golf course, but here the similarity ended because Tom is an exceptionally fine golfer with an exquisite swing who would have done really well if he had decided to concentrate on that sport instead of cricket.

Subsequent tours, both official and unofficial, increased my regard for him both as a player and as an individual. We have shared moments of triumph, such as when we retained the Ashes at Adelaide in 1954-5, and we have also shared moments of disappointment, like in 1958, though the main reason for our failure then was not the bent-arm controversy but the fact that we failed to play to our potential or as a team. However, above all else both of us have extracted enormous pleasure from touring and playing cricket.

Every time I see Tom at the crease one adjective immediately comes to mind: elegant. There have been few, if any, English players more attractive to watch over the past decade. Everything about his batting is graceful. It starts with his stance which is easy, upright and unmistakable. He has a top-of-the-handle grip, his backlift is high, his timing delicate, and he follows through with a flourish. This high backlift did on occasions prove his undoing against fast bowling in the early stages of his career in Test cricket, but it is also one of the main reasons why he possesses so much appeal for the spectator. A drive by a person with a short backlift may be as effective as one by Tom, but it never can be as exciting to watch. A cover drive by him, with full, graceful arc, represents considerably more than four runs; it is a thing of beauty, to be remembered and treasured.

But the most handsome batsmen do not always make the most runs. In county cricket Tom Graveney has always been a prolific scorer, but in Test cricket, when the going was hard, he was not always as successful as his ability warranted. When we toured Australia under Sir Leonard Hutton, Tom did not really come into his own until the end of the tour. In the final Test, with the series already decided, he scored a wonderful 100, while in the New Zealand Tests he overshadowed everyone with a series of innings of exceptional merit and brilliance. Technically, apart from a tendency to hit across the line when scoring on the leg side, Tom has always been a very correct player. What then, was the reason for his comparative failure at international level, until his triumphant reappearance on the international scene against the West Indies?

I have an idea that in his early days his temperament unconsciously resented the restrictions which have inevitably become part of so many Test battles whenever the opposition possesses a top-class attack. The knowledge that he could not afford to make a mistake affected his reactions so that he was unable to play his normal game. In the second Test of 1954 at Barbados he was at the crease for a very long time with little effect, and his tempo made even myself appear to be a fast scorer. On a beautiful track he forgot all his shots and allowed himself to be contained by two accurate spinners, Ramadhin and Valentine, who were not achieving much turn. It was a classic example of a player allowing a situation (we were facing a huge total) to blind his better judgment. In county and festival matches he has always looked truly Olympian so that it was difficult to understand why in a number of internationals he has appeared human and vulnerable.

Tom improved as a batsman after he left his native Gloucester. He had been appointed their captain and proved to be an adequate rather than an outstanding leader, perhaps because

17a Graveney

17b Bailey

17c May

18a Iverson

18b Alley

18c Lawry batting against England at the Oval in 1964 (Parks keeping wicket)

he tried to please everyone which is nearly always a fatal policy. At the time he was – other than as a maker of runs – comparatively inexperienced and in some respects rather naïve, while the idea of a professional skipper was only reluctantly being accepted by the county's hierarchy. In 1960 Tom led Gloucester, who had an undistinguished summer, although despite an injury, he comfortably headed their batting averages. At the end of the season the Gloucester committee decided to replace him by an amateur, C. T. M. Pugh, who possessed a strictly limited knowledge of the first-class game. Understandably this was a bitter personal blow to his pride and, predictably he resigned and decided to go elsewhere. I ran into him in London at this time and did my best to try to persuade him to settle his differences with his county, but to no avail. I gained the impression that the whole unfortunate business might have been avoided if only a little more tact and foresight had been employed, but this has seldom been an outstanding characteristic of county committees. Gloucester were naturally reluctant to release their most talented cricketer and this meant that he was forced to waste an entire season before he became eligible to play for Worcester. The undercurrents and the inevitable wrangling, publicity, accusation and counter-accusation left their mark on a basically uncomplicated, easy-going individual so that when Tom reappeared on the first-class scene it seemed that some of the fun in his batting had been replaced by an increased determination to score runs. He quickly settled down to become the most consistent player in the country. Thus a new, harder, more ruthless Graveney was born, but because of his style he remained a delight to spectators everywhere.

Of all the outstanding batsmen I have bowled against none has been as predominantly front-foot as Tom. This characteristic was encouraged by two factors. First, many of the Gloucester pitches on which he was trained were inclined to be slow and to take spin. In these conditions there is much to be said in favour of being on the front foot. Secondly, Tom is tall and

10

his height enabled him to ride a delivery which rose sharply even when on the front foot. Against fast bowling Tom largely employs a half-cock shot with the weight on his leading leg. To overcome the problem of scoring against a pace bowler who keeps the ball just short of the length he has, in addition to nudging and running the ball, developed a semi-push, semi-drive on the up, played late with the weight on his front foot; it is a most effective, highly individual and rewarding stroke.

What one first notices when bowling to Tom is his left leg thrusting firmly forward. It used to irritate me that if I managed to make a ball come back sufficiently to beat his very broad bat, it did not hit the wicket because the pad was in the way and my frantic appeal for l.b.w. was seldom of any avail. It is interesting to note that he is so expert on the front foot that he is even able to hook quick bowling from there. The one discernible weakness in his method is that it makes him slightly vulnerable to a top-class off-spinner, at least at the start of an innings. I always feel that there is a chance of having him caught out in the forward leg position, particularly if the ball should stop a little because this may well increase the influence of his right hand and because he tends to follow through even when playing defensively.

Like all great batsmen he has a wide variety of strokes, but relies largely on scoring his runs with straight bat shots in an arc between extra cover and forward short leg. This is the safest and surest method as one is employing the full face of the bat and is less likely to edge the ball.

In his younger days Tom was an extremely fine all-round fieldsman, better than average in most positions and possessing a very good pair of hands. As a slip, in his prime I would rate him as outstanding without ever quite attaining true greatness. In the deep he has always been reliable and takes the high catch baseball fashion with the hands reversed and the knowledge that if he fails to close them in time he will be hit on the forehead. He is an occasional bowler, whose most dangerous ball is the leg-break which does not turn.

One performance of Tom Graveney's against Essex at Romford many years ago gives a good indication of his batting mastery. On that occasion the wicket was so green that it would have served as a natural advertisement for an artificial fertilizer and the ball moved about in a most bewildering fashion. It was a seam bowler's paradise and Gloucester were removed for 153 of which Tom contributed exactly 100. In their second innings they were all out for 107. Once again Tom was the highest scorer with 67, and indeed was very unlucky to be out caught down the leg side off a genuine glance. In this match only two of his colleagues reached double figures, but what was even more impressive was the way he made his runs. Everyone else struggled and failed as the ball moved viciously off the pitch as well as swinging in the air, but Tom never appeared to be in any trouble. It was a classic example of how to bat under really difficult conditions, a triumph of technique and application, which only a great player could produce.

from THE GREATEST OF MY TIME *1968*

Brian Statham

MICHAEL PARKINSON

I first saw him in those distant days when people used to queue to see a cricket match. We were standing outside Old Trafford in the inevitable gloom waiting to see the Roses game and this slender youth walked by carrying a cricket bag.

'Who's yon?' said the old man.

'Our new fast bowler,' said the Lancashire supporter standing in front of us.

'Fast bowler,' exclaimed the old man. 'He's not big enough. He'll fall down before he reaches t'wicket.'

The Lancashire supporter looked sheepish and stared hard at the locked gates. There was nothing he could say because the youth who passed us by was certainly the unlikeliest looking fast bowler imaginable.

The old man wasn't letting it drop there. He sensed an opportunity to put the old enemy to shame.

'What's his name then?' he asked.

'Statham,' said the Lancashire supporter.

'He'll get some stick today,' said the old man.

Two hours later we were sitting behind the bowler's arm as the new boy, spindly and pale, prepared to bowl against the might of Yorkshire. As he measured out his run the old man said, 'He's not strong enough to run that far. Somebody ought to tell him.'

An hour later and we were a couple of very depressed Yorkshiremen. Statham had taken the first three wickets for next to nothing and we knew in our sinking hearts we had seen a great fast bowler in action.

Going back to Yorkshire the old man said, 'Tha' knows he's going to bother us that Statham.'

That was seventeen years ago and in that time John Brian Statham has done everything to prove the old man right. I have never forgotten my first sight of him all those years ago and have never forgone the chance to see him in action since. Watching him through the years has been a constant pleasure. In a changing world he has remained aloof from fashion's whims, unscathed by the advance of time. Even now, at the age of thirty-seven, the figure is as lean and as pliable as in his sapling years. There's the odd fleck of grey in the hair but the eyes are bright and youthful. I sought him out at Old Trafford to discover how many more seasons I might have the pleasure of watching him.

'About three more I reckon. I'd like to complete twenty years with Lancashire,' he said.

What then? 'Probably league cricket. Back to where I started,' he said with a smile.

In the seventeen years since he left the leagues to play for Lancashire, Brian Statham has established himself as one of the truly great fast bowlers. He hasn't got the subtlety of a Lindwall, the flair of Trueman or the blasting speed of Hall. His success is based on the two classic precepts of the bowler's art, length and direction. He is the most honest of bowlers. His avowed intention is to knock all three stumps down and he never disguises the fact. In a game slowly being strangled to death by the niggardly defensive tactics of a legion of second-class seam bowlers he stands out like a bold knight at the head of a peasant army.

The nearest this gentle cautious man gets to anger is when he talks about the modern-day seam bowler, 'Little phantoms' he calls them.

'They come on to bowl and they've no intention of getting a wicket. They just plop away all day, preventing the batsman from scoring, boring the crowd to death. It's wrong, terribly wrong,' he said.

He shakes his head and looks out of the dressing-room window across the sunlit green of Old Trafford. The years rest lightly on him and yet one feels that perhaps Brian Statham has not reaped their full harvest. The comparison with the fortunes of Fred Trueman is inevitable if only because of their great partnership. Trueman the businessman, Trueman the journalist, Trueman in the gossip columns, on the telly, Trueman in the gravy.

Brian Statham says: 'I'm happy. It's a question of what you want really. Fred's different to me. He likes the limelight. I think people should be what they are. I wouldn't go on television and talk about things I knew nothing about because that's not my job. Similarly you wouldn't ask Eammon Andrews to captain Lancashire would you?'

Statham is content to remain just a very good cricketer taking only what the game offers him and not expecting more. This and his exemplary conduct on the field and off made him the ideal man to rebuild the pride and faith in Lancashire cricket. It is a daunting task. The club has bled internally in the past from dissent among the players and the committee. It has been snubbed by the cricket lovers who see no reason to accept second best after many seasons of rich and splendid diet. At any age when, if there were any justice, he ought to be grazing in the outfield, Brian Statham is required to accomplish the most important task ever given to a Lancashire cricketer. He doesn't make any predictions. He simply says: 'We'll be all right. Just wait and see.'

In the three years we have left to us we ought to savour Brian Statham. The present legion of 'little phantoms' who are boring us all to death should be made to watch him for a full season and then given the choice of either emulating him or retiring. Those who mourn McDonald and the Ancients should seek solace in the sight of one of the few English cricketers still playing who can stand any comparison, and those of us who write about the game should always use him as the yardstick of our judgments. In any period of the game, no matter how enriched, Statham would be a treasure. Today, even in his twilight, he is simply priceless.

from SUNDAY TIMES *4–6–1967*

Fred Trueman

DERYCK COOKE

'*I think cricket should be played on the attack.*' – Fiery Fred.

Just before Ray Lindwall took the boat at Sydney in 1953, to come and demoralize England's batting as ruthlessly as ever, an Australian journalist described the great fast bowler, then 32, as 'a portly ghost of his former self'. Undeterred by this colossal howler, the press has ever since taken the curious habit of trying to *talk* fast bowlers out of Test cricket before their allotted time; and their greatest success to date, without doubt, has been their creation of the artificial atmosphere of alarm and despondency around the 33-year-old Fred Trueman, which led to his being dropped by England after this year's Leeds Test match.

It seems clear that the England captain, Dexter, is unhappy leading a team which does not include Trueman, and the figures indicate why. I am not referring to the dubiously informative 'bowler's average', which merely tells us how many runs the bowler bought each wicket for – though, even so, Trueman's excellent figure of 24 runs per wicket was at this juncture second only to Titmus's quite extraordinary 16.66 (contrast the figures of the two other quick bowlers – Coldwell 29.5 and Flavell 68). The heart of the matter is that Trueman had once again been the chief *destroyer*. To win, you have to get the other side out, and Trueman had taken more than a third of the wickets that had fallen to England's bowlers – 13 out of 36. Titmus was next with nine; Coldwell and Flavell had only six between them. Even more important, nine of Trueman's 13 victims were the accredited batsmen: Lawry (twice),

Simpson, O'Neill, Burge (twice), Booth, Redpath and Cowper.

In a quick bowler, the quality of penetration is far more important than the traditional average of runs per wicket, and infinitely more important than the 'economy average' of runs per over which causes so much concern today. It too can be measured in figures, as a 'penetration average' of *balls per wicket*: obviously the fewer the better, if the other side is to be ejected quickly. Judged from this crucial standpoint, Trueman is revealed as the most consistently destructive bowler in post-war England-Australia Tests – on either side. Trueman's overall figure of 56 balls for a wicket is surpassed only by Tyson (54), whose achievements were mainly confined to a single season (I exclude Meckiff's 53 in 1958-9, since he has now been exposed as a 'chucker'). Trueman's penetration average of 56 represents the harvest of six series over 12 years; and the comparable figures of his post-war peers are interesting: Lindwall 59, Miller 66, Bedser 68, Davidson 70, Statham 72, Bailey 77. The best figure for a single series since the War was Bedser's 41 in 1953. Next comes Bailey's 43 in 1950-1, Tyson's 43 in 1954-5, and Trueman's 46 – when do you think? During the first three Tests of 1964.

Figures are valid only if they reflect events faithfully. At Nottingham, Trueman promptly had the Australians 8 for 1 by bowling the newcomer Redpath. Then, after turning 61 for 3 to 61 for 4 by the inspired running out of a bewildered Booth, he turned 91 for 4 into 91 for 5 by trapping Burge leg-before. Again, after holding a stinging catch off Veivers of the kind which English fielders are all too prone to drop, to help Flavell turn 118 for 5 into 118 for 6, he exercised the fast bowler's traditional privilege of bowling No. 11 (Corling) for next to nothing. Australia all out, disastrously, for 168: Coldwell had done well, with three wickets, one every 44 balls, for 16 runs each; so had Trueman, with three wickets, one every 41 balls, for 19 runs apiece – plus a hot catch and an incredible run-out.

When rain ended Australia's second innings at only 40 for 2, for a drawn match, Trueman had taken no wicket – but he had thrown everything into trying to remove the dangerous O'Neill, challenging him by feeding his famed hook-stroke with short, rising balls on the leg-side, while Dexter left the square-leg boundary tauntingly untenanted. The plan misfired: O'Neill, instead of mishitting and getting caught near the wicket – as he was to do in the second innings at Lord's – treated the crowd to four superbly hooked fours off consecutive balls before Trueman gave it up and dropped back on a length. Take away this clearly calculated risk, and his 'expensive' economy average of 5.6 (28 runs off five overs) becomes his normal, reasonably economical one of 3 (12 off four overs) – in line with his overall 3.2 during the 1961 season.

At Lord's, Trueman again had Australia straight away 8 for 1; it was Lawry he bowled this time. And when Coldwell turned 84 for 3 into 84 for 4 by removing Redpath, Trueman swiftly made it 88 for 6, getting Burge leg-before and Simpson caught, square-cutting, for a duck. Shattering transformation! In the end Australia were all out, disastrously again, for 176. Trueman had five wickets, one for every 30 balls, at 10 runs apiece. Coldwell had one wicket for 51 in 130 balls. In the Australian second innings, neither Trueman nor Coldwell could get an early wicket, and Dexter persevered far too long with both, when the spinners were clearly called for. However, when rain ended the match as another draw, Trueman had taken his revenge on O'Neill, who this time mishooked a short rising ball on the leg-side to send a skier to backward short leg, where Parfitt made a neat catch. Watching Dexter in earnest conversation with Trueman when they walked back prior to this ball's being bowled, I wondered whether he was promising to carry the can back at the next selectors' meeting if the plan misfired again and O'Neill hooked Trueman for four sixes this time!

At Leeds, Trueman failed, for once, to take an early wicket, but he again accelerated a middle-order batting collapse – with

a typical piece of Truemanship. The young Cowper, replacing
the injured O'Neill, and coming in at 154 for 4 to face Trueman
in his first Test against England, was understandably nervous,
and Trueman easily bamboozled him with the old three-ball
trick: an easy one (two runs) to give him a sense of false
security, a vicious bumper to rattle him, and a lightning yorker
to spreadeagle his stumps. Unkind, no doubt, but Australians
must expect, as they have always given, a baptism of fire. With
the last accredited batsman now gone, except for the not-out
Burge, Titmus soon got Veivers and McKenzie, to make it
178 for 7, with Burge clearly struggling. Then came the
unhappy reversal, which, combined with England's poor
second-innings batting, lost us the match.

Dexter took the new ball, again – and when Trueman and
Flavell failed to get a quick wicket – dallied too long before
reverting to spin. Trueman was even more widely blamed
this time than he had been at Nottingham: he chose to feed
Burge's square cut, to try and get him caught immediately as
he had got Simpson for a duck at Lord's, but Burge kept the
ball down beautifully and smacked some resounding boundaries. As a result, Australia were all out, triumphantly this
time, for 389; Burge 160. Trueman had three wickets, one
every 49 balls, at 33 runs apiece; economy average four runs
per over. Not an inspiring analysis, but far from his worst-
ever. Flavell got no one out at all for 97 runs, in 174 balls,
economy average 3.3.

With Australia needing only 108 to win in their second
innings, Trueman did all that could be expected, getting Lawry
out quickly (3 for 1) before the spinners took over. But Titmus
and Gifford had been given far too few runs to play with by
the English batsmen; they were foiled by the monumental
patience of Redpath, and England lost by seven wickets.
Trueman had not had a good game, but this can happen to a
great cricketer any time. When discussing bowlers, we are apt
to forget that great batsmen also win tests, and inevitably at
the expense of the opposition's bowling.

The truth is that Trueman's actual results suggest no falling off in his Test cricket. His figures, after the third Test – 13 wickets out of 36, one for every 46 balls, at 24 runs apiece (economy average: 3.1) actually show a very slight improvement on his overall figures for 1961, which were 20 wickets out of 74, one for every 59 balls, at 27 runs each (economy average: 3.2). Why he has been dropped – apparently against Dexter's preference – is still unexplained. It would be unfair to try and deduce anything from the astronomical averages arrived at by Price, Rumsey and Cartwright on the feather-bed at Manchester – no doubt Trueman was glad to be well out of it; but even so, it seems hard to believe that, if he had been in the team, the Australians would have reached 201 before the first wicket fell (and that a run-out). The Australians must be secretly delighted.

Luckily, there is still time to invite him to play at the Oval and to join the winter team for South Africa.[1] In that country a really penetrating fast bowler is a must, especially now that England face the redoubtable Eddie Barlow and Graeme Pollock. The selectors must look to the future, of course, but in fact the merely quickish Price and Rumsey will be the age Trueman is now when the Australians are here again in 1968. . . . All we can hope for is that somewhere, in country lane or back alley, some unknown kid is even now hurtling up to a wicket in a ferocious effort to emulate – and if possible even outdo – the speed and fire and hostility of Fred Trueman.

from NEW STATESMAN *August 7–8–1964*

[1] He wasn't.

P. B. H. May

A. A. THOMSON

Peter May took over the England captaincy in 1955. He brought to the post certain fundamental advantages: for one thing, now that Hutton had retired, he was incomparably England's best batsman and, even then, very nearly the greatest batsman in the world. He was modest and courteous in demeanour and, though somewhat retiring, he was not difficult to like. Perhaps his greatest advantage of all was that he had received, so to speak, his basic training in stern schools: in county cricket under the ebullient Surridge, who was at the time in full spate, hurrying Surrey to the top of the championship and keeping them there; and his Test experience had taken place under Hutton, and this in itself was a rich education for a young man. Even though May retired through ill-health and for business reasons at an early age, he captained England forty-one times, which is more than anyone else had ever done. . . .

His first rubber as captain was played against the South African tourists in 1955, and was won by three games to two in a succession of hard struggles in which no quarter was given or taken. May himself batted superbly – in his prime there was nobody like him – and he still had the benefit of Compton's and Graveney's experience, but conquest was really clinched by the bowlers, by Statham and Tyson in the first two Tests and by Laker in the last.

The seasons of 1956 and 1957 were May's high summers of success, with England established on the heights, and May unchallenged leader of England. In neither year was the fight won without a struggle. The Australian team of 1956 was in no sense a feeble one and after a drawn first Test at Trent Bridge and a second, at Lord's, which was deservedly won by the Australians, the battle for the third was the vital point of the struggle. The Test itself was memorable in many ways, but especially for the return of Washbrook, who had not played for England since the 1950–1 tour of Australia, in which he had been only moderately successful. With three England wickets down for 17, May saw Washbrook striding purposefully to the crease. 'I have never felt so glad in my life,' he said afterwards, 'as when I saw who was coming.' Their stand was historic and before they were separated they had put on 187. England's batting position was assured and the bowlers Lock and Laker did the rest. The position of the teams was now all square with two to play. In the fourth Test, at Old Trafford, the most fantastic of all Test bowling performances took place, breaking records right, left and centre. England's leading batsmen did all that was wanted of them and Evans hit out with his usual exuberance. But the true triumph belonged to Laker, and his incredible toll of nine for 37 and ten for 53. There has never been anything like it and never will be. England once more had easily the best of a draw at the Oval and if heavy rain had not intervened, the Australians, who had already lost five wickets for 27 in attempting to get 228, would have hardly succeeded in saving the game . . . .

The magic of victory remained for one more season and England's win over a strong and widely talented West Indies side was, one might sadly say, England's last great achievement until a new England, stronger at such points as they are now lamentably weak, is securely built. But weakness had not yet done its worst and much of the credit for the strength that remained is directly due to the gifts and influence of May. The complete reversal of the result in the first Test at Edgbaston was symbolic of England's power of recovery and May was its most efficient instrument. Winning the toss on an amiable wicket, England fell flat for the miserable total of 186 before the cunning spin of Ramadhin, who took seven for 49.

By tea-time on the third day West Indies piled up a huge score, mainly through the punitive efforts of Walcott, Worrell and the lamented O. G. (Collie) Smith, and England, 268 to the bad, lost two wickets before the end of the day. One of the most welcome sights in all the cricket of the period was that of watching May come in at this point of peril and without ceremony attack Ramadhin with two searing cover-drives.

England, still in jeopardy, resumed on the Monday morning and Close, who had helped May to put on 48 useful runs, was out at 113. Before the West Indies captured the next wicket over 400 runs had been added. At first with resolution and then with zest, May and Cowdrey, the most gifted young English batsmen of their generation, proceeded to subdue and then to destroy the West Indies attack. They remained together the whole of Monday and when Cowdrey was caught in the deep he had made 154 and the stand lasted eight hours and twenty minutes. May went on to score 59 with Evans in another half-hour and, when he declared, England were 583 for four. His own magnificent total was 285 not out, worthy to be reckoned for a place among the finest of all Test innings. . . . At this point West Indies might have slipped quietly away to a draw, but so strong now was England's grip on the game that they were able to give the batsmen the fright of their lives, first through some thunder and lightning from Trueman and then some spin-bowling of diabolical cunning by Lock and Laker. Five wickets went crashing down for 43 and when time came West Indies had lost seven wickets for 72, while the fieldsmen were crowding menacingly round the bats of the two defenders who survived.

England won the next game at Lord's, which contained another handsome 150 by Cowdrey, who was now in magnificent form, not to mention some astonishing bowling by Bailey. . . .

The fourth and fifth Tests England won by an innings, with Loader as the destroyer at Headingley and Lock (eleven for 58) making hay at the Oval. Success in this splendid series marked the highest point of May's Test career.

The winter tour of South Africa that fell between his respective victories over Australia and the West Indies had been only partially conclusive, as each side had won two matches, with one drawn. His own batting on this tour, as a matter of fact, had been outstanding, except, strangely enough, in Tests. This is difficult to understand because in the three other rubbers in which he had been captain he had as a batsman stood head and shoulders above most of the others. . . .

England's decline and fall did not, of course, come immediately. The visitors of 1958 came from New Zealand and suffered both from the English weather and from injuries to some of their most talented players. . . .

The tour to Australia of 1958–9 was anticipated with confidence and its unsuccessful result was the cause of massive disappointment. The chosen team included many players who had formed the backbone of England's previously victorious side, but several of them, unfortunately, showed themselves to be either out of form or past their best. . . .

It was one of those rubbers which the victors thoroughly deserved to win, but the losers hardly deserved to lose by quite so much. The fifth Test merely had the effect of rubbing salt into the English wounds, as Statham and Loader were injured in a car accident before the game started. Cowdrey and Graveney again nailed their colours to the mast; Richardson hit hard, and Mortimore, who had been flown out as an injury replacement, played better than some of the recognized batsmen, but, with Laker and Bailey unfit to bowl, the end was inevitable and no one could deny that the Australians were genuine conquerors. . . .

Sadly, too, it marked the end of May's period of triumph, though he was to win a rubber against New Zealand at home the following summer, during which he batted magnificently. The Australian tour had been a heavier burden than anyone could have imagined, with its toll of injuries and its ill-natured controversies; its accidents and its individual failures. All these misfortunes seemed the worse, because his side had been widely tipped to win and because they had faltered. . . .

After the storm and stresses of the Australian tour the season of 1959 at home was a placid affair, with no echo of the alarums and excursions of the previous winter. Earlier in the year May married and did not turn out for his county till the end of the season's first month. He played for Surrey, in fact, in only seven matches. England won all five Tests with ease against the sadly weak opposition of an Indian touring side. May appeared in only three of them. . . . The fourth Test, at Old Trafford, provided an easy victory but sounded a warning note.[1]

With the start of the 1959–60 tour of the West Indies we are back in sombre vein. May, believing himself to have recovered more completely from the operation than was in fact so, went out to the Caribbean as captain, leading a team which included a number of players bent on winning their spurs. . . . What clouded the series from its earliest days was the serious recurrence of May's illness. He believed himself fit to play in the earlier matches and this courageous if misguided resolve was not shaken even when the operation wound opened up before the second Test. He played in horrid discomfort, known to no one but himself, making an excellent score in the island match against Barbados, which, as it happened, was the only game lost outright during the tour. He failed, however, in the first Test and did no more than moderately in the second, the successful batsmen being Barrington, Dexter and M. J. K. Smith. (This was the game in which Trueman bowled England to victory.) Against Jamaica May hit his only hundred of the tour, a beautifully accomplished piece of work, both swift and sound, though his friends afterwards suspected that it exhausted him unduly. In the third Test he made his highest Test score, a meagre 45, even though it was the next best to Cowdrey's 114 and 97. After this the facts of his illness became known and he was flown home for treatment. . . .

[1] May had to call off owing to illness and Cowdrey assumed the captaincy of the England side for the first time. May watched the first two days of the match. On the third day he underwent an internal operation.

The season of 1961 saw another Australian visit, led by Richie Benaud, who had captained his side with such consummate skill against May's men in 1958–9. . . . May came back into the team at last for the second Test at Lords. . . .

A win in the fifth Test would at least have halved the rubber, even if it had left the resting place of the Ashes unaffected, but England seemed incapable of reasserting any kind of grip. Three wickets went down for 20 and it almost looked as though the Old Trafford collapse was being 'continued in our next'. May's innings of 71 was one of the finest displays of the series offered by anybody; it was bold, purposeful and imaginative, and, with the help of Barrington, he put on 80 in an effort to knock the bowlers, and especially Benaud, off their length. For a time it looked as if they might have succeeded, just as he and Cowdrey had broken the spell of Ramadhin at Edgbaston four years before. But success was only partial. England were eventually all out for an indifferent total, which Australia, without great difficulty, almost doubled. . . . In cricketing terms the real delight of the whole innings was May's 33, which included seven fours; all of them superbly driven, as though in scorn of the whole proceedings. As matters turned out, this was his last Test innings, though a fortnight later I saw him hit a carefree hundred against the Australians in a Scarborough Festival match. . . .

He enjoyed a period of complete domination from the time he took over the captaincy until the unhappy tour in Australia of 1958–9 and the serious illness that brought him home from the West Indies in 1959–60 and kept him out of cricket for the whole of the following summer. While he remained fit and willing to play, nobody could seriously challenge his status as the best-equipped batsman in the world. He has undoubtedly been the most accomplished stroke-maker between Compton and Dexter. He was likable and well liked. His Test career was full of innings of which you could say: 'No captain ever served his side better. . . .'

from THE GREAT CAPTAINS *1965*

Sir Leonard Again

JOHN WAITE

Among the many pleasant opportunitities created by a cricket tour of Britain is that of meeting, off a cricket field and around a dinner table, such champions of the past as Sir Leonard Hutton, Denis Compton, Keith Miller and Godfrey Evans and discovering what kind of men and personalities they have grown to be now that their playing days are over. . . .

Now that the strain of measuring to Test cricket has been removed from their minds they are jollier companions than they were, men whose way of life must be the envy of many. They are not much interested in re-fighting their battles of long and not so long ago when they sit down to drink and dine. That will come later, in their old age. They now often discuss life and all its varied problems in a highly intelligent way and take to those discussions an outlook broadened by intensive travel to all parts of the Commonwealth, an outlook enlightened by contact with people that the average traveller would rarely encounter upon such intimate and open terms.

Sir Leonard, especially, has informed himself amazingly well upon such subjects as the situation of the Stock Exchange in Johannesburg, the American and his way of life, the financial future of Australia and the art of growing old as gracefully as possible in an age that renders that art increasingly difficult because most of the old values are vanishing.

Sir Leonard is taking to life the same incisive thinking which made him such a great batsman and so intelligent a captain. I remember walking behind him down some frighteningly steep, narrow steps at Old Trafford during the fourth Test and hearing a North Countryman calling, 'And how do you like living

down south, Sir Leonard?' Len, who was born in Pudsey like
his predecessor and tutor Herbert Sutcliffe, made his home near
London after his retirement from cricket and in some quarters
was criticized for so doing.

Quick as a flash he called back to his questioner, 'I love living
in the south. It gives me a chance to visit the north and appreciate just how much I am missing down in the south including
my oldest friends.'

What a superb answer and I believe a quite genuine one. Sir
Leonard impresses one as a most genuine person. Let me
provide proof of that, if proof is needed.

One night at the Queen's Hotel in Birmingham I and my col-
laborator Dick Whitington were sitting at a table in the dining-
room with Sir Leonard and a Johannesburg friend – that 'most
passionate' cricket-lover Wilfred Isaacs, who was in Britain to
watch the Test matches and to try to restore the faith of big
London business men in the future of South Africa.

We were close to the door of the dining-room and Denis
Compton dashed in to have a word with Wilfred Isaacs. I
understand that relations between Sir Leonard and Denis had
not been over affable since Denis published a book in which he
commented on Sir Leonard's captaincy. . . .

But Denis saw Sir Leonard just a second too late. There was
no avoiding this, perhaps first intimately close meeting they
had experienced for quite some time. So Denis smiled that
happy engaging smile of his and joined the party.

'Hullo, Len,' he called and took the nearest chair. 'Good
evening, Denis,' Len replied. Our conversation continued for
quite some time. Sir Leonard was expounding his sure belief
that cricket was the greatest game of all. Suddenly he turned to
Denis and said: 'You never loved a hard fight in a Test match,
Denis, did you?'

There was a silence. All present remembered many of the
sterling struggles Denis had staged with the bat when England
was in danger. Denis did not quite 'get' what Len meant by his
question and smiled from one to the other of us striving to

gather whether we had sensed what had escaped him. Len can be very difficult to understand; often, I feel, he is deliberately so. It is a by-product of his unusual Yorkshire sense of humour.

'No, I suppose I didn't exactly love them, Len,' Denis agreed – relieving the mounting tension.

'That's the difference between the southerner and the northerner. Up north cricketers absolutely revel in a fight. They prefer it to a match that lacks high tension,' Len said.

Then we all knew what Len was 'getting at' and smiles of relief were general.

What Sir Leonard meant was that Denis Compton could fight as hard as anyone when the occasion demanded but really was born to delight the happy crowds at a festival match at Hastings or Scarborough, not for a duel between the white rose of Yorkshire and the red rose of Lancashire. And that is very true. It was the Sutcliffes, the Leylands, the Kilners, the Washbrooks, the Stathams, the Truemans and the Tyldesleys who were born for the grim cricket duel, who felt, indeed, far more at home in one than in a carefree festival encounter.

What Len had intended by his question was complimentary to Denis Compton. Len knew we all appreciated that Denis's ability to fight had never been in question, knew that it was all the more creditable that a man with Denis's happy-go-lucky outlook could so many times have steeled himself to the crises that beset England's Test teams so frequently after the Hitler War.

'Perhaps I am too inquisitive a character,' Sir Leonard confessed to us later, 'but I wanted to be certain on that point.'

Nothing I gathered interests the modern Sir Leonard as much as character and he has tremendously keen insight into the kind of character most suited to Test match cricket.

I recall another dinner gathering when I asked him what he thought about certain members of the 1960 Springbok side. Characteristically he countered this with another question: 'What made you omit Jon Fellows-Smith from your fourth Test team and retain Colin Wesley in it?'

I said we had believed, rightly or wrongly, that Colin was likely to score more runs than Jon in the position of number eight batsman.

'But Fellows-Smith should be batted much higher on your list. He's a tremendous fighter. I think I would have batted him at number one and used myself as number four, had I been Jackie McGlew. Having captained teams from number one I believe it is wrong for a captain to have to take strike after he has spent a day or more trying to think out the opposition. There's only ten minutes between innings, you know. You hardly have a chance to clear your mind of one lot of worries before you go out to face a different set. When you have to face bowlers like Brian Statham and Freddie Trueman, it's not easy.'

'What do you think of Colin Wesley?' I asked.

'He's a nice boy, isn't he? But he's only a boy. If I'd had him in my dressing-room I'd have thought he was there for some other purpose than playing in a Test match. I'd probably have asked him by mistake to clean my boots or help me put on my pads. No, I wouldn't have *him* in my Test side, just yet.'

I found his statement most amusing as I'm sure would have Colin, had he been present. For Colin has a sense of humour, which, in its way, is almost as intriguing as Sir Leonard's. Len did not ask what I was laughing about. I think he knew.

Later I told Jon Fellows-Smith of this conversation and he replied, 'It would have been some shambles if I'd been asked to take strike against Freddie and Brian. Nevertheless it was a nice compliment.'

Quietly in himself I am sure he was mighty happy about what Sir Leonard had said.

When you reconsider so many of Sir Leonard's remarks you realize just how much commonsense and deep insight go into them.

One day I asked him what could be done to cure cricket of the ills that has fallen so unhappily upon it.

'Return to the old leg-before-wicket law,' he replied.

This rather astonished me, for I had heard that Sir Donald Bradman played a great part in the amendment of the law and indeed wanted it re-amended to take in balls pitched outside the leg as well as the off stump. The two cricketing knights, it seemed, were at odds on this question.

'You think the extension of the law to make l.b.ws possible from balls pitched outside the off stump has had all that effect?' I asked. The solution seemed an over-simplification of the problem.

'Positive of it. The new law stopped batsmen from playing the lap stroke.'

'The lap stroke?' I asked, wondering if Len had drunk one too many brandies.

'Yes, the *lap* stroke.'

'How do you spell it?' I asked, still incredulous.

'L-A-P, lap,' grinned Len. 'Haven't you heard of it?'

I confessed that I hadn't.

'Well, you should have seen Herbert Sutcliffe and Maurice Leyland play it before they changed the law. It's a kind of pull-sweep, played to the ball pitched well up just outside the off stump. Herbert and Maurice used to hit it hard and high over the gap between mid-on and mid-wicket. It was a great stroke for upsetting a tight field setting. Fancy your not knowing about it. They also used to play the hook off the back foot to the shortish ball outside the off stump. But they gave that up when this change in the law came in the mid-1930s.

'Yes, get back to that old l.b.w. rule and batsmen will play these strokes again. Then captains won't be able to hem them in as they do now. Everyone, who is forty years old and lived in Yorkshire as a boy, knows about the lap stroke. Play it now and miss and you are given out leg-before-wicket. It's the same with that hook to the ball just outside the off stump.'

I turned the conversation to Norman O'Neill, whom I then had not seen bat.

'He's a good player,' Len said with a faraway look in his blue eyes.

'No more than that? Richie Benaud tells me he's the greatest Australian since Bradman.'

'He's a good player,' repeated Len, refusing to be lured into eulogy. 'To be great you have to prove yourself on English wickets. Conditions are so different in this country. That's what makes it so hard for you fellows when you come over here. You're not used to it. You have to play forward here so much. Norman O'Neill is naturally a back player.'

'I thought back-play was important in England?'

'It is. But mostly I went forward. You have to go forward to Brian Statham, for instance. By doing so you narrow the angle and reduce the width of movement off the seam. It's the same for a soccer goalie.'

from PERCHANCE TO BOWL *1961*

Bill Alley

ERIC SHORE

Bill Alley is a phenomenon. Coming into county cricket at the age of thirty-eight, he tested credulity by making 3,000 runs four years later, and the next year, in 1962, stretched the imagination even further by scoring 1,915 runs, supported by a mere matter of 112 wickets.

Dreams are made of such figures, but there is nothing dreamy about William Edward Alley, born in Sydney, Australia, on February 3, 1919. He is a realist if ever there was one, his realistic view of affairs springing naturally from an eventful life embracing batting, close-wicket fielding, leg-spinning, wicket-keeping, medium-paced bowling, and work as a boilermaker's assistant, blacksmith's striker, car trimmer's mate, professional boxer, underground driller, and sorter-out of difficulties at a Sydney dance hall.

Of the last-named (spare-time) occupation, Bill quotes one interesting case. 'We never had fights inside the hall,' he says. 'When you told a bloke to get out, he would sometimes ask you when you knocked off. A meeting was fixed in the outside alley, and the first man to go down was the loser. Five Friday nights in a row I had to fight a Scotsman on these terms and we battered eight bells out of each other – claret all over. On the sixth Friday he came again, and I said: "Not you again." He said: "I'm not here to fight tonight, I wondered if you could fix me up a job as your assistant." He got the job when I left.'

He won 17 of his 28 professional fights by a knock-out, but adds ruefully: 'I often got a bigger hiding winning than I dished out to the other fellow.'

He started cricket at school when he was eleven, never played anything less than First Division cricket, and was never coached. He got into the under-21 Martin Shield Competition side when he was fourteen. Once he took all ten wickets with leg-spinners. He was so small that they wouldn't let him bat – it was considered too dangerous against fast bowlers on concrete wickets. Alley worked his way through grade cricket, and made his first big impact during the War, becoming the only man to make 1,000 runs for New South Wales in the single-day matches they ran then.

His record-making continued with Colne, in the Lancashire League, with five seasons in which he notched over 1,000 runs each. Four highly successful years with Blackpool followed; then he joined Somerset in 1957, playing a vital part in the county's resurgence as a cricket force. . . .

Nothing if not a man with forceful opinions forcibly expressed, Bill is emphatic about what is wrong with the game at the moment. 'Too much blankety interference from too many blankety blank officials mucking about with the laws every five minutes,' is his view. Longer contracts for younger players, he reasons, would also improve the attraction of the county game.

He reckons he has two or three years left as a county batsman, and would prefer to finish his career with Somerset. Certainly hordes of Somerset people and spectators all over the country would prefer this, too. He is the most popular Somerset player since the heyday of Arthur Wellard, with whom he shares numerous qualities.

His new bungalow, 'Down Under', is at Adsborough, just outside Taunton, and the two acres of land keep him happily occupied when away from cricket. His sturdy, uncomplicated batting style, his acute use of the new ball, the habit of picking up invisible flashes at gully, his constant flow of amusing, often derogatory patter, and his habit of looking as though he is immensely enjoying his own game and humour, have endeared him to masses of cricketing folk. Under it all is his deep pride in his skill, and a fierce determination to display it whenever possible.

A real character is our William. Somerset's warm affection for him was greatly enhanced when he decided to make his home in the county. Somerset and cricket at large will long remember his remarkable contribution to the game.

from PLAYFAIR CRICKET MONTHLY *June 1965*

W. M. Lawry

JACK FINGLETON

Bill Lawry was a tall, gangling Australian youth of twelve when he walked out to open an innings for the first time. His partner was a veteran and the opposition had a very fast bowler. 'You leave the fast bowler to me, son,' said the veteran. 'I'll look after him.'

The veteran wasn't as good as his word. The young William was called on to face the demon and the first ball laid him low – a nasty hit on the head. Bill Lawry's father was one of the first to rush to the middle and Bill, doing a good howl, as he himself describes it, wanted to leave the field. His father was adamant. Bill was to stay on and bat. So Bill, tears still in his eyes and already with a thumping headache, stayed on and batted.

Lawry says that was the beginning of his career – in a junior match in Melbourne. He thanks his father for making him carry on. Lawry thinks that had he retired, as he wanted, it would have had a marked effect upon his future and upon his feelings against a fast bowler. In the West Indies, several years ago, Lawry stood up as well as anybody against the terrors of Griffith and Hall. And he didn't think much of several of his team who, privately and later in print, complained bitterly against the West Indian tactics. 'We used to dish this stuff out ourselves in the past,' said Lawry, 'now it is our turn to take it.'

There is a little political yarn about Lawry, who was christened William Morris. His father was a great admirer of William Morris Hughes, an Australian Prime Minister of the First War and, to boot, a Labour Prime Minister. Hughes, however, split on his party over conscription and crossed to the non-Labour party to become its Prime Minister. Hughes was one of the founders of unionism in Australia and I am sure regretted in his later life leaving his former colleagues (I was one of Hughes' innumerable private secretaries – for a tumultous three months period – and he often chatted to me of past days). The story in the Lawry family is that Bill's father later regretted calling his son after Hughes but the story doesn't fit. Hughes did his political switch in 1916; Lawry was not born until 1936. I think Lawry's father must have forgiven Billy Hughes, the fiery Welshman, some part of his political change.

Lawry, the cricketer, is recognized as a leading Australian authority on pigeons. Most Sundays in England he spends with pigeon enthusiasts, being entertained by them and, seeing their birds. Pigeons and cricket had an early association for him. He played his formative years in cricket on the concrete path in the home back-garden that led down to the pigeon-loft. On recent visits to England, he has been invited to visit the Royal lofts.

Lawry worked the usual path up to Australia's Test team – the juniors, the state schoolboys' team, the club side, the inter-state side and then the Australian team. But his path to the top was sometimes a cobbly one. He got into the Victorian team and was then dropped for a period. He got back again – and was dropped early by Peter Philpott. This was the most important 'drop' in Lawry's career. He went on to score a double-century against New South Wales and this got him the last batting position in Richie Benaud's team to tour England in 1961. He trod on his wicket when the tourists played in Tasmania, on the way to England; he trod on his wicket in the next game at Perth and he trod again on his stumps in his first English innings, against Derbyshire at Chesterfield.

Lawry is an unexcitable person. He took with aplomb his choice for England. He was a plumber's apprentice and was working on the ninth floor of a new Melbourne building when the news came to him that he had been chosen for England and that a Pressman and photographer were below, wanting to talk with him and snap him. Bill didn't knock off work. 'Tell them to come up,' he said and so the Press party were swung up in the workman's lift to get their story.

His habit of stepping on the stumps hasn't quite deserted Lawry. He did it once against South Africa in a Melbourne Test and was given not out; he did it against M.C.C. for Victoria, again at Melbourne, and was also given not out. These things don't worry Lawry. He calmly went on batting in each instance while the opposition thought hard things of him. They thought, having gained the benefit of an umpire's blunder, he should have thrown his wicket away. Lawry doesn't agree. 'I am there to do my job; the umpire there to do his. I abide by his decision. If he says "out", then out I go. It's not my place to give myself out or to make an umpire look foolish.'

Lawry batted extremely well in England in 1961. He was one of the successes of the tour. He got his runs attractively with strong driving and hefty pulling, but he was a changed batsman when he came again in 1964. Or had the English studied and nobbled him? I think there is some truth in this latter theory because Lawry is unusual in that he moves forward, initially, to every ball. The English discovered this and pinned him accordingly by bowling just short of a length to him. Trueman, particularly, cribbed him by bowling around the stumps, angling the ball across Lawry's body.

To 1968, when he was chosen to lead Australia to England, Lawry always impressed me as a run-gatherer. I do not think the position of the game made much impression upon him. He regarded it his duty at all times to get as many runs as possible and I have seen him run a three as hard in an unimportant game as in a Test match. He loves batting. He always leaves, when out, with an obvious sigh of regret.

But when made touring skipper – he preceded this by leading Australia for several Tests against India just before coming to England – Lawry visibly changed his outlook. Together with Cowdrey, he vowed at Lord's in a dinner to commemorate the

200th Test between England and Australia that he and his team would play its part in making the series a successful and interesting one. He recalled that Hassett told him, before leaving Australia, that Lawry wouldn't be in the game in ten years' time but cricket would still be going on. Lawry said he realized it was his duty to see that the series, from the Australian viewpoint, was an outstanding one.

Lawry has a delicious humour and never hesitates to tell a story against himself. He said once that he didn't care much for an article in *Wisden*'s on himself. 'It's too near the truth,' said Lawry. He is not exactly a strict disciplinarian but his team knows who is boss. Following in the publicity roles set by Benaud and Simpson, his predecessors, Lawry is practically a mute when it comes to telling the Press anything. 'No comment,' is generally his terse comment although he will discuss things with those he trusts.

He fidgets when he is away from his touring side. When the Aussies were in trouble at Edgbaston in 1968, against Warwickshire, Lawry was constantly ringing the ground for scores. On one occasion he got through to an Australian Pressman who, when Lawry asked for the scores, said, aping Lawry: 'No comment'. Lawry, in a flash, said: 'It's not comment I want – it's the scores'.

When Lawry co-operated in writing a book with a Sydney journalist, Phil Tresidder, he agreed on the name 'Run Digger'. It aptly summed up Lawry. He has dug innumerable runs against all the countries: 1,909 at the splendid average of 50.23 against England (up to the end of the 1968 series); 792 at 41.68 against South Africa; 653 at 54.41 against India; 89 at 22.25 against Pakistan; 1,035 at 69.00 against the West Indies.

In that dinner at Lord's which I mentioned, Lawry followed in the speech-list after Sir Robert Menzies and Colin Cowdrey. Each had made a brilliant individualistic speech. It was a tough assignment for Lawry, the audience a big, brilliant and critical one. It didn't worry Lawry at all. He spoke splendidly, in a typical Australian manner, rich with humour.

Is there anything ahead of Lawry? He should lead Australia for a few more series, at least. He is now thirty-two but he continues a realist. He has done well in the business world, in a public relations capacity, but he remains a unionist. Each year he takes out his ticket in the Australian Plumbers' Union. And he maintains that Australian plumbers are second to none in the plumbing world. A rich and a likable character.

specially written 1968, revised February 1970

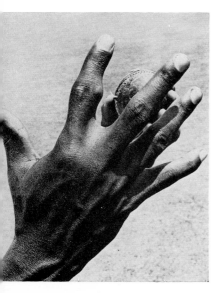

19a   *above left* Gibbs bowling against England at Old Trafford, 1966

19b   *left* Gibbs' fingers after ten years of Test cricket showing enlarged right index and middle fingers

19c   *above right* Graeme Pollock

20a *above left* Mushtaq Mohammed
20c *above right* Milburn
20b *left* Dexter

Gary Sobers

E. W. SWANTON

Gary Sobers is the best all-round cricketer – of my time, and I think of all time, captain of the winning West Indies teams against Australia and England, the maker of 5,172 runs in Test cricket, the taker of 130 wickets, and of 72 catches. Holder of the world Test record score of 365 not out. Holder of this, holder of that. One could simply go on reeling off the figures, but after one other hard fact I will turn to other things.

Eleven other cricketers in history have scored 1,000 runs and taken 100 wickets in Test Cricket, three Englishmen, seven Australians, and one Indian (Vinoo Mankad). But of these only Benaud's figures really compare with Gary's. He made 2,220 runs (less than half Sobers' total) and took 248 wickets (nearly double as many).

Yet although Gary entered the Test scene – as a boy of seventeen in 1954 – he's still only thirty-one, and could easily have the best part of ten more years to run. Gary, of course, is a prodigy, what we call a natural. Everton Weekes tells me he's a good footballer, and table tennis player. I know to my cost that he hits a golf ball for miles. On the cricket field there's no aspect of the game he doesn't excel at, except wicket-keeping, and in Malaya I once saw him make a pretty good fist of that. The only cricketer of my experience who compares with him in this complete versatility with a ball is Walter Hammond.

Gary was spotted as a boy of fourteen or fifteen by the present chief of the Barbados Police, Wilfrid Farmer, who promptly drafted him into the Police team. I rather think they tried to make him into a band-boy. Anyway before long he played an innings of 200 for the Police against Harrison College, and at the age of sixteen he was bowling slow left-arm and, incidentally, getting 4 for 50 – for Barbados against the Indians. The following year I saw him playing in his first Test against England at Kingston. Since then of course he has never been left out, and in fact has played in 57 successive Test Matches.

He has left his imprint on almost everyone, and one can only mention some of the landmarks, beginning with the prodigious 365, made in Kingston, to be honest against a rather depleted Pakistan attack. When M.C.C. came out in 1959–60 Gary averaged 100 against Peter May's side in the Tests. When he went to Australia the following winter he had a good tour, with two Test hundreds, but not quite an outstanding one.

I have always felt that the event that turned Gary from a very talented, often brilliant, but rather mercurial cricketer into the greatest was his three years with South Australia in the Sheffield Shield. It was there on Frank Worrell's tour that he first seriously bowled chinamen and googlies. It was in South Australia that he started bowling fast. To get an idea of his success there I need only to say that in the whole history of Australian cricket not one of their great all-rounders has ever made 1,000 runs in the season and taken 50 wickets. Gary did it two years running, and helped South Australia to their second Shield title in twenty-five years. The Australian experience tightened up Gary's cricket. He lost his carelessness. Some of the Aussies' toughness rubbed off on him.

When he took on the captaincy from the late Sir Frank Worrell one could not help wondering how the extra responsibility would affect his play – after all he was the mainspring of the side. As we now know the leadership, far from weighing him down, has brought out something extra. This was specially so in England in 1966 when his all-round contribution – 722 runs with an average of 103, 20 wickets at 27 runs each, with 10 catches thrown in – was something to which there is absolutely no parallel in Test cricket.

Beyond all this he has shown himself a naturally good captain who can read a situation well, and who handles his side with the same quiet, easy control as his predecessor. Gary obviously owes a very great deal to Frank Worrell from whom he inherited a splendid side with an excellent team spirit. It would be odious to make comparison of their respective merits as captains. Frank's calm under stress was something that no one else could quite achieve. I always think his reported advice to his team during that last over of the tied Test match at Brisbane was a classic – 'Don't worry, just relax!' But in one respect I think that Gary holds the advantage – Frank was rather inclined to be over-cautious. Gary is the more adventurous – as witness, for instance, his attacking answer to danger at Lord's when he and David Holford, his cousin, made that extraordinary stand to pull his side from the jaws of defeat.

That Lord's match was the crucial moment of the 1966 tour. The captain saw his side through it, and from then on it always seemed (to an Englishman at any rate) that the West Indies were going to win the series and clinch their title as World champion. Thanks to their captain they did.

The above was my assessment of Gary written three years ago in 1967. Since then he has had his ups and downs, and the game at top level has, perhaps only temporarily, lost its savour for him. His captaincy of a team in decline has not quite lived up to its early promise under Sir Frank Worrell's watchful eye, but basically my estimation holds good.

His up to date figures (at April 1970) now read as follows: In Test cricket he has made (to the end of the 1969 English season) 6,776 runs in 132 innings, average 58.92. He has taken 193 wickets at an average of 34.59, and caught 96 catches. In all first-class cricket he has scored 20,415 runs, average 56.08; taken 780 wickets, average 27.40; and accepted 292 catches.

A specially written sketch 1967, revised 1970

'Collie' Smith

IRVING ROSENWATER

Neither the cricket grounds of Lancashire nor those of the West Indies nor of any other part of the world will see 'Collie' Smith in action again. His tragic death following a road accident in Staffordshire last September [1959] removed from the cricket stage not only a player of a truly joyous temperament, but also one of the rarest combinations with which the modern first-class game has been blessed. For 'Collie' Smith, for all the exultant pleasure that he gave crowds wherever he played and for all the sparkling ebullience that he always exhibited, was a very gifted cricketer in his own right – fine enough to play in the highest class of cricket even if the exuberance and the smile had not been part of his make-up. But they were, and because of that he was able to add to his exceptional natural skill an adventurous approach in which he delighted especially in driving the ball with tremendous force, as much for his own entertainment as for that of the spectators.

As a hitter 'Collie' Smith was no wild and hopeful smiter. His hitting had the character of controlled power, which marked him primarily as a batsman of real quality. Indeed, he proved his quality amply and decisively by scoring hundreds in his first Test matches against both Australia and England, notwithstanding Lindwall, Miller, Statham and Trueman. He was perhaps one of the few batsmen who approached the qualities of the immortal 'Croucher', G. L. Jessop, for although Smith could not match Jessop's speed of scoring, he did combine the ability to hit hard, long and mightily with a genuine and undoubted high standard of batsmanship. In all classes of serious cricket, from the time he first played for the famous

Boys' Town in his native Jamaica, Smith realized what effect on a cricket ball could be achieved by the swift co-ordination of eyes, feet, wrists and sinews. When a measure of discretion was added, he could reduce most bowlers to despair. In one match, while still a youth, he watched an opposing bowler send down seven steady balls in an eight-ball over and then pulled the last delivery high into the sky for 6. This type of approach, often bordering on the audacious, endeared him to men and boys alike in all parts of the world, and if it often cost him his wicket prematurely he was nevertheless admired and respected as a match-winning cricketer.

It was his feats against the Australians in the season of his first-class début, 1954-5, when he played in a Test match less than two months after his first game for Jamaica, that spread Smith's fame throughout the world. Great names held little terror for him, and in the first innings he ever played against the mighty Australians – in which he gathered 169 runs – he smote a tremendous six off W. A. Johnston which sent the ball over the little red-roofed cottage where Ivan Barrow once lived adjoining the Melbourne Park arena. In a trial match preceding the Australian game, Smith scored a quick 108, including 15 in one over off Ramadhin. In only his second first-class game, for Jamaica against Trinidad at Kingston, Smith led his side to victory against the clock with an undefeated 58 in 57 minutes, which included the extra-ordinary proportion of 54 runs in boundaries – 9 fours and 3 sixes, the last of which was the winning stroke. It was during that season that the Australian critic R. S. Whitington, of the *Sydney Telegraph*, wrote that he had attended the birth of another Bradman, and if his estimate of Smith was perhaps rather hastily conceived, it at least showed the impact that the young, stocky Jamaican had made. As long ago as 1952, when Smith was quite unknown outside his immediate cricket surroundings, Ivan Barrow was so impressed by his natural ability that he unreservedly said that 'if there is ever to be another Headley, Smith is the one'.

It was certain that when the time came for the selection of those West Indians to visit England in 1957, Smith's name would be on the list. He had already toured New Zealand and in the Test match at Dunedin helped Everton Weekes rush on 50 runs in 25 minutes. In the season immediately preceding the English tour, Smith met with phenomenal success in the six important games that he played in the West Indies, scoring no fewer than 731 runs for an average of 81.22. (He also, incidentally, captured 24 wickets, including such batsmen as T. W. Graveney and D. V. Smith on three occasions each.) In the first innings he ever played on the Bourda ground at Georgetown – in the Intercolonial Quadrangular Tournament of October, 1956 – he scored, at a critical time, 109, which included two characteristic sixes, the second of them into the schoolchildren's stand, giving no doubt especial pleasure. And yet his captain, Alan Rae, pleased as he was, declared that 'Collie was not in real form'! Against the strong side brought over to Jamaica by the Duke of Norfolk, Smith struck 6 sixes in one innings of 118, and altogether 10 sixes, many of them powerfully long carries, in his three games against the visitors. In one of the trial matches at Port-of-Spain, arranged to help choose the side for England, Smith found himself at the tea adjournment with his score at 78 not out: on the resumption, in the course of a single Jessopian over, he went beyond his century by playing the six successive balls for 6, 2, 0, 4, 6, 6.

And so Smith came to England with a deserved reputation for powerful stroke-play and adventurous cricket. In the opening first-class match of the tour, on the beautiful ground at Worcester, Smith opened his first-class scoring in England typically enough by hitting Berry for 6: he then hit 2 further sixes in his innings of 68, and when he was eventually out – caught on the long-off boundary – the ball was hit so hard that the unfortunate fieldsman, Outschoorn, suffered a split finger. This was the beginning of an exciting tour for Smith, on which his hard hits were seen on nearly every ground on which he appeared. Special mention should be made of one or two matches, first that against Nottinghamshire at Trent Bridge at the end of May. The first day's play was dominated by Garfield Sobers, who scored a double-century, but shortly after six o'clock Smith walked out to join him at the crease, and in the last 55 minutes' play actually outscored Sobers (who had been in since the first ball bowled) by hitting 67 of the 117 added: the aggressive pair scored their side's last 88 runs in 40 minutes, the score advancing from 401 to 431 in only 10 minutes. It was in the second innings that Smith played a most incredible innings – one of the fastest in the history of the game – by scoring 46 not out, including 2 sixes and 6 fours, out of the 50 added while he was at the crease, in only 12 minutes. During this time Asgarali, who was certainly well set with 126 when Smith came in, managed to score only four singles. Later on in the tour, at Chesterfield, Smith played one of his most spectacular innings by making 133 against Derbyshire. Apart from 18 fours, he struck 4 soaring sixes, one of them (off Gladwin) shattering five tiles on the pavilion roof and another landing on the concrete shore of the boating lake: two more fell into the crowd crouching for safety near the sight-screen. In his next match Smith scored his magnificent 168 against England at Trent Bridge, when one of his sixes (off Laker) again broke some tiles, this time on the roof over the ladies' balcony over long-on. At the end of the tour, in the festival games, Smith played with great abandon and at Hastings, against L. E. G. Ames' XI, his 79 at more than a run a minute came in 24 scoring strokes, including 6 hits for six, two of them out of the ground. In his first and only appearance at Scarborough he ended the first-class tour just as he had begun it – by opening his account with a six, the ball soaring high into the packed gallery. It may be interesting to note some of the fastest partnerships in which 'Collie' Smith shared during his tour of 1957:

47* for 6th wicket in 20 minutes
   with G. S. Sobers *v.* Oxford U., Oxford

50* for 4th wicket in 12 minutes
    with N. Asgarali *v.* Nottinghamshire, Nottingham
79* for 7th wicket in 55 minutes
    with F. M. Worrell *v.* Essex, Ilford
89 for 5th wicket in 60 minutes
    with F. M. Worrell *v.* Cambridge U., Cambridge
93   for 3rd wicket in 40 minutes
    with G. S. Sobers *v.* Sussex, Hove
100* for 4th wicket in 38 minutes
    with C. L. Walcott *v.* Kent, Canterbury
107 for 4th wicket in 68 minutes
    with R. B. Kanhai *v.* L. E. G. Ames' XI, Hastings
117* for 4th wicket in 55 minutes
    with G. S. Sobers *v.* Nottinghamshire, Nottingham

As was to be expected, Smith's vitality and approach attracted the attention of clubs in the Lancashire League. He joined Burnley in 1958 on a two-year contract and proved himself one of the most popular professionals in the League. 'He is happy hitting fours, but happiest hitting sixes,' said Bruce Pairaudeau, the West Indian batsman and former Burnley amateur. And the Lancashire crowds were not disappointed. Some of his hits were historic and will be remembered for all time by those League enthusiasts who saw them. He was responsible, last May, for what was described as the biggest hit ever seen at the Turf Moor ground, Burnley, when he made a tremendous soaring drive from the Belvedere Road end which sent the ball over the stand and into the centre circle of the adjoining football field. He thus joined the 'immortals', those illustrious few —not more than four in number—who have accomplished this prodigious drive. In that same dynamic innings, against Accrington, he hit another six over the wall and out of the ground and reached his century in only 78 minutes to enable his side to win in a hectic fight against the clock. On the following day he scored yet another hurricane century – bringing his total for one week-end to 215 without being dismissed – against Lowerhouse at the West End ground, when he struck one ball so hard that he cracked the bat and also hit an on-drive which smashed through a pane of glass in a window of the tea-room, which no doubt startled the many occupants who were there at the time. He also once made a hit over the houses at Bacup, but for sheer prolificness of scoring Smith will be best remembered for his astonishing innings of 306 not out for Burnley in a Worsley Cup match against Lowerhouse at their West End ground last June. This was one of the most remarkable pieces of sustained hitting ever seen on a Lancashire League ground, and the popular West Indian easily exceeded the previous record score for a Lancashire League player – 225 not out by Everton Weekes for Bacup against Rawstenstall in 1958. Smith, in his astronomical score, frequently kept youngsters occupied when he struck balls out of the ground, and there were two instances when the ball entered an adjoining park three times in succession. He gave several chances in his innings – which was the first time he had reached a double century in any class of cricket – but such was the power behind his drives that that probably saved him from being caught. He was credited with 56 boundary shots, all of them fours, for there are no sixes on Lowerhouse's small ground – otherwise his total would have been more gigantic still.

His exuberance on the field and his kindliness off it will now be seen no more. However, as a Burnley admirer, Mr E. L. Herbert, said shortly after Smith's tragic death: 'Of this one may be sure – that if cricket is played in Elysian Fields it will not be long before Collie is joining some illustrious partner in a split-second single, or is sending a ball soaring high over the Golden Gates.' Indeed, Smith the ebullient will for ever remain the gay cavalier, the genial Hotspur of cricket.

from THE CRICKETER *Spring 1960*

Wesley Winfield Hall

IRVING ROSENWATER

It would have been a tragedy had Wesley Hall not come to England with the West Indian side [in 1963]; but those who knew his loyalty to the game – as well as his abundant love of bowling – thought little of the rumours that surrounded his name at the start of the year. When he flew in from Barbados to join the rest of the team in London, he was obviously happy to be with his colleagues again and was fit and anxious to start on another tour, despite the habitual cold in the head with which the English climate always seems to greet him!

He is a magnificent athlete. He stands 6 feet 2 inches and, like many West Indian sportsmen, has a broad back and loose, long limbs. With a ball in his hand, he does not like batsmen. To many he is considered the fastest and fittest of modern bowlers. For the past four years he has had virtually no rest from cricket, playing continuously either in England or Australia, as well as managing to tour Africa and the Far East with an international side in 1962. His reputation today is high: he is undoubtedly one of the world's great crowd-pulling cricketers, for the hostility of his bowling and his dynamic fervour on the field are in the truest tradition of West Indian cricket.

Not long before he played against Dexter's team for Queensland in November 1962, Hall's speed of bowling was mechanically timed. The result showed that his deliveries came down at 91 m.p.h. – about the same speed reached by Tyson at his fastest. He ominously warned M.C.C. that he would have no fielder further from the bat than first slip! But Hall has not always bowled fast. In his early days in Bridgetown he hardly bowled at all, for he was a batsman-wicketkeeper with a few centuries to his credit in minor cricket. He played in this capacity for his school, Combermere, until he was eighteen, and it is amazing to reflect that when he first came to England as a fast bowler in 1957 he had never taken a single wicket in first-class cricket. Indeed, he had then played in only one first-class match – against E. W. Swanton's side in 1956, when he failed to take a wicket and saw Graveney make a faultless 154. Hall has rarely been as nervous as he was on that occasion: it had only been a matter of weeks since he first began bowling fast.

He was the youngest member of the 1957 party in England and of the forty West Indians who have come here on the three post-war tours to this country. His selection that year was a surprise, not least to himself. When the names of the touring side were announced by the selectors, the method they chose was to place them in alphabetical order on the Port-of-Spain score-board on the last evening of the final trial. When the name of Hall appeared he was literally speechless with a mixture of relief and astonishment. He did not, alas, fulfil his admirers' hopes in 1957. He did not play in any of the Tests, though he gained his first experience of what Test batsmen could achieve when he fielded as a substitute through the whole of England's mammoth total of 583 for 4 declared at Edgbaston. Back home in the West Indies he again was not chosen for any of the Test matches played against Pakistan in the early months of 1958 and when, a day after the series ended at Port-of-Spain, the West Indian selectors announced the side to tour India later that year, Hall's name was not unnaturally omitted from the list. That might have been the end of Hall's career in major cricket. He had not yet played in a Test and his latest experience of first-class batsmen had seen him hammered unmercifully by Hanif Mohammed and his brother Wazir in the Barbados match at Bridgetown. But here it was that fate stepped in. Frank Worrell announced he would be unable to lead the side to India due to studies, and a replacement was required. Hall had bowled well in two matches against Jamaica at Kingston in July–August 1958, but a batting place was open. It was given to J. K. Holt, jun. The selectors, however, paid a fine compliment to Worrell by deciding to replace him with *two* men, and thus Hall was the final choice for the tour. By such narrow margins are events determined.

What Hall achieved in India and Pakistan in the five months from November 1958, is now history. It should be remembered that he went to India as the third fast bowler of the side to Gilchrist and Taylor, but emerged as the most fearsome opening bowler West Indies have possessed since the days of Martindale and Constantine. In his first match on Indian soil, at Motibaug Palace, Baroda, he took 7 for 84 with sustained hostility, completing a 'pair of spectacles' for V. S. Hazare. Before he made his Test debut he said that he was sure he would carry away many recollections from the tour – and in fact he carried away 46 Test wickets as well, including 11 wickets against India at Kanpur (which won him a prize) and a hat-trick against Pakistan at Lahore, the first-ever for West Indies in a Test.

England's batsmen in the Caribbean in 1959-60 will remember Hall as a massive man with a classical action. To his genuine speed he allied remarkable stamina – and a full measure of bouncers in company with Chester Watson which caused Cowdrey and Pullar to wear bumper-proof vests in the Test at Sabina Park. Hall again ended the series with the best bowling aggregate on either side.

He was now established as a key member of the West Indian attack. Selection for Australia on the tour of 1960–1 was a mere formality. He had just taken 100 wickets in his first season as a league professional in Lancashire, and three days after the final match in September he set sail on the R.M.S. *Strathaird* with his fellow West Indian professionals from Tilbury for Fremantle. The impact he made on Australian crowds is now almost legendary. His bouncing, 30-yard run to the wicket; his explosive delivery of the ball from almost

6 feet 8 inches; his disconcerting lift from the pitch and his systematic hostility all made him a great favourite with spectators. In the course of that inspiring tour Hall dismissed O'Neill, Simpson and Harvey for 'ducks' and took more wickets than any of his colleagues in both the Tests and all first-class games. Near the beginning of the tour, at Perth, Neil Harvey said that Hall was as fast as any bowler he had ever faced, including Tyson. He was not slow to acknowledge the help of his captain. 'Bowling under Worrell's captaincy,' said Hall at the end of the tour, 'is a bowler's dream.' His admiration for and loyalty to Worrell are factors which compelled Hall's presence in England in 1963.

Australia lured him back again for their past two domestic seasons, when he played for Queensland in the Sheffield Shield and did coaching in the State. His number of first-class wickets in Australia totals 116 (av. 26.78)—by a coincidence the exact number of wickets he had captured for West Indies in Test cricket up to the start of the English tour. His actual figures in Australia over the last three seasons are:

		Overs	Maidens	Runs	Wickets	Average
1960-1	For West Indians	260·4	22	1,109	40	27·72
1961-2	For Queensland	203·5	30	871	43	20·25
1962-3	For Queensland	255	30	1,127	33	34·15

Though he is known to the world as a fine fast bowler, Wesley Hall can also bat. He has not altogether forgotten his youthful skills as a run-maker, and even in Test cricket he has more than once batted in the comparatively respectable position of number 7. In the famous tied Test at Brisbane in December, 1960, he scored a hectic 50 in 69 minutes, thrashing Meckiff and Davidson in a whirlwind onslaught. He scored another Test 50 – this time not out – against India at Port-of-Spain in 1961–2, adding 98 (unfinished) for the tenth wicket with Worrell, a last-wicket record for West Indies in Tests. Three weeks earlier he had hit the Indians for 88 in their colony match with Barbados. In one of the trial matches before the 1957 side for England

was announced, he hit 77 and shared a ninth-wicket stand of
134 with F. C. M. Alexander, and spectators at Hove will recall
the tremendous hit he made off R. G. Marlar in 1957 when he
sent the ball clean out of the ground at the sea end. In 1962,
as well as taking most wickets for Accrington, he scored most
runs for the club: and in the match against Bacup at the end of
August he not only scored 79 but took all 10 wickets for 28
runs! Three years ago he failed by only 4 runs to score a
century against East Lancashire. In Australia in 1961-2 he
scored 98 for Queensland Colts against Sandgate-Redcliffe at
Brisbane, and in a one-day game during the 1962-3 season he
actually scored 103 (including 8 sixes and 9 fours) for an
international side which included A. V. Bedser: on that
occasion Hall kept wicket to the former Surrey and England
bowler. In his final innings for Queensland in the Sheffield
Shield in March 1963 he scored 50, including 6 fours and a six,
out of 66 in an hour against Victoria at Brisbane. His century
reached in 65 minutes at Fenner's in May 1963 – the fastest of
the season in first-class cricket – was a thrilling spectacle in
which Hall revelled as much as the excited spectators.

Off the field, Hall is a charming man. He likes calypsos and
likes to talk cricket. He likes to think of the circumstance of
fate which enabled him to play for West Indies. He is also a
deeply religious man. He disliked having to play cricket in
Australia on Christmas Day, and both on and off the field he
wears a tiny gold crucifix suspended from a chain around his
neck. When playing for Queensland against the M.C.C. he
bowled a ball which lifted and hit the Rev. David Sheppard on
the hip; as he bowled Hall's crucifix jerked up and hit him in
the right eye. As Hall stood rubbing his eye and Sheppard his
hip, the Reverend remarked: 'Let that be a lesson to you,
Wesley. You should bowl only half-volleys to me and everything would be all right!'

It is never Hall's intention to bowl half-volleys. 'It is my
job to get wickets,' he once declared, though – successful as
he is – he is always aware that his primary task is to retain his

place as West Indies' opening bowler. For that reason he will
practise at every opportunity and will play in as many matches
as his captain will allow him. He is only 26 and a Test target of
200 victims is not outside his reach. He added to his tally in
1963 with some magnificent bowling in the Tests against
England. W. E. Bowes described Hall's first two overs in the
first innings at Old Trafford as the fastest bowling he had seen
in his life. (This was not forgetting Larwood or Lindwall.)
Hall himself says that his fastest spell was at Melbourne in the
New Year Test of 1960-1, but for sheer sustained endeavour
his performance at Lord's in 1963 must be very high on the list.
At the end of that Test the West Indian manager, Berkeley
Gaskin, said that Hall 'must be as fit as a Stradivarius violin'.
'The next two days I was a sort of walking corpse,' said Hall,
and if the truth be known he was never quite the same bowler
thereafter. But the enthusiasm and wonderfully rhythmic
gathering of momentum remained with him to the end of the
tour, and those who saw him at the Oval in the tourists'
farewell match in mid-September will still recall his boundless
energy when he bowled and his beautiful and agile swooping
on the ball from his full height while racing round the boundary-
edge. The metal plate on his right toe-cap was more worn than
it was in May, but Wesley Hall had rendered a devoted service
to West Indian cricket in 1963. For that – and for his skill in
his chosen art – he is admired by countless West Indians, and
by many others.

from JOURNAL OF THE CRICKET SOCIETY,
Vol. II, No. 2 *January 1964*

Lance Gibbs

HENRY BLOFELD

Lance Gibbs is a quiet unassuming man, but with bright eyes and a keen and narrow face. They hint at the instinct and awareness which has made him a spin bowler to rank with those other great West Indian spinners, Ramadhin and Valentine. His slow and rather awkward stride as he walks from gully to gully while the shine is disappearing from the new ball is misleading. When a batsman plays the ball three yards to his right and sets off for a run or his captain throws him the ball he moves and looks like a setter who has scented game.

Gibbs is the first great off-spinner that the West Indies have produced. He was an important member of Worrell's side in the early 1960s and of Sobers's since, but because his art does not lend itself to histrionics or headlines, one of the least noticeable.

By the time of his thirty-fourth birthday he had played in 39 Tests and had taken 171 wickets. These figures are not only ample proof of his ability, but also they entitle him to rank with Laker and Tayfield and in many ways Gibbs is a more interesting bowler than either.

Laker was the supreme example of the orthodox English off-spinner. The slow, deliberate run in, the big delivery stride which unfolded almost in slow motion, the slight flick as ball went spinning out of his fingers, and the huge off-break. Tayfield was different. He had a short lop-sided run, a high quick delivery, clever variations of flight, an unvarying length, but not much spin. Like Gibbs he was a product of hard wickets.

Gibbs learnt his cricket in Guyana, or British Guiana as it then was, which is a land where off-spinners are as difficult to find as palm trees in England. He worked out instinctively the problems of the hard unresponsive wickets where an off-spinner has to beat the batsman in the air and he has developed a style of his own.

When Gibbs has delivered a ball he waits impatiently for it to be returned to him and then he walks quickly back to the end of his run. He comes fast to the wicket for a spinner, kicking his enormously long legs up high as if he were taking part in a trotting race. The momentum of his approach continues through his action.

His right arm comes fast through a high action and this enables him to conceal so well his variations of flight and pace. Gibbs never lets the batsman relax. He never bowls the same ball twice running and he is constantly changing the speed and the angle of his run up and even if the batsman diagnoses the run up the action will probably conceal something else. He is like a conjuror who puts lots of torn paper into his hat. It is going to appear in one piece, but the shape is anyone's guess.

But there is more to Gibbs than just flight. He spins the ball a lot with his long sinewy fingers at the same time as maintaining good control of length. These fingers are so strong that he is also able to throw in a leg-break with an imperceptible change of action and at Gibbs's speed it is a dangerous ball.

Gibbs is an attacking off-spinner in all conditions. He is always trying to get the batsman out and he never settles for a defensive role.

One of Gibbs's two weaknesses is his West Indian temperament. When success is being hard to come by he can lose hope and also he can be hit out of the game. Tayfield bowled as if he knew he would always win in the end, but with Gibbs there can come a time when he appears to lose interest and he just goes on turning his arm over.

He is so natural a cricketer that when he meets problems he may not understand them as fully as a player who is not so naturally gifted and at times he has had to struggle. As fine a bowler as Gibbs should take a hatful of wickets around England, but he did not have much success at the start of his playing for Warwickshire. If he takes a long cool look at the problem he must come up with the right answer as he is too good a bowler not to. It is a matter of temperament.

Gibbs also has a weakness of method and this has never been more obvious than on the first day of the first Test at Port-of-Spain in January 1968. On a wicket which was taking spin slowly Gibbs and Cowdrey fought out a fascinating duel through a long hot afternoon.

When Cowdrey came in he was surrounded by short legs and two of them remained for most of the next three and a half hours. Gibbs went through his full repertoire of flight and pace changes, he spun the ball, he pushed it straight through and he bowled the leg-break, but Cowdrey kept him out. For hour after hour Cowdrey stretched his left leg far down the wicket and let the off-break turn on to his pad, when he had to play the ball, it was with bat tucked away behind the pad and the short legs went on waiting.

If Gibbs had been able to bowl round the wicket the balls which Cowdrey was taking on his pad, sometimes as many as four an over, would have had to have been played. For two short spells he went to that side of the wicket, but it unsettled him. He could not pick up the right line and his length suffered. Cowdrey batted out the day. If Gibbs had dismissed him early it might have had the greater effect on the series than the taking of just one wicket. But then Laker and Tayfield had their weaknesses too.

specially written

Mushtaq Mohammed

H.G.

A dark-haired, swarthy youngster delighted English cricket-lovers in 1962 with displays of attractive and mature batsmanship which would have done credit to an established player twice his age. Mushtaq Mohammed, one of a noted family of cricketing brothers, once of India but now – after that country's partition – of Pakistan was the lad concerned. The lad is certainly a correct description of this remarkable stripling. He was ten months and seven days younger than record-books showed him to be!

Wisden has Mushtaq's signature to his verification of the date of his birth as November 22, 1943, instead of the hitherto accepted date of January 15, 1943. Mushtaq, a well-educated and intelligent youth, explains the discrepancy by saying that many of his family's documents were lost in the migration from India in 1948, and that the birth-rate of 15–1–1943 was unofficially given him for school purposes in Pakistan. His mother and his eldest brother Wazir – the Pakistan Test cricketer of the 1950s – have, however, assured him of his November birthday and the family have always celebrated it. Mushtaq, a modest boy, had not previously troubled about altering his published birth-date, but the disclosure makes him more of a prodigy than ever.

He was only 13 years and 41 days, not 13 years and 352 days, when he became the youngest player to appear in first-class cricket, and 15 years and 124 days, instead of 16 years and 70 days, when he gained the distinction of being the youngest cricketer to play in a Test Match. The matches in question were for Karachi (Whites) against Hyderabad, on January

2, 3, 4, 1957, and for Pakistan against West Indies in the Third
Test Match, at Lahore, on March 26 to 31, 1959. He was only
17 years and 82 days, not 18 years and 28 days, when he took
his place in cricket history as the youngest batsman to score a
Test century – 101 against India in the Fifth Test, at Delhi, on
February 12, 1961.

Cricket came naturally to Mushtaq as it did to his four
brothers, Wazir, Raees, Hanif – holder of the world record individual score of 499 – and Sadiq, all of whom have played in
first-class cricket. Their father, a military man who had to stay
behind in India when partition occurred, was not a cricketer of
any particular standing, but their uncles, who looked after
them when they reached Pakistan, and their mother, who came
with them, were extremely keen sports-enthusiasts. The
mother became a champion Badminton player, and her ambition to see her children develop into sportsmen of note
inspired them.

The story of Mushtaq would not be complete without telling
of the progress of his brothers. Wazir and Raees had learned to
play cricket while the family were still in India, but Hanif,
fourteen when India was divided, and Mushtaq, five years of
age, were taught all their cricket in Pakistan. Hanif advanced so
rapidly that in the space of three years he was playing alongside
Wazir and Raees in the National Cricket Championship of
Karachi.

So Mushtaq, encouraged by his mother and relatives, had
plenty of incentive to follow in the footsteps of his older
brothers. When eleven, Mushtaq, who attended the Christian
Mission High School at Karachi, played in his first representative match for the School First XI, and he went from stage to
stage as his physique and technique improved. He practised
with his brothers, and also received valuable instruction from
Abdul Aziz, the well-known coach, who was also largely
responsible for Hanif's correct batting methods. With the
growing-up of Sadiq – a left-hand bat – the five brothers set a
record in 1961 when all played together in a first-class match in

the Ayub Zonal Trophy. Raees, Hanif and Mushtaq were on one side, Karachi Whites, and Wazir and Sadiq on the other, Karachi Blues.

With so much evidence before them about the cricket skill of Wazir, Raees and Hanif, the Pakistan selectors were quite ready to give another brother his chance.

On his first-class debut in 1957, Mushtaq scored 87 and took five wickets for 28 with his leg-spin bowling, but he did little when first called on by his country two years later. He was, in fact, given his place as a leg-spin bowler, but he sent down only six overs, for 34 runs, without taking a wicket and scored 14 and 4. The Selectors chose Mushtaq again – this time for his batting – when Pakistan visited India in 1960-1. He finished second to his brother Hanif in the averages for the drawn 15 first-class matches comprising the tour, and by making his maiden Test century at Delhi, when India were on top, he helped to save the game and the rubber for Pakistan. Mushtaq rates this innings of 101 as his best. Realizing that the prestige and reputation of his country was at stake, he was determined to make a 'do or die' effort and his resolution brought reward.

Mushtaq had sampled English pitches when he made a junior tour with the Pakistan Eaglets in 1958 – he often kept wicket then and opened the batting – and he gained first-hand knowledge of senior English bowling in the 1961-2 winter when M.C.C. visited Pakistan. Mushtaq was selected for the three Test matches, but apart from a splendid innings of 76 in the First Test, at Lahore, where he shared with Burki a fourth-wicket stand of 153, he achieved nothing of note. Still, in the same season he gave his countrymen a rare taste of his liking for free stroke-play by hitting 229 not out – his highest score – for Karachi Whites against East Pakistan. He reached his hundred before lunch. There was, therefore, little hesitation on the part of the Selectors to pick him, together with Hanif, for the 1962 visit to England. With Hanif handicapped by knee trouble, Mushtaq had the opportunity to come into the

limelight, and considering the generally disappointing performances of his team he did exceptionally well to head their batting
aggregates in all first-class games with 1,614 runs. The next
highest tally was 320 runs fewer.

Mushtaq demonstrated his fluent stroke production in the
first game at Worcester where he scored 55 and 86 not out. He
went on to trounce the Cambridge bowlers for 176 and in the
First Test, at Birmingham, made 63 in good style. He was out
for 7 and 18 in the Second Test at Lord's, and for 27 and 8
in the Third Test at Leeds, but he hit Hampshire for 108 at
Bournemouth before adding to his growing reputation with
splending innings of 55 and 100 not out in the Fourth Test at
Trent Bridge. As in his rubber-saving effort against India at
Delhi, Mushtaq once more subordinated his attacking pro-
pensities to the necessity of saving the match. For five and a
quarter hours he defied everything his rivals could bring
against him and he enjoyed the great satisfaction of helping
Pakistan to snatch the game out of the fire. So, at eighteen, he
had the honour of being the only player in history to score two
Test centuries before reaching the age of twenty. Mushtaq
concluded his Test displays by scoring 43 and 72 in more
characteristic style at the Oval and Pakistan though having
lost the series, were happy in the possession of a grand player
for many years to come.

For one so young, Mushtaq is quite composed at the crease,
and a twirl of the bat between strokes is his only idiosyncrasy.
He is not so slight in build as he appears, for although he stands
only 5 ft. 7 in. he tips the scale at just over 12 stone. His strength
– and quickness of foot – is particularly evident when he moves
inside the line of the ball to hook, and his stroke gives him just
as much pleasure as does his entertaining off-side repertoire of
cover-drives, square-drives and cuts. His preference is for fast
bowlers. As for fielding, anywhere in the region of cover or in
the deep affords Mushtaq the chance to exhibit his ability in
this department of the game.

Thus Mushtaq has added lustre to the wonderful record of

his family who have so far given three players to Pakistan Test cricket. There will be another in due course, if Mushtaq's estimate of his youngest brother's prowess comes true. Mushtaq forecasts that Sadiq will grow into a really dashing batsman as good as, if not better than, any other son of their much-loved mother.

from WISDEN *1963*

Graeme Pollock

K. G. DIMBLEBY

Graeme Pollock was always an advanced child. He started walking when only seven months old. Before he reached eighteen months he had played cricket for the first time – and in his own way.

He and his four-year-old brother, Peter, were playing with a bat on the back lawn of their home in Durban. Their mother, a keen sportswoman, joined in the game. She showed Graeme how to hold the bat as a right-hander, and walked away to bowl to him. When she turned, she discovered he had taken up a left-hander's stance. So she said, 'No, Graeme, you must hold the bat this way,' and positioned him as a right-hander. But again when she turned to bowl to him, he had changed to a left-hander's stance.

This happened three times – and then she realized the youngster was not just being perverse, but was a left-hander when it came to batting. In this he follows his father, Mr A. M. ('Mac') Pollock, now editor of the *Eastern Province Herald* in Port Elizabeth, who was still up north on service when that game of cricket was played on the back lawn in 1945.

'Mac' Pollock, who kept wicket for the Grey High School First XI in Port Elizabeth, and later for Free State, batted left-hand, but in all other aspects he is a right-hander. Graeme bats left, but bowls, writes and plays tennis with his right.

When he was only nine, the fair, long-legged youngster scored a century for the Junior Grey Under-11 team against Union High School in Graaff-Reinet. Taking complete command of the bowling in a manner that was later to thrill the crowds in South Africa and Australia, he cracked 7 sixes and

12 fours – 90 in boundaries – in an innings of 117 not out. Youngsters who played in that game still recall how some of the sixes landed in an adjacent graveyard.

Now, only ten years later and only just out of his teens – he was twenty on February 27, 1964 – he has been described by Ron Roberts, one of the foremost of the contemporary cricket writers, as 'without doubt the most exciting young batsman in the world today'.

The Australian critics – some of whom had been a bit sceptical when listening to the advance stories about the young player from South Africa – are now falling over themselves to find suitable superlatives. They refer to 'the boy wonder' . . . 'fabulous' . . . 'another Frank Woolley' . . . 'the best off-drive since Hammond' . . . 'as hard a hitter as Ted Dexter'.

Jack Fingleton wrote recently after Graeme Pollock's century in the Third Test: 'South Africa now possesses one of the great batsmen of the modern age . . .'

This is high praise indeed, but those who have followed the career of this young genius are not surprised that he has already blasted his way into the record books of cricket in a country which is renowned for its tough assessment of a man's ability.

Like the young lady in the musical, *Annie Get Your Gun*, it's a case of 'doing what comes naturally' for Graeme Pollock. And breaking cricket records has become almost a matter of routine. Scoring that century in Graaff-Reinet at the age of nine was by no means his only outstanding feat while at the Junior Grey. In another game he took all ten wickets.

When he moved to the Grey High School, he became the youngest boy ever to play for the First XI. He was only twelve when he was first selected, but the game, against St Aidan's, was washed out by rain. The first time he actually took part in a match for the First XI, against Graeme College, was on his thirteenth birthday. Runs flowed from his bat at an incredible rate in school games, his perfect timing sending the ball to all parts of the boundary. He hit centuries against several schools.

In a senior house match he scored a double century in about an hour.

Another record came his way in Nuffield Week with an innings of 152 for Eastern Province – then the highest score by a Nuffield player. He captained the S.A. Nuffield XI.

Small wonder that a woman who at one time spent most afternoons watching games at the Grey predicted that Graeme Pollock would be the youngest person to play cricket for South Africa. Her prediction did not prove correct, for Graeme was 19 years 8 months old when he first wore the coveted green cap last October in the Springbok's first game in Australia. The youngest was Carlstein, 19 years 4 months when he played in the Fifth Test against Australia in Port Elizabeth in 1958.

There are many who consider Graeme should have been blooded against the New Zealanders in the 1961-2 season when he was seventeen. He took 78 runs off the Kiwi's bowling in Eastern Province's first innings, and 50 not out for South African Colts against the tourists in East London.

One of the first persons to recognize Graeme Pollock not only as a future Springbok but also one of the greats of cricket was George Cox, the Sussex batsman who coached at the Grey. But he also realized that it was no use trying to coach him in the orthodox manner. As Cox has been quoted as saying, it was a case of: 'To heck with the canons of the game. This chap is a natural. Let him be.'

Graeme came under George Cox's watchful and admiring eye again in 1961 soon after leaving school. While on a visit to Britain with his parents he stayed with Cox. . . . Graeme played six games for the Sussex Second XI, which includes the budding young professionals, and gained valuable experience on the different types of wickets in England. He also played for the Duke of Norfolk's XI against Sussex in a charity game at Arundel and bowled Dexter.

It was during this season that his brother, Peter, toured England with the Fezelas – a tour that proved to be a prelude to his gaining Springbok colours as a fast bowler against the New Zealanders the following season.

Tom Dean, the former Hampshire player who took over as coach at the Grey in 1957, held a watching brief over Graeme Pollock's progress in his last three seasons at school. 'A cricketing freak or genius' is how Dean describes him. And he adds: 'If ever I saw the likes of him again I would be more than lucky. One of the most vivid recollections I have of his repertoire of strokes is a six he hit against St Aidan's College from the school end of the Grey field. It was hit *over extra cover*, and the ball cleared the trees, went over College Drive and landed in the garden of a house on the other side of the road. I will never forget it.'

Tom Dean is a leg-spinner and has bowled hundreds of balls to Graeme Pollock in the nets so should know what he is talking about when he says: 'A leg-spinner will never get him out. You've only got to drop the ball about six inches short and he hits it wherever you haven't got a fielder. Look what he's done to Richie Benaud.'

Dean confirms that Graeme has 'a wonderful temperament' for cricket. Quiet and unassuming with an almost shy smile, he does not really suffer from nerves before a big game. It's hard to believe that any batsman does not have 'butterflies' before going in, but if Graeme does feel at all that way, those few practice shots he plays while striding to the wicket seem to sweep away all nervousness. He sleeps no less soundly before a game and still has to be wakened by his mother in the morning.

He has no superstitions or lucky charm, but does develop a fondness for certain bats while looking upon others with disfavour.

The purists will not approve of his stance. 'As soon as one looks at Graeme Pollock, one begins to think of how he could be improved,' wrote Fingleton after watching him score 122 in the recent Third Test in Australia. 'His stance at the crease is an ugly one. He holds his short-handle bat at the bottom of the handle. As he stands well over six feet, he has to pop his posterior in the air to fit everything in and he forms an ugly, elongated, upside-down figure as he stands awaiting the ball. In such a stance his head is far away from his feet. He cramps himself, one says, on the leg-side and, indeed, he is cramped on that side and, if he has a weakness, it is just behind square-leg. But suddenly he blazes forth with ferocious, fiery off-drives that surge across the turf . . .'

But why worry about his stance. It's what happens when he plays the ball that counts. And in that Third Test century he cracked 17 fours and one six. His second 50 was made in only 57 minutes off 17 scoring strokes.

Bill O'Reilly, the former famous Australian Test bowler who has been a leading cricket writer for some years, was moved to describe this effort as 'the most brilliantly punishing Test innings I have ever seen.'

Graeme obeys a fundamental tenet of batting by treating every ball on its merits and taking full advantage of loose ones. But because of his uncanny ability, he is able to make loose balls out of deliveries that would be regarded as good by most other batsmen.

The result is a greater flow of scoring strokes which send the ball rocketing between fielders who are left flat-footed. And Graeme has the knack of finding gaps in the field which makes life even more embarrassing for the fielders.

His achievements at a tender age inevitably resulted in early maturity as a cricketer – and selection when only sixteen to play for Eastern Province in Currie Cup games. He was chosen to represent his Province in 1960, his last year at school, his debut being delayed by matriculation examinations until December 9 when he played against Border.

He was not the youngest cricketer to play for Eastern Province, but he was certainly the most accomplished for his age. He started his first-class career auspiciously by making 54 against Border. A few weeks later, when still sixteen, he scored 102 against Transvaal and established his first South African record by becoming the youngest player to score a century in Currie Cup games.

His first season in Currie Cup cricket produced 384 runs in eight innings (average 48). He had ten innings in the 1961-2 season, but was not quite so successful, scoring 346 runs (average 38). The 1962-3 season saw the flower of his ability burst into full bloom, his 11 innings in Currie Cup games totalling 596 runs (average 54.2). These scores included 111 and 98 in a key game against Transvaal and 137 against Western Province.

But the most memorable day that stands out above all others in a season studded with success is March 18, 1963 – the final day of the game between an Eastern Province Invitation XI and the Cavaliers. It was an historic occasion for Eastern Province cricket.

The touring team included several leading Australian players – Benaud, O'Neill, McKenzie, Hoare, Sincock and Martin. In reply to the Eastern Province XI's first innings of 263 (Graeme Pollock 2), the Cavaliers declared at 401 for 9. When the Eastern Province XI had lost three wickets for only 41 runs on the morning of the last day, the visitors were justified in thinking they were set for an easy win. Some of them were probably thinking in terms of a round of golf in the afternoon.

But they had reckoned without Graeme Pollock, who had only recently celebrated his nineteenth birthday. If one can be excused the pun, he treated the bowlers in cavalier fashion and clouted them to all parts of the field in the most devastating exhibition of batting ever seen in Port Elizabeth.

An incredible transformation came over the game. By lunchtime the young batsman had reached his century. After lunch the tempo of his innings increased still further, and a great cheer went up from the wildly excited crowd, which had swelled as the news of his onslaught spread, when yet another boundary took his total past the 200 mark.

His undefeated innings of 209 in 201 minutes, which included 154 in boundaries (3 sixes and 34 fours), enabled the Eastern

Province XI to declare at 355 for 5. At the close of play the Cavaliers were on their knees with 8 wickets down for only 76 runs. At one stage in his magnificent innings, Graeme Pollock hit 6 fours off six balls from Hoare.

Ron Roberts, who organized the Cavaliers tour and was one of the best informed cricket critics, declared: 'I have not seen a batsman of his age play an innings of such sustained aggression.' But Benaud and the other leading Australians in the touring team seemed reluctant to give full credit to Graeme's outstanding display. They tended to say in effect: 'Yes, he's very good, but . . . we also have some outstanding young 'uns in Australia . . .' And there seemed to be a hint of: 'We'll know how to deal with him in Australia.'

Since then Graeme has blasted the restraint out of their praise. By the time he left with the Springbok team in October to tour Australia and New Zealand, he had scored 1,566 runs (average 54) in only three seasons of first-class cricket. Now he is well past the 2,500 mark.

Soon after the tour of Australia started, in a game against a Combined XI at Perth, which included Benaud and other Test players, he scored what was described as 'a blazing yet wonderful century'. His first 100 runs came in 88 minutes (18 fours) – the same time he had taken to score his second hundred in the double century against the Cavaliers in Port Elizabeth.

Among those who watched this feat was Sir Donald Bradman, who told Graeme afterwards: 'If ever you score another century like that, let me know in advance so that I can be there to watch it.'

Sir Donald has been lucky. As convenor of the Australian selection committee, he watched Graeme hit centuries in the Third and Fourth Tests.

When asked what he thought of Graeme now, Benaud is reported to have replied: 'Well, he has made four hundreds against me already. What would you think?' He has also rated Graeme as the best left-handed batsman he has seen since Neil Harvey in his heyday.

Graeme's 175 in the Fourth Test at Adelaide was lauded as perhaps the greatest Test innings ever played by a teen-age batsman. In addition to other records, it gave him the distinction of having made two centuries in his first six Test innings – something even Sir Donald Bradman did not achieve. Sir Donald's second Test century came in his seventh innings.

Before the start of the Fifth Test, Graeme had scored nine centuries in less than four seasons of first-class cricket – a rare achievement in the world and unique for a South African.

A well-known sports writer who has closely followed Graeme's career since he came to Port Elizabeth at the age of four, says that since scoring that 117 not out in Graaff-Reinet as a nine-year-old, he has hit at least 50 more centuries in first-class, first league, friendly and school games.

By way of relaxation, this young star shares other teen-agers' enjoyment of hit parade music and modern dancing. But unlike his brother, Peter, who taught himself to play the guitar, Graeme does not play any musical instruments.

The Pollock brothers enjoy playing snooker, and during their first visit to Adelaide had a game against Sir Donald Bradman and a friend. They claim to have beaten the Australian pair, mainly because Sir Donald went in off the red a few times.

Graeme has thrived on his sporting family background and his prowess is by no means limited to cricket. In addition to playing cricket for Free State, his father won provincial hockey colours. His mother, formerly Edith Howden, played tennis for Durban. Her brother, Bob, represented Natal at Rugby, cricket and hockey. Her uncle, Jock Howden, was a former President of the South African Cricket Association.

At school Graeme took a leading part in Rugby, athletics and tennis. He succeeded Cliff Drysdale, now a leading tennis Springbok, as singles champion at the Grey and held the title for two years. The young Test cricketer gave up Rugby after leaving school. He is now a keen hockey player.

Apart from scoring a century in a Test match, Graeme

achieved another ambition when he returned home. He has always wanted to own an Alsatian dog. Recently his parents bought one for him. The puppy was a present for his twentieth birthday on February 27, 1964.

from THE CRICKETER *8–5–1964*

Colin Milburn

JOHN REASON

There is no doubt that the greatest gift to cartoonists since the emergence of F. S. Trueman has been the arrival of Colin Milburn as a Test cricketer.

As Roy Ullyett was quick to observe, Milburn is so amply proportioned that he can even bring about a very total eclipse of M. C. Cowdrey if he happens to pass in front of him. After faithfully drawing the wicket-keeper's view of England's Test captain for so long, Ullyett must be glad of the change.

Milburn says he weighs $17\frac{1}{2}$ stone. He also maintains (stoutly, of course) that he has a waist. As one who has closely observed the various phases of Milburn down the years, both on the cricket circuit and at the Northampton Rugby Football Club, I beg leave to question both statements.

I think that he is ignoring (heavily, of course) all contact with a weighing machine. I very much doubt whether he would get any change out of 18 stone at the moment, and, once it had reached his chest, I doubt whether a tape measure would so much as waver from a steady reading of 47 inches until it approached his knees.

This presents his tailor with almost insuperable difficulties. On more than one occasion this season Milburn's trousers have been unequal to their task. They even split in a Test match.

In addition to all these engaging virtues, Milburn is such a rich character that he is savoured by everyone in the game; he is also a happy man, and he approaches batting in a Test match in exactly the same way as he approaches all his batting – as if his only thought is to score the runs in fours and sixes. What more could the cartoonists want?

Milburn is no johnny-come-lately to the slogging business either. 'I've always been a slogger,' he says, 'and my father was a slogger before me.'

Milburn *père et fils* played for Burnopfield, which is a mining village seven miles from Newcastle. Father works for the N.E. Electricity Board, and Milburn was in the same village team by the time he was thirteen. Father just taught him how to hold the bat and let him get on with it. That is all the tuition he has ever had. Milburn cannot remember when he first hit a six, it was so long ago. He is only twenty-four now [1965].

When he was seventeen, in 1959, he played for Chester-le-Street in the Durham Senior League. In just two months he scored two hundreds and was chosen to play for Durham County against the Indian tourists. With Desai, Surendra Nath, Nadkarni, and Borde bowling to him, he made a hundred. He did not take too long about it, either.

Neither did Northamptonshire. On the recommendation of Bill Coverdale they had already given him a trial when he was sixteen, but as soon as he made that hundred against the Indians Northamptonshire put him on the staff.

He left Stanley Grammar School one Easter. The next week he was playing cricket for a living. This was just as well, because he had never wanted anything else. He still doesn't.

First he had to qualify for Northamptonshire, then he had to establish himself in the team. Qualification took a year. The second part took rather longer.

'Of course I was an all-rounder then,' he says, with his face very nearly straight, and his bowling arm goes through the county cricketer's familiar motions of bowling the inswinger and the out-swinger. (No seamer *ever* bowls a straight ball in county cricket.)

'I gave up bowling, though,' he adds. 'It was my back, you know.'

He times the punch line as accurately as Jack Benny.

'It was a mug's game, too.'

His very white teeth show in a great sunburned melon of a

grin. He does not mention that his abilities as an all-rounder were sufficient to take him to the final of the single-wicket competition at Lord's two years ago. On that occasion Mr G. O. Allen very properly rebuked him for throwing away an easy chance in the final. Mr Allen obviously wanted him to win. Milburn has that effect on people.

He batted at number six or seven in the county side to start with, then in 1963 he went in at number three. He started to open the innings half-way through last season, and he much prefers it. 'I don't like sitting around,' he says. 'I like to get on with it.'

Milburn has certainly done that. This season he has made hundreds against Derbyshire, Sussex, Leicestershire, Nottinghamshire, and the West Indies, and he was first to make 1,000 runs. He has scored the fastest hundred of the season so far, and he failed by only four runs to make a hundred in his first Test match. He has three times hooked Wes Hall for six.

This, then, has been the season in which he has established himself, but he still thinks that the best innings he has ever played was against Derbyshire at Buxton in 1962. It was a poor wicket, and when he went in Northamptonshire were 20–4. Les Jackson had just taken four wickets for four runs in about 10 balls.

Colin Milburn and Mick Norman then put on 150 and Milburn made a hundred. When they got out, the last six wickets fell for seven runs.

Talking of his build, Milburn confesses that he has always been 'pretty solid'. He has dieted seriously on three occasions, starving himself and dehydrating, but he has never been able to lower his *avoirdupois* below 16½ stone.

'When I first came down to Northampton they got me on these training runs,' he recalls, 'but I'm just not built to run a long way. I'm all right on a short sprint, but after about half a mile the others left me behind, so I thumbed a lift on a milk float. We sailed past the rest of the boys a bit further up the road.'

Milburn is much too convivial to spend his life dieting like a flat-race jockey. Socially, Northamptonshire are one of the quieter counties, but Milburn is a shining light. He radiates zest and humour. In his first year as a regular county player he arranged parties for all the teams visiting Northampton and they love him for it.

Umpires love him too. I can remember hearing his praises sung by 'Lofty' Herman and others long before anyone else was singing them. He plays the game as they used to – for fun, and not as a job of work.

This has a lot to do with his appeal. He does not conform. He is not grey and arid. He is not as others. He does not find a thousand and one reasons why it is technically impossible to hit the ball. He takes that big, booming, bottom-hand of his out there, and, if Wes Hall bowls him a half-volley first ball in a Test match he will try to belt it for four.

And, of course, he is a different shape. Fat men are funny men, and Milburn has an irresistible streak of Oliver Hardy in him.

He failed his driving test twice. Once he drove the wrong way up a one-way street, and the other time he so incensed a bus-driver that the bus-driver stopped his bus in the middle of Northampton, climbed out, and threatened to punch the examiner on the nose.

'I was not confident of passing the test,' admits Milburn. He has not driven since.[1]

He went to South Africa last winter with Fred Rumsey to do some schools coaching in East London. Milburn decided he must try his hand at the aquatic sports.

'I saw these athletic looking blokes kneeling on their surf-boards and paddling out,' he says, 'and then turning round and coming back on a big wave, so I thought I'd have a go. I couldn't even get on the surf-board. Every time I tried, it capsized.'

His attempts at water-skiing were even more discouraging.

[1] Written 1966.

He got down in the water, with his skis at the high port, and hung on to the rope just as it said in the instruction book, but when it came to pulling him up out of the water the speed boat was as unequal to the task as his trousers were at Old Trafford. He stayed in precisely the same position as he had been to start with, and boiled slowly through the Indian Ocean submerged at a depth of about 4 ft., water-skis and all.

'It didn't half pull on my arms,' he said.

Other players who were at the Scarborough Festival last year are still laughing about the occasion when Milburn, perspiring somewhat from his exertions, decided to cool himself down by spraying himself all over with one of the new volatile deodorants.

His bottom hand was as heavy on the spray button as it is on a cricket bat, and he fairly covered himself with the stuff. As the deodorant started to evaporate and cool his skin, his expression was as blissful as Nero's might have been at one of his better orgies. This lasted about 10 seconds. Then a spasm of doubt crossed his face. This was followed very rapidly by, first, a look of alarm, and then a shout of pain. As the liquid bit into his skin the effect was as corrosive as acid.

Milburn leapt across the dressing-room to one of the capacious wash-basins, turned on both taps and simply sat in the basin while the water swirled round the more pertinent parts of his person. It says much for the sanitary ware at Scarborough, for the plumber's wall fixings, and even for the wall itself that each and severally they were able to stand the strain.

Milburn might have been a first-class Rugby player. He used to play in the centre, where I imagine he brought a new concept to the tactic known as 'breaking', but then he settled down to play as a prop in the front row of the scrum.

His ambition was to tour Australia with M.C.C. (it still is), and 18 months ago he told me that if he did not win a place in the 1965-6 touring party he would probably take up Rugby seriously. As it turned out, he did not, because he accepted the coaching appointment in South Africa instead, but I cannot help thinking that Rugby football has lost a considerable force.

As a batsman, Milburn is held in high regard by his contemporaries. Most of them think that he is easily the best of the new wave of sloggers who are opening the innings in county cricket, and this is surprising when you remember what R. W. Barber did in Australia.

Technically, Milburn can prop if he has to, and as Tom Graveney told him on the night before he made his hundred in the second innings at Lord's, he should use his ability in defence to build a big score.

Graveney was at pains to point out that Milburn must not change his aggressive style. 'It is just that you cannot slog *every* ball in a Test match,' he said.

Milburn nodded and took his bottom hand off to bed early. The next day he played the best innings I have ever seen from him. He knew that if he failed his Test place was in danger but on that day he needed less luck than ever before in a big innings.

He is fearless, which is why he fields at short leg and why he loves playing fast bowling. 'They can only hit you,' he shrugs, but he admits that, as yet, he has not developed a taste for off-spin.

He knows, too, that he only has to fail twice for his critics to say, 'You can't have a man who bats like that opening the innings for England.'

He knows that they are probably saying it already, even though his Test match average is 50, and even though it is often the *rate* at which a side scores its runs which is decisive.

Never mind. It will be fun as long as it lasts.

from THE CRICKETER *1966*

Envoi

Mr Dexter and I

A. A. THOMSON

I once knew a man who never saw Hobbs make a century. All his watching life he kept hearing about the great man's hundreds – eventually they added up to 197 – but none of these polished performances took place within my unlucky friend's personal observation. Every time he went to watch Surrey or England Hobbs would make one of his rare modest scores and this series of unhappy coincidences continued for so long that it almost seemed as if he had only to put down his money at the turnstile to ensure disaster for his hero. Now my friend was a sensitive citizen. He recognized that his very presence in the vicinity had a cramping effect on the Master's genius, and so he decided to stay away. Indeed, to the end of his days, he was firmly convinced that it was only through his consistently unselfish absence from the Oval and other relevant spots that Hobbs was able to retire from first-class cricket with the rather tidy total of 61,221 runs in the books. And, most poignant of all, Sir Jack, a kindly soul, as everybody knows, has never even heard of my friend's existence. All of which proves that the great will, quite arbitrarily, do their stuff for some people and not for others.

In my necessarily more modest way I have, until this season, suffered a similar searing experience with Mr E. R. Dexter. I had in the past few years heard high praise of his cricket but I had regularly failed to witness any *Wisden*-worthy deeds on his part. I had heard that in his last year at school, when he was captain of cricket, he had a batting average of nearly 80. (But, after all, Radley was a rowing school, anyhow.) Then, of course, at Cambridge he was a golf blue. (That might put you

against a chap, don't you think?) True, they told me, he played
a bit of cricket, too, collecting seven hundreds, two of them
against Lancashire, essentially a bowling county. But on the
occasions when I watched Cambridge he would not make a
century for me. (As a mild supporter of the other place, I did
not complain at the time.) One must believe the scorebooks,
but there was something incredible in his bowling in that
fantastic Gentlemen v. Players match. Just as 1957 saw the
centenary of the Indian Mutiny, so 2057 will recall Dexter's
analysis in the Players' first innings at Lord's:

5 overs   2 maidens   8 runs   5 wickets

He had taken only 18 wickets altogether in first-class cricket
and now he had encompassed the Players' destruction for
the lowest score they had ever made since before W.G.'s
time.

So it went on. The next year he was awarded his first
English cap which he christened, I was told, with a bright half-
century. He scored another vital 50 in the Varsity match, but
(inevitably) on the day I was not there. When he flew to
Australia on an S.O.S. call, his batting average in Tests was
4.50. (There have been seasons in village cricket when I have
done as well as that myself.) Then, flying on to New Zealand,
he played an innings of 141 and a Christchurch friend of mine –
I have spies all over the Commonwealth – wrote to say that
this was one of the most dazzling knocks he had ever seen. But
Christchurch is a long way off.

In 1959 Dexter scored over 2,000 beautiful runs, but still not
for me. It was his first full season for Sussex, and a grand one,
but so potent was the power of my evil eye that I watched him
make 1 against Lancashire, o against Hampshire, o against
Kent, o against Essex and another o against Middlesex. His
duck against Kent at Hastings was the result of a ferocious
first-ball slash which found gully's hands, instead of knocking
gully's head off. In that magical summer Dexter compiled
seven lordly centuries; under my baleful eye his highest score

was 8. The chorus acclaiming his greatness swelled louder and louder, but, right up to the end of the season, I felt more inclined to amend the poet's lines:

> *If he be not great for me,*
> *What care I how great he be?*

I was within a bail's length of abandoning the struggle. If Dexter could make 2,000 runs, I argued, in spite of the handicap of my watching, I had better stop away altogether next year and give him a chance of his 3,000. This theory was confirmed during the winter. I could not, for economic reasons, if for no other, spend the winter in the Caribbean, and so no sinister influence of mine prevented him from being one of the major successes of the tour.

The thing that broke my altruistic resolution was the early visit to Hove of my own county. My duty to greet the champions was greater than my duty to stop away. It was during this game that I enjoyed my first and only personal contact with Mr Dexter and oh, as Wordsworth says, the difference to me. In his innings against Yorkshire he played with a power that almost amounted to sovereignty. Nursing Sussex through a sticky opening, he assumed complete control. There was no reckless hitting, his defence was firm and clean, but never dull. His strokes formed a gallery of pictures 'out of the book' an older and more illustrious book than we have looked at lately: easy, effortless drives that flew between cover and extra cover with the approximate speed of light; good-length balls that were returned with interest past the bowler into the south stand; glittering cuts so late as to be positively posthumous. At 96 he was caught off a tremendous skier and in the end Sussex won the match. A freakish result in the sense that the defeated side did not lose a single wicket until well into the third afternoon, but a fair victory, nevertheless. Not merely did Sussex win; they went on winning, and this was highly creditable to somebody because, apart from my lion-hearted namesake, Sussex are not reckoned a mighty bowling side.

There is something in coaching; there is undoubtedly something in captaincy.

From that day I seemed, almost dramatically, to lose the power of my evil eye. I saw him score 111 at Worthing against Gloucestershire and again I watched the majestic strokes: easy, almost languid, infinitely graceful and, except for the most enchanting late cuts, almost all in front of the wicket. In the Bank Holiday game against the old enemy, Middlesex, Dexter did it (for me) a third time in an innings that for sheer aristocratic quality surpassed anything I had seen for years. With Don Smith, whose robust 80 was entitled to the highest praise, Dexter took the score from 42 for 4 into the three-hundreds and after tea the Middlesex fieldsmen, trying to stop drives which bit like serpents, may well have remembered where Dexter was born, and thought hard thoughts of the Viper of Milan. MacLaren, said Neville Cardus, did not hit the ball, he dismissed it from the presence. Woolley, said J. M. Barrie, whispered his wishes to the ball and it understood. And in 1960, whenever I see Dexter batting, I feel that, for a time at least, there is no impertinence in recalling great names and great phrases. Whatever I may think, I do not often shout that there is nobody today like the old 'uns. Even if true it is irrelevant, and, in any event, it seems churlish to keep rubbing it in. With Dexter at the wicket, I am certain that cricket is the same game as I used to see in the brave days of old.

In G. M. Trevelyan's *History of England* there is a much-quoted passage which lauds the English eighteenth-century way of life when 'squire, farmer, blacksmith and labourer, with the women and children, come to see the fun, were at ease together and happy all the summer afternoon . . .' He also laments that in France peer and peasant never came together in that way. Yet if a French duke of the *ancien régime* had learnt to bat – and what a pity none of them ever did – I toy with the fancy that he would have batted just as Dexter bats today; with *élan* and *panache*, with delicacy and supreme power, extravagantly, elegantly, a little disdainfully, above all, *ducally*. That touch of disdain in his style sometimes gets him out to a haphazard stroke. Against Northamptonshire I saw him clean bowled at 17 after an innings which enshrined, like jewels in a small case, two of the noblest cover-drives seen by mortal eye since Hutton's, or even Hammond's best. What makes it possible to mention his name in the same sentence as those of the immortals is his appearance of having all the time in the world to make his stroke – any stroke. Hobbs had three strokes for every ball and Trumper, his countrymen tell us, had five. Dexter undoubtedly has a minimum of two. Further than that I dare not go, but I will say this: that, with May temporarily out of cricket, there is at the moment only one individual name that will draw people – crowds and connoisseurs alike – into a cricket ground. The name of Edward R. Dexter.

I have never spoken to Mr Dexter in my life, but if I mentioned a personal contact, I did not lie. The contact occurred during the Yorkshire match on May 7, 1960, when a ball, on-driven at jet-propelled speed, struck me on the shin as I sat in front of the Hove pavilion, as heaven is my witness. This blow raised within minutes an enormous bruise similar in kaleidoscopic brilliance to the colours of some of the Picasso pictures now on exhibition at the Tate Gallery, though to be fair to all of us – Dexter, Picasso and me – my leg, even after such punishment, still looked more like a leg than most of Picasso's models' legs, if you see what I mean. The size and opulent vividness of the bruise are tributes to the sheer power of the stroke, for it appeared to be nonchalantly made. Now Mr Dexter and I are *en rapport* and he cannot do anything wrong for me. It just shows what personal contact can do!

from THE CRICKETER *September 1960*

Acknowledgements

Acknowledgements and thanks are due to the following authors and publishers for the use of copyright material:

To Gerald Duckworth and Co. Ltd for the extract from *W. G. Grace* by the late Bernard Darwin;

To George G. Harrap and Co. Ltd for 'F. R. Spofforth' and 'Jack Iverson' from *Australian Bowlers* by the late A. G. Moyes;

To Mr Alan Gibson and *Playfair Cricket Monthly* for 'S. M. J. Woods';

To Mr Vijay Merchant and the K. S. Duleepsinhji Commemoration Volume Committee for 'K. S. Ranjitsinhji' by K. S. Duleepsinhji from *Duleep: the Man and his Game*;

To Sir Neville Cardus and the respective publishers: Guardian Newspapers Ltd for 'R. H. Spooner'; *Playfair Cricket Monthly* for 'C. G. Macartney', 'Ted McDonald', and 'Maurice Leyland'; Collins Publishers for 'Walter Hammond' and 'A. V. Bedser' from *Close of Play*, and 'Roy Kilner' from *The Summer Game*;

To Mr Ian Peebles and Museum Press Ltd for 'S. F. Barnes' from *Talking about Cricket*;

To Hutchinson Publishing Group Ltd for 'P. F. Warner' and 'P. B. H. May' from *The Great Captains* by the late A. A. Thomson;

To Lord Constantine for 'L. S. Constantine' from *The Changing Face of Cricket* by Learie Constantine and Denzil Batchelor (Eyre & Spottiswoode);

To Frederick Muller Ltd (on behalf of John Miles Ltd) for 'Victor Trumper' from *Bat and Ball* by Thomas Moult;

To J. M. Dent and Sons Ltd and the respective authors for the following extracts from *Cricket Heroes* published by Phoenix House: 'J. W. H. T. Douglas' by Charles Bray; 'Sir Jack Hobbs' by E. W. Swanton; 'E. Hendren' by Brian Johnston; 'M. W. Tate' by John Arlott; and 'H. T. Bartlett' by Alan Ross;

To Mr John Arlott and the respective publishers: J. M. Dent and

Sons Ltd for 'C. P. Mead' from *Hampshire County Cricket* (Phoenix House); Longmans, Green Ltd for 'Walter Hadlee' and 'T. G. Evans' from *The Echoing Green*; and Times Newspapers Ltd for 'Sir Frank Worrell';

To Alan Ross Ltd for 'F. E. Woolley' and 'D. R. Jardine' from *Cricket Prints* by the late R. C. Robertson-Glasgow;

To Mrs C. S. Marriott for 'C. H. Parkin' from *The Complete Leg-break Bowler* by the late C. S. Marriott (Eyre & Spottiswoode);

To Mr Ray Robinson and Collins Publishers for 'E. A. Paynter', 'Fast Bowlers 1921-46' and 'S. J. McCabe' from *Between Wickets* and 'Mushtaq Ali' from *The Glad Season*;

To Mr C. L. R. James and Hutchinson Publishing Group Ltd for 'L. N. Constantine' and 'George Headley' from *Beyond a Boundary*;

To Sir Donald Bradman and Hodder & Stoughton Ltd for 'W. J. O'Reilly' from *Farewell to Cricket*;

To Mr Jack Fingleton and Collins Publishers for 'Don Bradman' from *Brightly fades the Don*; as also to Mr Fingleton for 'W. M. Lawry';

To Mr Keith Miller, Mr R. S. Whitington and Latimer House Ltd for 'Bodyline' from *Bumper*;

To Mr Gerald Brodribb and William Heinemann Ltd for 'A. W. Wellard – Hitter of Sixes' from *Hit for Six*;

To Epworth Press Ltd for 'Sir Leonard Hutton' and 'Cyril Washbrook' from *Hutton and Washbrook* by the late A. A. Thomson;

To Mr Trevor Bailey and *Playfair Cricket Monthly* for 'W. J. Edrich' and 'Denis Compton'; as also to Mr Bailey for 'Tom Graveney' from *The Greatest of my Time* (Eyre & Spottiswoode);

To Mr Ian Johnson and Cassell & Co for 'Keith Miller' from *Cricket at the Crossroads*;

To Mr J. M. Kilburn and William Heinemann Ltd for 'Ray Lindwall' from *Cricket Decade*;

To Mr Bert Sutcliffe and W. H. Allen for 'J. R. Reid' from *Between Overs*;

To Mr Jim Laker and Frederick Muller Ltd for 'Trevor Bailey' from *Spinning around the World*;

To Mr Michael Parkinson and the *Sunday Times* for 'Brian Statham';

To Mr Deryck Cooke and the *New Statesman* for 'Fred Trueman';

To Mr John Waite and Kaye and Ward Ltd for 'Sir Leonard Again' from *Perchance to Bowl*, © Nicholas Kaye Ltd, 1961;

To Mr Eric Hill and *Playfair Cricket Monthly* for 'Bill Alley' by Eric Shore;

To Mr Irving Rosenwater and *The Cricketer* and *The Cricket Society* respectively for 'Collie Smith' and 'Wesley Winfield Hall';

To Mr E. W. Swanton for 'Gary Sobers';

To Mr Henry Blofeld for 'Lance Gibbs';

To Sporting Handbooks Ltd for 'Mushtaq Mohammed' from Wisden's *Cricketers' Almanack*, 1963;

To Mr K. G. Dimbleby and Mr John Reason respectively and *The Cricketer* for 'Graeme Pollock' and 'Colin Milburn';

To *The Cricketer* for 'Mr Dexter and I' by the late A. A. Thomson.

Lastly the Editor would like to acknowledge his own publishers Eyre & Spottiswoode for reproducing 'C. B. Fry' and 'A. A. Mailey' from *The Game goes on*.

Index of Authors